Job Feedback:
Giving, Seeking, and Using Feedback for Performance Improvement

SERIES IN APPLIED PSYCHOLOGY

Edwin A. Fleishman, George Mason University
Series Editor

Teamwork and the Bottom Line: Groups Make a Difference
Ned Rosen

Patterns of Life History: The Ecology of Human Individuality
Michael D. Mumford, Garnett Stokes, and William A. Owens

Work Motivation
Uwe E. Kleinbeck, Hans-Henning Quast, Henk Thierry, and Hartmut Häcker

Psychology in Organizations: Integrating Science and Practice
Kevin R. Murphy and Frank E. Saal

Human Error: Cause, Prediction, and Reduction
John W. Senders and Neville P. Moray

Contemporary Career Development Issues
Robert F. Morrison and Jerome Adams

Justice in the Workplace: Approaching Fairness in Human Resource Management
Russell Cropanzano

Personnel Selection and Assessment: Individual and Organizational Perspectives
Heinz Schuler, James L. Farr, and Mike Smith

Organizational Behavior: The State of the Science
Jerald Greenberg

Police Psychology Into the 21st Century
Martin I. Kurke and Ellen M. Scrivner

Benchmark Tasks for Job Analysis: A Guide for Functional Job Analysis (FJA) Scales
Sidney A. Fine and Maury Getkate

Stress and Human Performance
James E. Driskell and Eduardo Salas

Improving Training Effectiveness in Work Organizations
J. Kevin Ford, Steve W. J. Kozlowski, Kurt Kraiger, Eduardo Salas, and Mark S. Teachout

Assessment and Measurement of Team Performance: Theory, Research, and Applications
Michael T. Brannick, Eduardo Salas, and Carolyn Prince

Job Feedback: Giving, Seeking, and Using Feedback for Performance Improvement
Manuel London

Job Feedback:
Giving, Seeking, and Using Feedback for Performance Improvement

Manuel London
State University of New York at Stony Brook

LEA LAWRENCE ERLBAUM ASSOCIATES, PUBLISHERS
1997 Mahwah, New Jersey

Lawrence Erlbaum Associates, Inc., Publishers
10 Industrial Avenue
Mahwah, New Jersey 07430

Cover design by Kathryn Houghtaling

Library of Congress Cataloging-in-Publication Data

London, Manuel.
    Job feedback: giving, seeking, and using feedback
for performance improvement / Manuel London.
        p. cm.
    Includes bibliographical references and index.
    ISBN 0-8058-2474-X (cloth : alk. paper). — ISBN
0-8058-2475-8 (pbk. : alk. paper)
    1. Employee motivation. 2. Feedback (Psychology)
3. Performance standards. I. Title.
    HF5549.5.M63L66 1997
    658.3'14—dc20   96-35237
                                                CIP

Books published by Lawrence Erlbaum Associates are
printed on acid-free paper, and their bindings are chosen
for strength and durability.

Printed in the United States of America
10 9 8 7 6 5 4 3 2 1

Contents

Foreword

Edwin A. Fleishman
Series Editor

There is a compelling need for innovative approaches to the solution of many pressing problems involving human relationships in today's society. Such approaches are more likely to be successful when they are based on sound research and applications. This Series in Applied Psychology offers publications that emphasize state-of-the-art research and its application to important issues of human behavior in a variety of societal settings. The objective is to bridge both academic and applied interests.

Feedback is generally acknowledged as an essential ingredient for effective management. It goes along with other important management practices, such as designing meaningful jobs, building teams, providing training and development, setting goals, and appraising performance. Together, these functions constitute a human performance system.

We know from psychological research that people need knowledge of results in order to accomplish performance goals and improve their performance over time. Unfortunately. feedback is often the weak link in the management process. Managers feel uncomfortable giving feedback, especially when it is negative. They don't know how to make feedback a constructive experience. They don't know how often to give feedback and how specific to make it and not sound self-serving. They worry that the person receiving the feedback will be defensive, ignore the message, or blame the messenger. Even when feedback is positive, managers may fear that a "pat on the back" may go to a subordinate's head or antagonize the subordinate's coworkers. On the receiving end, employees often shy away from feedback. Perhaps they don't ask for feedback because they are afraid it will be negative or because they think they will be perceived as looking for praise.

Such psychological and social dynamics suggest that managers need a better understanding of the importance of feedback and ways to make it constructive. Giving and receiving feedback are skills that need to be acquired and practiced. In this book, Manuel London describes how feedback works. He offers practical ideas, based on research, for improving the effectiveness of feedback in organizations. Dr. London is particularly well qualified to write this book. He has worked on human resource programs at AT&T for 12 years and has studied and written about career insight, management development, and 360-degree feedback programs.

In this book, Dr. London covers the gamut of feedback-related processes by describing how people give, seek, and use performance feedback. He examines how givers of feedback process and evaluate information and prepare the message for delivery. He considers how the receivers of feedback react to and use the information. He shows how this happens informally during the normal course of daily events. He also shows how effective feedback processes can be incorporated into formal human resource programs, such as perform-ance appraisal, upward and 360-degree surveys, and assessment centers. Feedback to groups is also covered to show how feedback can enhance their coordination and cooperation.

In today's world of organizational downsizing and change, people cannot assume the organization will take care of their development needs. Supervisors and organizational systems provide the resources for individuals to take responsibility for their own development. As such, people need to learn how to ask for feedback and use the information for self-assessment, development and career planning, and for monitoring their progress. London shows how employees can get feedback not only from supervisors but from peers, subordinates, and customers. The manager's role is not just to give feedback, but to help the receiver make sense of the feedback in relation to other information about. for instance. changing business strategies and performance expectations. Managers and their subordinates can be held accountable for giving and using feedback.

The book argues that improved feedback processes are needed in organiza-tions. Moreover, these processes should be integrated into a comprehensive human performance system. In this context, feedback supports and links job design, goal setting, training, and appraisal. This highly readable book will be particularly valuable for human resource professionals, industrial and organ-izational psychologists, and trainers as they design and fine tune management systems and development programs. It can also be used by managers and employees to understand how feedback operates and how to improve the ways they give and use feedback.

Preface

Feedback is an anomaly. People have a general sense that feedback is good to give and receive. But, many people avoid it like the plague. They are uncomfortable telling others they have done well, and they feel even more uncomfortable telling others they have performed poorly. Some people would just as soon not know how they did, and they dodge evaluations of their performance and opportunities to learn how they can improve.

This is not necessarily irrational. After all, sometimes people give feedback in a dysfunctional way—for instance, to deliberately hurt others' feelings and destroy their self-confidence. Or, this may be the unintentional result. Others give or request feedback to influence how people see them.

I know from personal experience that managers often shy away from giving feedback and have trouble dealing with subordinates' performance problems. I learned this when I was a manager of human resource and training units at AT&T and later when I was an administrator at SUNY-Stony Brook. I also found this to be true in my consulting work in large and small organizations, such as a national manufacturer of textiles, a major communications firm, a government agency associated with national defense, a 200-employee engineering firm, a regional agency with more than 600 employees providing care and training for handicapped individuals, and a community library employing more than 200 part-time people. Managers in these various organizational settings rarely took time to give feedback. Most managers recognized that giving feedback is an important part of the manager's role, but they did not do it! They tended to let poor performance slide by rather than nip it in the bud. They would ask me in puzzlement how to cope with poor performing subordinates and how to improve marginal performers. Subordinates would complain that their managers rarely told them how they were doing.

My interest in feedback arose from my research on the employment interview with Milton Hakel and performance appraisal with Richard Klimoski during my days as a graduate student at Ohio State University. I especially wanted to know how people perceive and make judgments about each other. I incorporated this interest in my work on career motivation at AT&T with Douglas Bray. We defined three components of career motivation: career insight (having information about oneself and the organization), career identity (the goals one wants to accomplish), and career resilience (one's ability to overcome career barriers; see, e.g., London, 1985). As such, feedback is an essential ingredient of an employee development program, as people use information about themselves to formulate career goals.

Several years after studying career motivation and designing management development programs in ways that would strengthen managers' career insight, identity, and resilience, I began work with Arthur Wohlers and, later, James Smither on a method to give managers information about how others see them. Called 360-degree feedback, this is a multisource rating survey that collects ratings about managers from their subordinates, peers, and supervisor. The managers also rate themselves. The technique has several goals: It is a source of information to help managers determine areas for development. It is a way to communicate to employees what elements of management are important and that different constituencies have different views of the manager's role. It contributes to a continuous learning environment with annual (or more frequent) administrations of the survey calling attention to the managers' need to track their improvement in areas that are key to effective boss–subordinate, peer–peer, and customer–supplier relationships.

At SUNY-Stony Brook, I have continued my research on 360-degree feedback and applied the process in consulting projects in different types of organizations. I also began to flesh out the underlying psychological mechanisms and cognitive processes by which people use feedback. In a recent book, I examined self- and interpersonal insight—how people learn about themselves and others in organizations (London, 1995c). My model of how people process information about themselves and others suggests that some information is processed mindlessly. It might reinforce our existing self-image, but it does not suggest ways we can change and improve. Other information is processed mindfully. For this to happen, the information must set off an alarm in some way. This happens when unexpected performance results do not fit existing categories of the way we view ourselves. A process that guides or forces people to pay attention to feedback may also be a wake-up call. As we process the information mindfully, we make attributions about its causes and ways we can control or improve our behavior. Hopefully, this leads to constructive strategies to enhance performance.

After I completed my book on self- and interpersonal insight, I realized that the concepts could be applied to improve feedback. I wanted to make my ideas practical and accessible to human resource practitioners and training professionals as well as students in these fields. I thought that this should be especially important in today's increasingly changing organizations where high performance expectations and fair treatment are critical to success. In particular, I thought that I could build on my work on career motivation, 360-degree feedback, and self- and interpersonal insight to address how people give, seek, and use feedback and how to design better feedback systems. This is my goal in this book. I believe that people can learn to be more insightful about themselves and better observers of others. I draw on theory and research to address issues of practical concern. In doing so, I hope to contribute to the development of sound performance feedback strategies in organizations. I examine the many ways that organizations and individuals benefit from constructive feedback. I view feedback as a key to performance management, and I show how feedback affects learning, motivation, and interpersonal relationships.

I am indebted to several colleagues whose work is represented here and cited at appropriate places. Edward Mone and I have written about how human resource systems can be designed to contribute to organizational change. Feedback is a central ingredient to our view of a comprehensive human performance system. I value Ed as a friend, colleague, and co-author, and I continue to learn a great deal from his organizational insights. James Smither and I have written a number of papers on multisource ratings that shaped my thinking about this increasingly important management tool. Jim is an innovative and careful researcher who has taught me about melding research and practice. Gerrit Wolf, my colleague at Stony Brook, continues to be an inspiration for creative ideas about management. I have benefited from his optimistic, can-do philosophy. An anonymous reviewer was extremely helpful in highlighting the important elements of the manuscript and suggesting how to organize the material to improve the book's usefulness. Last, but not least, I am indebted to my wife, Marilyn, and sons, David and Jared, who are never shy about giving me constructive feedback.

—*Manuel London*

1

Introduction

Meaningful feedback is central to performance management. Feedback guides, motivates, and reinforces effective behaviors and reduces or stops ineffective behaviors. However, although feedback is an important management tool, many people feel uncomfortable giving and receiving feedback. They may give feedback as a way to reinforce their self-image or manipulate how others see them rather than improve others' or their own performance. Givers of feedback may be destructive or hurtful intentionally or unintentionally. In addition, they may be biased by factors unrelated to actual performance and, as a result, convey useless information. Receivers of feedback may be apprehensive about being evaluated, defensive in the face of negative feedback, and/or apt to ignore information that could improve their performance.

People often use negative terms when they observe and describe others, whereas they use positive terms to describe themselves (Langer, 1992). As a result, feedback may be detrimental. No feedback at all may be better in such cases: Feedback is not effective regardless of the content and manner in which it is given and regardless of the receiver's sensitivity to the information. Support mechanisms are needed to ensure that feedback is worthwhile.

Such mechanisms focus on:

1. *The recipient's ability to comprehend the feedback:* The extent to which it conforms to the recipient's cognitive processing capabilities (e.g., it is not too detailed), causes the recipient to think about the task from others' perspectives, and can be applied to improve job performance. These conditions depend on the control and credibility of different sources and the clarity, reliability, and validity of the information they provide. It may also depend on organizational standards and expectations for behaviors associated with different perspectives connoted by the information, and the availability of coaching and role models for how to apply the feedback.

2. *The recipient's sensitivity to feedback:* The extent to which the recipient wants to learn and is able and motivated to process information from different sources.

1

3. *Context:* What is happening in the organization and the demands and stressors experienced by those who give and receive feedback. Such conditions differentiate the recipient's role in relation to that of others and suggests reasons (and rationalizations) for differences in perspectives.

4. *Accountability mechanisms:* Ways the organization holds people responsible for giving and using feedback. These mechanisms may include requiring the recipient to explain and justify the use of feedback, encouraging employees to recognize that people may have different viewpoints about the same event, expecting raters to provide accurate and meaningful ratings, and rewarding improved performance.

In this book, I examine how people give, seek, and use performance feedback. I describe processes by which givers of feedback perceive and judge performance, and I outline information processes by which receivers of feedback absorb (accept, deny, or ignore) and apply feedback. I consider formal sources of feedback including performance appraisal, multisource (upward and 360-degree) survey feedback methods, and assessment centers. I also examine the ways individuals and groups receive informal feedback. This includes guidelines for how to give effective feedback under different conditions and how to hold people accountable for giving feedback.

I focus on the receiver of feedback by considering self-assessment, seeking feedback, and reactions to feedback. Several chapters provide questionnaires that employees (and readers) can use to evaluate themselves. This includes self-assessment of performance and sensitivity to feedback from others. I emphasize that individuals need to be proactive in getting feedback, and I show how to increase feedback. I describe how employees can draw on horizontal and lateral relationships in organizations as sources of feedback in addition to information from one's supervisor. I also suggest how to hold people accountable for using feedback.

I consider ways managers become coaches and developers of their subordinates—how they establish long-term, growth-oriented relationships that enhance individual and group performance. I give special attention to ways managers use feedback to increase coordinated behavior in groups and generate win–win resolutions to conflict. I also show how goal setting permits people to get feedback about their own performance relative to their goals.

Overall, the book demonstrates how managers can be more effective in gathering and processing performance information about subordinates and feeding back this information in a way that is nonthreatening and leads to productive changes in behavior. Also, it shows how employees can gather, accept, and use meaningful performance information to change their own behavior. In doing so, the book suggests how human resource practitioners and training professionals can help managers give and use feedback more effectively.

SOME BACKGROUND

Industrial and organizational psychologists have devoted considerable atten-tion to studying and guiding formal performance appraisal processes, but less attention to feedback delivery and use. However, psychologists have long recognized the value of feedback to enhance job challenge, increase motiva-tion, and facilitate learning when the information is meaningful and given in a helpful way. Knowledge of results is a critical psychological component of motivation that stems from performance feedback inherent in the task or job. Moreover, feedback is an important element of career motivation. Insight about oneself and the environment affects the stability and direction of one's career behavior. Such insight stems from performance feedback and informa-tion about potentially fruitful career directions. Also, feedback is an important element in learning. We know that people learn by modeling others, trying new behavior, and receiving feedback on how well they are doing.

Despite these potential positive benefits of feedback, an extensive analysis of research on feedback programs found that on average, feedback interven-tions have only a moderately positive effect on performance (Kluger & DeNisi, 1986). Thirty-eight percent of the effects found in the literature were negative! Kluger and DeNisi (1996) theorized that the negative findings occurred when managers gave feedback that threatened their self-esteem and generated a defensive reaction. Feedback works well when it informs employ-ees about their behaviors and shows them what they need to do differently to improve. Also, feedback is motivating when it evaluates employees' perform-ance and reinforces their positive behaviors (e.g., it says, "You're doing well. Keep up the good work!"). However, feedback that focuses on employees' personal characteristics ("You're not smart enough to do this job" or "You need to work as hard as Fred") focuses employees' attention on themselves rather than on their behavior. This is distracting, to say the least, and invites defensiveness. This also suggests that some managers do not know how to give constructive feedback.

That people do not like to give negative feedback is not surprising. They know that the recipient is likely to be defensive or hurt. However, many people avoid even patting others on the back for good performance. Some managers seem to feel embarrassed or threatened about giving favorable feedback that a subordinate or coworker deserves. Employees sometimes request feedback, but they usually do not do so when the results are likely to be negative and they cannot avoid accepting blame.

Unfortunately, many managers do not know how to give feedback, let alone how to coach and develop subordinates. Some do not even see giving feedback as part of their jobs. Indeed, they may view performance discussions as a distraction from day-to-day operations. They decry the expense of individual development that may result from feedback discussions, and they fear losing an employee's loyalty and friendship from negative feedback. Managers' reluctance to give feedback is especially problematic in organizations faced with tight resources and employee cutbacks. Standards of performance are increasing in these firms, and more and higher quality work is expected of everyone who remains. Marginal performance cannot be tolerated for long.

Elements of Feedback

Performance information may be *objective*, resulting from clearly visible performance output. Moreover, the amount and type of information may be under the control of the performers who can select the information they want about how well they are doing. On the other hand, performance information may be *subjective*, arising from formal and informal evaluations made by others. Such information may be sought deliberately by the performer. Or it may be delivered by the performer's supervisor or coworkers even when it is not sought and may even be unwelcome. The performer may be receptive or defensive depending on factors such as the favorability of the feedback, the source's intention to be constructive, and the performer's self-confidence. The source's willingness to give feedback depends on factors such as the source's ability to communicate, the source's comfort with giving a performance evaluation face to face or in writing, and the source's ability and desire to coach the performer in using the information to improve performance. Giving feedback may also depend on organizational expectations to deliver perform-ance feedback as part of the management process.

Unfortunately, feedback has its dark side. For instance, managers may avoid giving feedback or may deliberately give destructive feedback. I cover the psychological, social, and situational antecedents of these all too common occurrences. I show how people give and seek feedback in ways that manage others' impressions of them. I relate destructive feedback to harassment and other forms of treatment abuse and discrimination on the job. I show how to encourage constructive feedback and develop functional feedback and growth-oriented interpersonal relationships and discourage destructive feedback and dysfunctional interpersonal relationships.

Human Resource Programs

Mindful of human resource practice, I present examples of feedback methods integrated with different appraisal techniques. I also offer guidelines for improving the value of feedback and its use by recipients. This should help managers who struggle with the difficulty of discussing another's performance face to face with the individual. I show how improved feedback processes can be integrated into more effective and comprehensive human performance systems.

Psychological and organizational barriers that intervene in giving effective feedback are discussed. I show how to design feedback systems for collecting reliable and telling information about performance from multiple sources and viewpoints, and I present ideas for program development that can be used in managerial assessment and training.

The book is intended to be valuable for designing employee development programs, training supervisors in performance management, establishing more challenging jobs, building an integrated human performance system, and creating environments that enhance employees' career motivation. The book covers ways to provide interdependent group members with information that increases their coordination and cooperation. I also demonstrate how to hold managers accountable for giving and using feedback.

OVERVIEW OF THE BOOK

The book is divided into five sections: (a) characteristics of feedback, (b) sources of feedback, (c) giving feedback, (d) using feedback, and (e) ways to enhance the effectiveness of feedback.

The first section draws on theory and research to build a foundation for later chapters. Specifically, chapter 2 outlines a model to understand the antecedents and consequences of effective and ineffective feedback. The model focuses on characteristics of the source, recipient, and situation that affect how information is conveyed, received, and used. The model considers both feedback *content* (for instance, its favorability and specificity) and feedback *process* (e.g., how and when it is given). This approach applies basic social psychological theories on person perception and information processing to feedback processes between two individuals, between one individual and a group, and between groups. The approach also draws on literature about interpersonal expectations—how sources generate self-fulfilling prophecies and how recipients regulate their own behavior to prove or disprove others' opinions. In addition, the approach considers such processes as evaluation apprehension, self-image development, and self-attributions in seeking and accepting feedback.

In chapter 3, I explain how people receive and use feedback about themselves and how they process information about others. I outline the cognitive processes of how people encode, store, and decode information prior to giving feedback. In addition, I describe how rater motivation, observation skills, perceptual biases, and empathy for others influence rater accuracy.

The section on feedback sources begins with chapter 4's review of traditional supervisor performance appraisal rating and multisource feedback surveys. The chapter shows how different rating methods and performance appraisal systems encourage the supervisor to be a coach and developer of employees rather than a monitor and judge. I emphasize the employee's responsibility for the appraisal and using the feedback for development and performance improvement.

Chapter 5 considers other systematic sources of feedback: assessment centers, computerized assessment, simulations, and organizational analyses. These methods give employees the opportunity to learn about themselves and experiment with new behaviors.

Section C turns to giving feedback. In chapter 6, I explain what it means to be an effective coach and developer. I show how some organizations reward these roles while others discourage them. Organizations that train and reward managers in how to coach and develop subordinates are likely to be more successful than organizations that ignore or actually punish managers who pay attention to subordinates' development.

The seventh chapter covers effective ways to give feedback. I show how people can improve their observation skills, become more accurate raters, and be more supportive and constructive in giving feedback.

Chapter 8 focuses on the performance management process and, in particular, the performance review discussion between supervisor and subordinate. I outline steps for conducting the review and then discuss some recommendations, such as linking feedback to goal setting, separating the salary and development discussions, using self-appraisals, and eliminating grading. The chapter concludes with a section on how to manage marginal performers.

Section D examines how employees use feedback. Chapter 9 considers how people react to informal sources of feedback that come from one-on-one discussion and observation. I discuss feedback seeking and its relationship to managing the impressions others have of us. I suggest how to ask for and receive constructive and meaningful feedback.

Recognizing how people react to feedback, chapter 10 considers how to create an organizational culture that encourages receiving and using feedback. This includes fostering self-assessment as a way to help individuals compare themselves to others and evaluate themselves relative to performance standards and expectations. I give special attention to multisource feedback and self-ratings as methods to enhance employees' sensitivity to, and ability to take advantage of, feedback from others.

The final section outlines ways to improve the usefulness of feedback. Chapter 11 considers a frequently used but little understood concept—accountability. The chapter describes forces and mechanisms that increase managers' accountability for giving and using feedback. Also, it suggests interventions to enhance accountability to different sources of feedback.

In the last chapter, I describe how feedback can be beneficial in changing work settings. I discuss issues surrounding electronic performance monitoring technologies and open learning methods that allow people to direct their own learning at their own pace. I consider cross-cultural and diversity training and the learning demands of new jobs and work group structures. Overall, I show why giving and receiving constructive feedback will continue to be important to individual performance and organizational success.

In summary, this book shows the value of meaningful feedback. Feedback is an important component in job design, career motivation, self-assessment, and self-concept development. Feedback is important to managing in times of increasing organizational complexity. It is important for strong self-esteem and accurate attributions of positive and negative outcomes. Also, it is vital for effective performance management—directing behavior, overcoming marginal performance, and reinforcing excellent performance.

I

CHARACTERISTICS
OF FEEDBACK

2

How and Why Feedback Works

Consider some facts about feedback. Feedback is the information people receive about their performance. It conveys information about behaviors, and it conveys an evaluation about the quality of those behaviors. Giving feedback is "the activity of providing information to staff members about their perform-ance on job expectations" (Hillman, Schwandt, & Bartz, 1990). Feedback is an important part of the educational process. Test grades let students know what they have achieved and what they have to learn to do better next time. People at work give feedback to reinforce others' good behavior and correct their poor behavior. The recipient of feedback judges its value and determines whether to accept and act on the feedback, reject it, or ignore it. Feedback has different purposes at different career stages. It helps newcomers learn the ropes, midcareer workers to improve performance and consider opportunities for development, and late career employees to maintain their productivity. Managers are an important source of feedback because they establish perform-ance objectives and provide rewards for attaining those objectives. Other sources of feedback are coworkers, subordinates, and customers.

This chapter, reprinted in part from an article I wrote on giving feedback (London, 1995b), describes why people feel uncomfortable about feedback. I consider the benefits of feedback and provide some initial suggestions for ensuring that feedback is worthwhile. I draw on the scientific literature to learn about the characteristics of feedback, feedback providers, and feedback recipients that may determine whether feedback is effective. Finally, I distin-guish between constructive and destructive feedback purposes, styles, and behavior.

FEELINGS ABOUT FEEDBACK

Consider how you respond to feedback. Would you agree with the following statements (from Fedor, Rensvold, & Adams, 1992)?

- I like being told how well I am doing on a project.

- Even though I may think I have done a good job, I feel a lot more confident after someone else tells me so.
- Even when I think I could have done something better, I feel good when other people think well of what I have done.
- It is very important for me to know what people think of my work.

Now, do you perceive a risk in asking for feedback? Consider how you would respond to the following items (from Ashford, 1986).

- I think my boss would think worse of me if I asked him or her for feedback.
- I would be nervous about asking my boss how he or she evaluates my behavior.
- It is not a good idea to ask my coworkers for feedback; they might think I am incompetent.
- It is embarrassing to ask my coworkers for their impression of how I am doing at work.
- It would bother me to ask my boss for feedback.
- It is not a good idea to ask my boss for feedback; he or she might think I am incompetent.
- It is embarrassing to ask my boss for feedback.
- I think my coworkers would think worse of me if I asked them for feedback.
- I would be nervous about asking my coworkers how they evaluate my behaviors.
- It is better to try to figure out how I am doing on my own rather than ask my coworkers for feedback.

Even someone who shies away from seeking feedback directly may still crave it. How would you respond to the following statements (from Ashford & Tsui, 1991)?

- I find myself eavesdropping on other supervisors to get different points of view about my performance.
- I pay close attention to how my supervisor acts toward me to figure out where I stand.
- I keep my ears open in case my supervisor has any more information about my performance.
- I pay close attention to the feedback my supervisor gives to my coworkers in my group.

Feedback is a touchy issue in organizations. Of course, people like being told when they are doing well, but they probably do not take the risk to request feedback unless they are pretty sure the information will be positive. Indeed, they may ask for feedback in a way that ensures they only get favorable information. In general, people are apprehensive about being evaluated. They fear failure, and they would just as soon not know what others think of their performance rather than receive painful information even if it could help them. Learning from feedback often requires overcoming a mental block—the tendency to rationalize, ignore, or avoid feedback.

Many people feel the same way about giving feedback as they do about receiving it. Some managers see little practical value in the performance feedback discussion. They foresee primarily aversive consequences from giving negative feedback (Napier & Latham, 1986). Managers generally view the feedback discussion as an unpleasant situation to be avoided, postponed, and handled hurriedly (Kopelman, 1986; Meyer, 1991). So unless they want to deliberately abuse someone, they shy away from giving negative feedback. They know it puts the receiver on the defensive and leads to an uncomfortable situation at best. Being tactful and clear at the same time is difficult. They may also feel embarrassed about giving positive feedback. Feeling they are laying bare inner feelings; they worry that they will be perceived as ingratiating. They may believe that saying something positive now makes it harder to say something negative later. Or they fear that the receiver will expect a reward they cannot provide.

Consider a few examples. Some of these are examples of feedback in action, some represent failures in feedback giving, some represent desire for feedback, and some represent problems of *not* giving feedback.

- A sales manager who recently lost his job in the latest company down-sizing asked his boss, "Why me?" The boss gave him several examples of customers who had complained. The manager wondered why his boss did not mention these problems earlier.
- A supervisor wanted to let a subordinate know he did a great job on the project, but she did not want the subordinate to expect a raise the supervisor could not provide. So she did not say anything at all about the subordinate's performance.
- A graphic designer liked working with a particular client because the client was clear about what she liked and did not like. The client was usually satisfied, and told the designer so. Other clients would accept a job with little comment. But some of them would not return with new business, and the designer was never sure why.
- A company started a new program that asked subordinates and coworkers to rate every manager each year. However, managers tended to ignore the feedback reports. They did not have a chance to rate top management, and they saw no reason why they should pay attention to how their subordinates evaluated them.
- A young manager with only 2 years experience after college felt she should have a clearer career direction. She wished she had a plan that would move her ahead in the business. She did not know what kind of

future she had with the company. She envied a colleague in another department who had frequent discussions with her manager about career opportunities. Her friend had a good idea of what she would have to do to be promoted, and she even had a career plan that indicated the types of assignments she should have during the next 5 years.

- One of the first lessons learned by newly appointed members to a quality improvement team was that total quality management requires data on customer satisfaction. The team developed indexes of performance quality and a tracking mechanism to collect and analyze the information.
- Self-managing work teams in an automobile parts plant reviewed their production data at the end of each day. They tracked results weekly to evaluate fluctuations in performance and test the effectiveness of improvement methods.
- Negotiation team members in a labor dispute met after each bargaining session to discuss the opposing team's reactions to offers and counteroffers presented during the session.

These examples show that performance feedback comes in many forms. Moreover, feedback is important to individual and group performance. Now consider *why* it works.

BENEFITS OF FEEDBACK

Research on feedback indicates a number of reasons why it is so important to enhancing work outcomes. Feedback has the following effects (based on literature reviews by Ilgen, Fisher, & Taylor, 1979; Larson, 1984; London, 1988; and Nadler, 1979):

1. Feedback directs behavior; that is, it keeps goal-directed behavior on course.

2. Feedback influences future performance goals, essentially creating objectives for achieving higher levels of performance in the future. Employees know what they can do well, and how much better than can do if they try harder.

3. Positive feedback is reinforcing in and of itself. Even if it does not lead to some material outcome, such as more money, people appreciate knowing when they have done well. Such feedback heightens their sense of achievement and internal motivation.

4. Feedback increases employees' abilities to detect errors on their own. They know what performance elements are important and what levels of performance are expected. As such, feedback sets standards of performance, and employees learn to evaluate themselves against these standards.

5. Feedback enhances individual learning. Employees realize what they need to know and what they need to do to improve. Seeking self-knowledge is a prerequisite for, and motivator of, growth and improvement.

6. Feedback increases motivation by demonstrating what behaviors contribute to successful performance.

7. Feedback helps people clarify their beliefs about the effects of their behavior. They learn the extent to which their good behavior contributes to rewards and their poor behavior contributes to being deprived of these rewards or being punished in some way. They also learn what aspects of the situation beyond their control influences these outcomes.

8. Feedback increases the salience of the information and the importance of the feedback process. People used to receiving feedback learn to seek it out. Also, they know how to ask for feedback they can use. In a group setting, feedback focuses group members' attention on the same performance elements and provides all group members with a common perspective. This is helpful when group members depend on each other to complete the task, have different roles, and want their teammates to like them.

9. Feedback increases in the amount of power and control employees feel. This applies to both the source of feedback and the recipient. Providers of feedback understand how information can improve others' performances. Recipients of feedback recognize how information helps them take control of their own performance. Regular feedback helps them feel they can cope with performance problems by being able to make incremental changes in their behavior and see the effects.

10. Feedback increases employees' feelings of involvement in the task. They recognize how they contribute to the task, and they feel a sense of task ownership and importance.

11. Feedback about individual performance coupled with information about environmental conditions and opportunities helps employees form a career identity that is challenging and potentially rewarding.

12. In negotiations, feedback is a mechanism for evaluating offers.

13. In decision making, feedback about the results of the decision helps groups and individuals recognize cognitive biases (e.g., the tendency to overly weigh information that is worded negatively) and avoid these biases in the future.

In summary, feedback has value because it directs and motivates behavior. It has reward value in and of itself. It provides paths for career development. It contributes to increased self-awareness and willingness to engage in self-assessment. It enhances supervisor–subordinate relationships, fosters group development, and improves service quality and customer responsiveness. However, the benefits of feedback depend a great deal on how the feedback is delivered. In the next section of the chapter, I offer some advice for giving feedback.

EFFECTIVE FEEDBACK

Despite the potential advantages of feedback, it is not automatically beneficial. Certain conditions improve its usefulness. The literature suggests dimensions for effective, constructive feedback:

1. Feedback should be clear and easily understood. Moreover, it should be interpreted similarly by the source and recipient. The recipient should not leave the meeting thinking that the feedback was positive when the source meant the feedback to be constructive directions for improvement.

2. The content of the feedback should be specific and easily understood. It should take into account the recipient's ability to comprehend and absorb the information. Too much information or data that are too complex may be distorted, ignored, or misunderstood.

3. Feedback should be frequent. Giving feedback should be a common practice, not an unusual occurrence that seems to have momentous implications. Moreover, it should be timely so that the recipient knows just what behaviors and performance outcomes are in question. Feedback should occur immediately, or at least soon, after the behavior or performance about which feedback is given.

4. Feedback should be relevant to elements of performance that contribute to task success and that are under the recipient's control. For instance, information to help group members work together more effectively should deal with group process, such as information about interpersonal relations or climate.

5. Feedback should come from a credible source—one that is taken seriously and believed to be accurate. Recipients will have a difficult time denying or ignoring such information.

6. In some cases, the source of feedback should be confidential. This is true especially if the source is dependent on the recipient (as subordinates are on their supervisor).

7. Feedback should be accompanied by explanation and use so the recipient understands the source of the feedback and how it can be applied to improve task performance. The source of the feedback should not take it for granted that the recipient will know what to do with the feedback. Also, support mechanisms should be available to help the recipient profit from the feedback. These may include training or special job assignments that allow the recipient to practice and improve.

Understandably, supervisors are hesitant to give poor performance feedback to subordinates they like. Poor performing subordinates receive less feedback than high performing subordinates (Larson, 1986). However, when managers give poor performance feedback, they tend to be more specific than when they give positive performance feedback in order to be as helpful as possible to the poor performer. Managers delay evaluating and giving feedback to moderately low performers, and they evaluate them with more positive distortion than they evaluate moderately high performers (Benedict & Levine, 1988). *Positive distortion* includes selective transmission of bad news by providing only neutral messages and avoiding unpleasant portions. Inflating the ratings decreases the possibility that feedback will be negatively received. Moreover, distortion increases when the raters feel they will be publicly accountable for the feedback (i.e., subordinates know who is giving the negative feedback).

In general, people are more willing to give feedback and guide its effective use when the recipient can control the results, the results are positive, the source and recipient get along well, and the source and recipient agree (Larson, 1984). Also, people are more willing to give feedback when the information is salient (perceived to be important by the recipient and source), the feedback is tied to organizational rewards such as a pay raise, the source of feedback is dependent on the recipient in some way (e.g., for excellent performance), the source is responsible for providing the data (it is in the source's job description), and there are positive norms in the organization for giving feedback (e.g., other managers do it and it is widely accepted as part of the management role).

The Source's Reactions

Feedback is a dynamic process between source and recipient, and giving feedback affects the source as well as the recipient (Larson, 1984). For instance, supervisors say that they like subordinates to whom they give positive feedback and dislike subordinates to whom they give negative feedback. Also, giving feedback may increase the ease with which supervisors recall specifics about subordinates' behavior. In addition, giving feedback may increase supervisors' feelings of control over subordinates, especially if subordinates actually improve their performance. However, supervisors may perceive they have less control over subordinates if the feedback is followed by declines in performance.

Subordinates realize when their supervisors prefer to avoid giving negative feedback. Employees who believe they are performing poorly use feedback seeking strategies that minimize negative performance feedback as a way of maintaining their positive self-esteem (Larson, 1988). As a consequence, they receive less negative feedback than may be warranted. This makes worse an already poor relationship between the supervisor and subordinate. As the performance problem persists, the supervisor is likely to see it as more severe, and the supervisor becomes increasingly angry and resentful toward the subordinate (Baron, 1988). When the feedback is public, supervisors will try to be consistent, making it harder to correct the situation by giving accurate feedback.

CONSTRUCTIVE AND DESTRUCTIVE FEEDBACK

Constructive feedback is specific and considerate (Baron, 1988). It attributes poor performance to external causes, such as situational factors beyond the subordinate's control. Also, constructive feedback attributes good performance to internal causes, such as the subordinate's effort and ability. This assumes, of course, that these attributions are appropriate. The feedback does not blame people for negative outcomes that are not their fault, and it recognizes people for their accomplishments. When a problem or weakness is evident, suggestions are made for improvement. Sample statements from the feedback source include "I think there's a lot of room for improvement," "You did the best you could under the circumstances," or "You should give more attention to . . . " *Destructive* feedback is the obverse, including general comments about performance, an inconsiderate tone, poor performance attributed to internal factors, and possibly threats. The feedback source might say, "You didn't even try," "You can't seem to do anything right," or "If you don't improve, I'll get someone else to do it."

In several laboratory studies, Baron reported that undergraduates receiving destructive feedback expressed lower self-efficacy on subsequent tasks than those receiving constructive feedback (Baron, 1988). Destructive feedback led subordinates to feel more anger and tension and to report that they would handle future disagreements with the source of feedback through resistance and avoidance instead of collaboration and compromise. Further, Baron found that employees believed that poor use of criticism was a more important cause of conflict than some other factors, such as competition over resources or disputes over jurisdiction. Later research found that trainees who received feedback that attributed their performance to factors within their control had higher task efficacy and improved learning (Martocchio & Dulebohn, 1994).

Abusive Behavior

We can learn about the nature and effects of destructive feedback from studies of abusive behavior (cf. Bassman, 1992). Although abuse in the workplace may not be as blatant as that in other settings, it still occurs and can be destructive to employees' careers and self-esteem. Moreover, it may take the form of illegal behavior (e.g., sexual harassment or treatment discrimination). Profiles of domestic abusers include feelings of being weak and powerless (Fleming, 1979). They are unable to tolerate frustration, have a low level of impulse control, frequently are overly emotionally dependent on their victim, and exhibit excessive jealousy. They have two sides to their personality: a nice person to the outside world (the pillar of the community) while exercising a form of domestic terrorism at home. Couples who deal ineffectively with conflict use aversive control strategies (e.g., criticism) as ineffectual ways to alter each other's behavior. Abusive, destructive behavior is learned, and often abusers come from families with a history of similar behavior.

This pattern may also hold for abusers in the workplace including supervisors who give abusive feedback. The supervisor's power may lead the supervisor to manipulate the subordinate, losing sight of the subordinate's feelings and abilities. The hierarchical power of the organization means that supervisors who harass subordinates are in control of a variety of resources. This makes abused employees similar to other victims of abuse (Bassman, 1992). The victim's oppositional or succumbing reactions reinforce the abuser, creating a gradually escalating series of punishing behaviors. Such a cycle may apply to supervisors who are insecure about their own power. Powerless authority figures use coercive methods to provoke resistance and aggression. This prompts them to become even more coercive, controlling, and restrictive (Kanter, 1977). Such aversive control strategies tend to multiply over time and tend to be reciprocated, resulting in long-term costs and dysfunctional relationships (Jacobson & Margolin, 1979).

Examples of Constructive and Destructive Feedback

Table 2.1 lists examples of behaviors associated with constructive and destructive feedback. The behaviors depend on the nature of the relationship between supervisor and subordinate. In the table, I distinguish between three types of relationships: those characterized primarily by control, reward, or affiliation. In *control-dominated relationships*, the supervisor's motivation is to control, or be in a position of power over, the subordinate. In *reward-dominated relationships*, the supervisor uses available rewards to affect the subordinate's behavior. In *affiliation-dominated relationships*, the supervisor wants to maintain a friendly relationship with the subordinate. Each of these dominant role relationships helps us understand different types of constructive and destructive feedback. Keep in mind that negative feedback can be constructive or destructive depending on how it is presented. Positive feedback may be destructive under some circumstances, for instance, if the value of the positive behavior is minimized or undervalued by the source.

Characteristics of control include power, negotiation, demeanor, tone, and values. The source's intention in constructive, control-dominated relationships is to empower the recipient and concentrate on ways they can both win. The source is respectful and patient and adheres to the *Golden Rule*: "Do unto others as you would have them do unto you." The source's intention in destructive, control-dominated relationships is to be domineering. The source behaves as if this were a zero sum game in which only the source or recipient can win and one of them must lose. The source is curt and expects the recipient to "Do as I say, not as I do."

Characteristics of reward-dominated relationships are behavior continuity, confidence building, evaluation/reward, attribution, timing, and focus. The source's intention in constructive, reward-dominated relationships is to encourage and reinforce a can-do attitude. The source praises the recipient, attributing favorable outcomes to the recipient's behavior and ability and negative outcomes to environmental factors beyond the recipient's control. Feedback is given soon after the behavior occurs, and the focus is the task itself. The source's intention in destructive, reward-dominated relationships is to discourage the recipient. The recipient's confidence is diminished, if not

TABLE 2.1
Feedback Characteristics and Behaviors

Feedback Characteristics	Feedback Intention	
	Constructive	*Destructive*
Control-Dominated Relationships		
Power	Empower	Domineer
Negotiation stance	Win-win	Win-lose
Demeanor	Show respect	Confront
Tone	Be patient	Be curt
Values	Enact the Golden Rule	"Do as I say, not as I do"
Reward-Dominated Relationships		
Behavior continuity	Encourage	Discourage
Confidence building	Have a can-do attitude	Belittle/Disparage/Ridicule/ Demean/Use name calling
Evaluation/ Reward	Positively reinforce Praise	Negatively reinforce Withhold positive rewards
Favorable attribution	Attribute internally	Attribute externally
Negative attribution	Attribute externally	Attribute internally
Timing	"Do it now" (immediately)	Delay/procrastinate
Focus	Focus on task	Focus on person
Affiliation-Dominated Relationships		
Expression of feelings	Be controlled	Vent emotions
Communication	Be open Encourage two-way communication Be clear Communicate face-to-face	Be close lipped or engage in one-way communication Be confusing Be indirect Communicate "behind-the-back"
Revealing self	Be self-disclosive	Be self-protective
Bias	Provide fair and equal treatment Give more attention	Be unfair Discriminate Withhold attention
Overall		
Focus	Focus on recipient	Focus on self
Behavior	Be tolerant and patient Be supportive	Be intolerant and impatient Be abusive
Rationality	Make decisions that are clear and logical ("20-20" rationality)	Make decisions that are confused or misguided (corrective "lens" needed)

destroyed, through belittling, disparagement, ridicule, and demeaning words and actions (e.g., labeling or name calling). Positive reinforcement is withheld and negative reinforcement is given. Favorable outcomes are attributed to external causes whereas negative outcomes are attributed to the recipient's behavior or ability. Feedback is delayed and the focus is on the recipient as a person rather than the task.

Characteristics of affiliation-dominated relationships are expression of feelings and, more generally, communication. The source's intention in constructive, support-dominated relationships is a controlled expression of their feelings. Communication is open, two-way, clear, frequent, and face-to-face. The source reveals information about him or herself as a way to gain confidence and trust and provide a level playing field for honest discussion of the recipient's strengths and weaknesses. The source strives to be fair and treat recipients equally. The source provides the recipient with considerable attention and may deliberately or unwittingly increase or foster learning (a positive Pygmalian effect; Eden, 1992). The source's intention in destructive, support-dominated relationships is to vent, personally benefiting from emotional catharsis regardless of its effects on the recipient. Communication is closed and one-way. Messages are oblique and confusing. In general, communication is infrequent and indirect. Feedback is given indirectly by talking behind the recipient's back. The source is self-protective and secretive about his or her own characteristics, not wanting to reveal information that may suggest weaknesses and lack of dependability. The source discriminates unfairly in evaluating and providing information to recipients, demonstrating personal biases that are unrelated to the needs of the task or organizations. The source provides the recipient with little attention and may deliberately or unwittingly prevent learning (a negative Pygmalian effect; Oz & Eden, 1994).

Characteristics of all types of relationships (whether based on control, reward, or affiliation) are focus, behavior, and rationality. Constructive relationships are typified by the source's focus on the recipient of the feedback. The source's behavior is tolerant and supportive. Also, the source's rationality is "20–20," meaning that the source has a reasonably accurate and complete picture of his or her feedback intentions and the recipient's likely reactions. Destructive relationships are typified by the source's focus on him or herself. The source's behavior is intolerant and, in the extreme, abusive. And the source's rationality is myopic—that is, generally shortsighted and careless as to the short- and long-term effects on the recipient. The source is likely to attribute the feedback to the welfare of the recipient ("I'm doing this to challenge the individual—get him or her moving"). "Corrective lenses" are needed to at least stop the destructive behavior and hopefully move to a more constructive mode. Such interventions, described later, may include training, a behavioral reinforcement schedule, methods to increase self-awareness, or removal from the situation.

CONCLUSION

This chapter recognized that employees do not like to give or receive feedback. Yet, feedback has many benefits in directing, motivating, and rewarding job behaviors that are important to high performance. In particular, it is critical to the goal-setting process as a way for employees to track their progress and set new goals for further achievement. I described characteristics of effective feedback and ways to avoid destructive feedback.

This chapter raises the following points:

1. People generally do not react positively to feedback. It is natural to be apprehensive about being evaluated. Also, people worry about how others will react to feedback.

2. Feedback directs, motivates, and rewards behavior. It is the basis for development and career planning. Moreover, it contributes to building effective interpersonal relationships.

3. Effective feedback is clear, specific, frequent, and relevant to important job behaviors.

4. Feedback is a dynamic process between source and recipient. Also, giving feedback affects both the source and the recipient.

5. Constructive feedback attributes poor performance to external causes, such as situational factors beyond the subordinate's control, when the external attribution is warranted. That is, it does not blame people for negative outcomes that are not their fault. Also, constructive feedback attributes good performance to internal causes, such as the subordinate's effort and ability. That is, it recognizes when an individual should be praised for positive outcomes.

6. Destructive feedback is abusive. Although the word "abusive" may seem extreme as a description of workplace behavior, it occurs, and can be destructive to employees' careers and self-esteem.

7. The nature of the boss–subordinate relationship determines how feedback is manifest. Constructive feedback in control-dominated relationships empowers the recipient and concentrates on ways the recipient and source can both win. It increases the recipient's sense of independence and self-control. In reward-dominated relationships, it encourages and reinforces a can-do attitude. It increases goal clarity and challenges the recipient to do better or overcome disabilities or barriers on their own. In affiliation/support-dominated relationships, it allows a controlled expression of feelings. It leads to increased mutual trust and confidence.

The next chapter provides the foundation for a better understanding of feedback. It examines factors that influence how people process information about themselves and develop a self-concept.

3

Processing Information About Ourselves and Others

This chapter explains how people receive and use feedback about themselves and how they process information about others. I draw on research in psychology that explains the accuracy of interpersonal perceptions. (For an in-depth review of this literature, see London, 1995c, chapters 3, 4, and 6.) I consider the cognitive processes of how people encode, store, and decode information prior to giving feedback. Also, I show how rater motivation, observation skills, information distorting biases, and empathy for others influence rater accuracy.

SELF-INSIGHTS ABOUT HOW WE EVALUATE OTHERS

In general, people do not have a good idea about how they form impressions of others (Reilly & Doherty, 1989; Slovic & Lichenstein, 1971). For instance, research shows low relationships between the attributes interviewers say are important in evaluating job candidates and those that are derived from statistical analyses (correlations of a rater's evaluations of a ratee on a series of performance dimensions with the rater's evaluations of the ratee's overall performance; Nisbett & Wilson, 1977). When raters are given these statistically derived weights, they develop a better understanding of how they evaluate others, and they are able to learn how to form more accurate judgments (Summers, Taliaferro, & Fletcher, 1970; Surber, 1985). Moreover, they are more insightful about the importance they place on specific performance dimensions after they have had time to practice in similar situations with clear feedback about the quality of their judgments (Reilly & Doherty, 1989; 1992). Over time, raters become fairly good at accurately identifying the weights they use and how they go about making decisions about others. They become even better after they receive an explanation about their cognitive processes when making a decision (e.g., the weights they use and why).

23

Recognition of how people evaluate others is one indicator of insight. Another is the extent to which self-perceptions match others' ratings. This is discussed next.

AGREEMENT BETWEEN FEEDBACK AND SELF-PERCEPTIONS

The gap between self-ratings and feedback from others (e.g., subordinates, peers, superiors, or customers) helps people determine the need to behave differently. People are most likely to recognize the need for change when both self and other (e.g., subordinate) ratings tend to be unfavorable. However, they may not see the need to change when feedback from others is unfavorable and self-perceptions are favorable. This is when change may be needed most, but it is also when defense mechanisms, such as denial, come into play. Managers who experience failure tend to inflate their self-ratings as a way to salvage their self-concept (McCall & Lombardo, 1983). Managers who experience success (e.g., receive a promotion) tend to agree with their coworkers assessments of them (McCauley & Lombardo, 1990). That is, they are likely to see their strengths and weaknesses in the same way that others see them. However, people who judge themselves more favorably than others do are likely to be poor performers. This happens because they do not get along with those who are rating them or they do not understand the expectations others have for their behavior. People who evaluate themselves more unfavorably than others evaluate them often have inconsistent levels of performance. They are concerned about improving their performance, but they are not likely to attempt hard tasks or set difficult goals (Bandura, 1982).

People who consistently evaluate themselves higher or lower than others rate them have little insight into their strengths and weaknesses. They are unlikely to use performance feedback to alter their self-image and behave differently (Ashford, 1989). Nevertheless, feedback can improve the accuracy of their self-image over time. Eventually, unfavorable feedback will decrease the extent to which one overestimates one's self-image (Atwater, Rousch, & Fischthal, 1992). Until that point is reached, overestimators set goals that are too high for their capabilities, thereby increasing their chances of failure. They won't see the need for training until it is too late. Underestimators—those who evaluate themselves less favorably than others see them—set goals that are too low for their capabilities. They won't get a chance to test their abilities and improve their self-concept.

Self-Assessment Accuracy

Consider the possible combinations of agreement between self-ratings and ratings from coworkers and agreement between self-ratings and objective performance indicators. Coworkers and self-evaluations might be the same but both may not agree with objective measures. This could happen when ratings by others are affected by employees' attempts to manage others' impressions of them. In another case, self-ratings may agree with objective performance indexes but not with others' ratings. This would occur because employees know themselves better than raters know them (Ashford et al., 1992).

A natural tendency is for people to over-estimate their own performance. Nevertheless, how people evaluate themselves is important to them and their employer. Self-assessments help people understand their work environments and the demands placed on them. They generally desire to evaluate themselves accurately and avoid self-delusion.

How We Think Others See Us

People tend to think others see them in the same way they see themselves (Shrauger & Shoeneman, 1979). That is, there is high agreement between how people rate themselves and how they think others rate them. However, there is less agreement between self-ratings and the way others actually rate them. People make judgments about how others evaluate them by both the feedback they receive and how they see themselves (Kenny & DePaulo, 1993). This is why people overestimate the agreement between their self-evaluations and how they think others see them. Not surprisingly, people who are more egocentric tend to think that others see them in the same way they see themselves (Fenigstein & Abrams, 1993). But if they believe that those rating them control valued rewards, such as pay raises, they are more accurate in judging how others see them (Kenny & DePaulo, 1993). Thus, supervisor ratings become more salient to employees when the organization uses the ratings to make decisions about salary increases or promotions.

Some people have very strong self-perceptions. They have the sense that others perceive them quite clearly and have good insight into their personalities. When asked to guess how others see them, these individuals think about how they see themselves. They evaluate their own performance and suppose that others will evaluate them similarly. Some people consider carefully their own performance as a way of guessing how others view them. Such observations do not necessarily change self-perceptions, but they do influence how people believe others view them. Actually, over the course of many interactions, an individual's self-perceptions are likely to influence how others see him or her. This is especially likely for people with high self-confidence who convey to others what they think of themselves in a clear and convincing way.

Other people consider how others react to them when they are asked to evaluate themselves. Rather than look inward, they look outward. These individuals are likely to develop self-evaluations that agree with others' ratings of them. In this sense, self-image is a product of the reflection people see of themselves in observing others. For these individuals too, exuding a confident self-image may cause others to see them positively, and a negative self-image may cause others to see them negatively. So, there is likely to be a dynamic interaction between self-perceptions and others' ratings.

People are able to perceive differences between others. That is, they can agree among themselves about others' behaviors. They observe the same behavior, consider the same available information, and come to the same conclusions (Fenigstein & Abrams, 1993). But people are less adept at recognizing how others see them. After all, they have a vested interest in their self-concept and in hoping that people evaluate them favorably. When they get feedback, they initially explain it in a way that agrees with their self-image. If the feedback persists in diverging from self-image, the self-image may bend in the direction of the feedback. This will happen more rapidly if the person giving the feedback is also making decisions about valued outcomes.

Feedback that is misleading, incomplete, or not accurate will have dysfunctional consequences. For example, lenient feedback to people who overestimate their performance will reinforce their positive self-image and maintain their low performance. Ambiguous or incomplete feedback to individuals with low self-image will not improve the view they have of themselves.

Personal Qualities That Influence Self-Assessment

Individual characteristics may affect how people rate themselves. For instance, intelligence, internal locus of control, and achievement orientation are positively related to the accuracy of self-evaluations (Mabe & West, 1982). People are less subject to biases in self-ratings when they are higher in intelligence, believe that they can take actions to produce positive outcomes, and desire to achieve. Biases in self-ratings include the tendencies to be lenient, attribute poor outcomes to external conditions, and the need to impress others. Introversion and being interpersonally sensitive are positively related to accuracy of self-perceptions of leadership (Rousch & Atwater, 1992). Also, leadership success tends to be positively related to realistic and less lenient self-evaluations of leadership (Bass & Yammarino, 1991).

The way people evaluate others is also associated with characteristics of the rater. Similarity between the rater and ratee on dimensions such as education, race, gender, and other elements of background are related to rating others more accurately. Not surprisingly, raters who know the ratee better are more accurate. As a result, subordinates may be better able to rate a manager's supervisory behavior than the manager's boss. In addition, there is a higher relationship between self-ratings and ratings by others in organizations that encourage supportive interpersonal relationships (e.g., evaluate managers on their teambuilding and communication skills) compared to organizations that pay little or no attention to interpersonal relationships and may even promote poor work group dynamics (e.g., through poor communication and inadequate explanation of role relationships; Yammarino & Dubinsky, 1992).

COGNITIVE MODELS
OF PERFORMANCE APPRAISAL

Principles from social cognition and cognitive psychology have been used by researchers and theorists to explain raters' cognitive processes in performance appraisal. These processes involve receiving, interpreting, and recalling information about subordinates' performance (Ilgen, Barnes-Farrell, & McKellin, 1993). Research has been helpful in the design of appraisal systems and generated better understanding of how rater characteristics foster rating accuracy. However, practitioners and researchers need to give attention to three areas: "(a) the content of cognitive variables, (b) the work group and organizational factors that influence these variables, and (c) the design of appraisal systems that incorporate cognitive principles" (Ilgen, et al., 1993, p. 362). For example, the nature of the rating environment may influence ratings. When raters feel confident that they can be open and honest without jeopardizing themselves, ratings are less likely to be lenient (Padgett & Ilgen, 1989). Such rater confidence may improve when raters are encouraged to document their observations over time prior to the rating.

Automatic Versus Careful Cognitive Processing

When raters observe behavior, they compare it to pre-conceived impressions or images (Beach, 1990). If their observations conform to their expectations, their observations are automatically categorized and not considered further. This state of mindlessness is characterized by an overreliance on categories and distinctions from the past. As a result, raters are oblivious to novel or alternative aspects of the situation (Langer, 1992). Their observations fit into an existing cognitive category, and no additional thought is needed to interpret them. However, if their expectations were not met, then they need more careful (deliberate or controlled) cognitive processing to understand the observation (Sanders, 1993). The raters then ask themselves a series of questions: Is there a need for more information? Might the observed outcomes be caused by the situation rather than the individual being evaluated? If yes, could the individual being evaluated have changed the situational conditions to alter the outcomes? The answers will determine whether or not the raters attribute the outcome to the situation or to the individual being rated. If the observation is attributed to the individual, then the favorability of the observation will affect the favorability of the evaluation. If the observation is attributed to the situation, then the favorability of the observation will not influence the favorability of the evaluation.

People placed in the task of evaluating others are likely to start with the assumption that the behavior they observe is intentional. This occurs because the rating situation focuses attention on the ratee. If the ratee is experienced, the raters assume that performance outcomes resulted from the ratee's actions, not particularities of the situation. However, experienced raters tend to recognize and take into account situational constraints that may influence performance. They also take into account the reasons the ratee gives for the performance outcome. Regardless of the reason, however, the more serious the performance outcome, the more raters are likely to attribute the outcome to the ratee rather than the situation (Mitchell & Wood, 1980; Murphy & Cleveland, 1991).

Raters' evaluations are influenced by social and situational factors. For example, a supervisor's ratings of a subordinate are likely to be more favorable when (based on Judge & Ferris, 1993):

1. The supervisor has more opportunity to observe the subordinate, and so close observation by the supervisor will motivate the subordinate to work harder.

2. The supervisor has a low span of control and so has more opportunity to know and work with the subordinate.

3. The supervisor has more experience and so has learned that unfavorable ratings are not worth the trouble they cause and that ratings are not error free.

4. The supervisor believes the subordinate's self-perception is favorable and so the supervisor feels pressure to conform to the subordinate's wishes.

5. The supervisor likes the subordinate and so would feel a sense of incongruity by giving the subordinate a low rating.

Effects of Rater Motivation on Rating Accuracy

Motivated raters are more accurate because they are more careful in paying attention, encoding, recalling, and integrating information about the ratee. In one study, giving raters a monetary reward for being more accurate increased accuracy (Salvemini, Reilly, & Smither, 1993). In this experiment, one third of the raters was offered the incentive before observing the performance of ratees on a video tape. Another third was offered the incentive after viewing the tape but before making the ratings. A third of the raters received no incentive offer. Having the incentive before making their observations increased their accuracy in rank ordering ratees. The incentive was given early enough in the evaluation process to affect the full range of cognitive precesses—attending to, encoding, and recalling behaviors. Learning about the incentive after the observations could influence only the recall and integration processes. As a result, these raters were likely to process information automatically during the attention and encoding stages, and they were not as able to recall the specifics of this information later when they were motivated to make accurate evaluations.

Encouraging Recall

Because a number of factors may decrease rater accuracy, controlling these factors may improve accuracy. For instance, if we know that rater biases and motivation affect ratings, we can attempt to eliminate the biases (or at least make raters aware of them) and enhance motivation to be accurate. Perform-ance appraisal researchers usually assume that ratings are a function of the rater's memory of specific observed behaviors and that memory and rating accuracy are positively related (Feldman, 1981). However, ratings may be based on previously formed impressions instead of memory of recent obser-vations. Therefore, the effects of preconceived impressions may be lessened if raters are requested to recall recently observed behaviors before making their ratings (Woehr & Feldman, 1993).

Effects of Rater Expertise

Expert raters are those who have been trained to avoid biases and have experience making accurate ratings. Hence, expert raters are likely to agree with each other and agree with objective performance indicators (Funder, 1987; Zalesny & Highhouse, 1992). However, experts may disagree among themselves if situational characteristics are perceived differently—for in-stance, one rater believes that situational conditions were a major determiner of performance and another rater arrives at a different conclusion. Also, the way the expert rater recalls information may depend on the rater's similarity to the ratee. Thus, experts may be subject to biases and differentially influ-enced by situational conditions. Even trained raters may make the mistake of jumping to a conclusion with little investigation (Kelley, 1972).

Attribution Biases

A common bias is attributing favorable events to ourselves and unfavorable events to factors beyond our control (Herriot, 1989). Another is believing that other people have the same expectations, beliefs, and attitudes that we do. We tend to blame our poor actions on the environment. However, when other people behave the same way, we tend to attribute the behavior to their dispositions. Generally, we underestimate the effects of situational conditions on others and overestimate dispositional factors. A reason may be that we pay attention to our environment when thinking about ourselves and pay attention to others and ignore the environment when evaluating others (Storms, 1973). Additional attributional errors include assuming mistakenly that we behave the same way regardless of the situation, believing that others face the same situational conditions that we do, and thinking that we have enough informa-tion to form an accurate evaluation.

Impression Management

People are concerned about managing the impressions that others have of them. They do this by using such strategies as ingratiation, intimidation, exemplification (i.e., being a model of exemplary behavior and dedication), supplication (supplicants try to have others pity them and help them with their troubles), and face saving (Copeland, 1993; Gardner, 1991). Trying to affect the impressions others have of us is not unreasonable. It is natural to put our best foot forward. After all, we want social approval. Also, impression management tactics can be effective. Subordinates who try to manage the impressions supervisors have of them receive higher ratings from the supervisors (Wayne & Kacmar, 1991). In addition, supervisors are less critical of subordinates who use impression management (Dobbins & Russell, 1986). People who are good at ingratiating themselves with others tend to be better liked and receive more pay raises and favorable performance appraisals than their coworkers (Gardner, 1991). Unfortunately, being overly ingratiating is likely to make a negative impression on others.

Nonverbal cues are important to the way we learn about others. Such cues include eye contact, facial expression, distance, and gestures (Gifford, 1994). Some cues are inherent in a person's being, such as race and gender, whereas other cues are transitory and under the individual's control (e.g., gestures, eye contact, and interpersonal distance). People use these cues to manage the impressions others have of them. Also, impression management includes saying things that flatter others or oneself or conform to others' opinions.

People are more likely to engage in impression management when they think it will be beneficial. So, managing a supervisor's impressions is likely to be viewed as important because supervisors control valued outcomes. However, managing subordinates' impressions is likely to be viewed as less important. This may change when subordinates are asked to provide upward ratings of the supervisor. However, if these ratings are solely for developmental purposes (that is, managers can use them to identify areas for improvement, but the ratings have no direct consequences), then managers may not try to influence the impressions their subordinates have of them. Of course, the managers may feel differently if upward feedback is incorporated into the evaluation process and used to make salary or promotion decisions about the managers.

Expected Behavior Patterns

The way we perceive others may be influenced by expected patterns of behaviors called *scripts* or *schemas*. These are well-learned behavioral sequences that comprise typical reactions to environmental conditions (Abelson, 1976). The schemas we hold about the way people behave under certain conditions tells us what information and events to monitor for feedback. The initial information we get about a person suggests relevant schema. This causes us to arrive at conclusions that influence our later perceptions. Cues that distinguish the ratee from other people are especially likely to gain our attention and prompt a schema. We are primed to use some schemas. For instance, people who view themselves as high–achieving categorize others on the basis of competence, labelling them competent or incompetent. We use schemas that fit how we feel at the moment. As a result, when we are in a good mood, we are likely to be favorably disposed to others and rate them positively. Conversely, when we are in a bad mood, we are likely to rate others more harshly.

The next section considers further how raters' characteristics influence their evaluations.

INDIVIDUAL CHARACTERISTICS AFFECTING EVALUATIONS

Our skills and personality tendencies influence how we perceive other people. This section discusses observation skills, self-monitoring tendencies (our sensitivity to the environment), and empathy as individual difference variables influencing person perception.

Observation Skills

Being a skilled observer is having the ability to understand the effects of individual characteristics, situational conditions, and the effects of situations on people (Boice, 1983). Some people are better observers than others because they are able to monitor and recall cues in various situations. Good observers generally are experienced observers, similar to the people they are observing, high in self-awareness, high in cognitive complexity, and socially intelligent. Moreover, they are able to make swift and accurate judgments of other people. Admittedly, this is not the same as acquiring an in-depth understanding of those observed, but it is enough to predict future behaviors.

Self-Monitoring

As discussed in the last chapter, high self-monitors are those who are sensitive to others' reactions to them. They have an understanding of others' behaviors. For example, high self-monitors are more accurate than low self-monitors in making judgments about others' emotions (Snyder, 1974). Being high in self-monitoring helps employees in job situations that call for interpersonal sensitivity, such as a gender-nontraditional jobs (e.g., men in the nursing field; Anderson, 1990; Anderson & Thacker, 1985). These employees must perform well, but also must show that they belong in the role. They benefit greatly from the adaptive self-presentation skills of high self-monitoring.

Empathy

Empathy is the ability to understand others' feelings and emotions. People who are high in empathy can take the perspective of others and understand the situations in which they find themselves while remaining at a social distance from those observed (Stinson & Ickes, 1992). Such individuals are able to distinguish between factors in the environment that influence a person's behavior and aspects of the person's past that influence his or her behavior. Empathy is not just a matter of intelligence. People are likely to be empathetic in understanding the emotions of those they know well. One study found that well-acquainted partners were more understanding of each other's emotions than strangers (Stinson & Ickes, 1992). This may occur because friends exchange information and disclose their feelings to each other. In addition, of course, friends have a more detailed understanding of each other's lives. They are also likely to share knowledge structures. As a result, friends are more accurate than strangers in being able to read another person's thoughts and feelings about imagined events in another place or time.

CONCLUSION

This chapter began by exploring what people know about how they evaluate others. In general, they do not know much. This led to a discussion of variables that influence agreement between self-perceptions and feedback from others. I described some cognitive models to help understand the performance appraisal process in light of possible situational constraints and motivational dynamics that influence rater accuracy. I considered how impression management influences evaluation and self-perception processes. I also considered how individual characteristics, such as observation skills and empathy, influence judgments of others.

Here are the major learning points from the chapter:

1. We are not good judges of our evaluation processes.

2. Agreement between our self-perceptions and others' perceptions of us is important because we are more likely to change our behavior when we accept others' evaluations of our weaknesses. Our self-perceptions tend to agree substantially with the way we believe others see us. However, agreement between our self-perceptions and the way we are actually viewed by others is much lower. Nevertheless, self-perceptions can change with direct feedback.

3. Cognitive processes of person perception indicate that when we observe another's performance, we compare it to our expectations. If our expectations are met, we automatically process and categorize the information, and the observation is not considered further. If our expectations are violated, we initiate more controlled and thoughtful processing that may lead to a change in our perspective and evaluation of the individual.

4. Our evaluations of others will be more accurate and probably more favorable when we have had more time to observe them.

5. Our skills and personality tendencies may influence how we perceive other individuals. However, although appraisals tend to be biased, they can be made more accurate with the right support.

6. In asking for and giving feedback we intentionally or unintentionally manage the impressions other have of us.

7. Our observation skills, self-monitoring tendencies (sensitivity to the environment), and empathy affect how we evaluate others. Observations skills can be learned and improved.

The next chapter begins a review of sources of feedback. These are ways organizations provide feedback formally and informally, and ways individuals should consider in their search for constructive feedback.

II

SOURCES OF FEEDBACK

4

Appraisals and Evaluation Surveys

Feedback can come from any number of sources. It can come directly from the tasks we do as we track the pace and quality of our work. It can come from reports, such as monthly sales figures. It also can come from other people—supervisors, subordinates, peers, and customers. This chapter concentrates on this latter source. I describe formal sources of subjective feedback—in particular, the traditional supervisor performance appraisal rating, multisource feedback, and survey feedback (employee attitude surveys). I describe ratingless appraisals as a way to encourage the supervisor to be a coach and counselor rather than a judge. Also, I cover self-assessment as a way to highlight the employee's responsibility for performance tracking and using the feedback for development and improvement.

PERFORMANCE APPRAISAL DYNAMICS

The supervisor is the traditional source of performance appraisal and feedback. Most organizations require at least annual appraisals. The appraisal process usually entails a feedback discussion. During the discussion, the supervisor explains the appraisal to the subordinate and asks for the subordinate's signature to attest that the appraisal was explained to the subordinate (not that the subordinate necessarily agrees with the appraisal). Some appraisal forms may provide space for the subordinate to write his or her own opinion.

Perceptions of Fairness

Organizational norms may influence the extent to which employees are concerned about rating each other fairly. Such norms of reciprocity occur when, for instance, subordinates who get favorable feedback from their manager feel obligated to rate the manager favorably on upward feedback. Midlevel managers who rate their bosses and their subordinates and are rated by both in a multisource rating program may create a "Golden Rule" response

37

set. That is, they may rate others as fairly (or highly) as they hope to be rated. This may inflate their ratings of their bosses and decrease the leniency of their self-ratings.

Rating Formats

The traditional rating form consists of a series of items, each of which is rated on a numerical scale with scale points described by adjectives, such as *very good* or *exceeds expectations*. Considerable research attention has been given to rating formats in an effort to find procedures that yield the most accurate ratings. Consider the difficulty of the performance appraisal task: "Raters are faced with observing, storing, recalling, integrating, and judging the effectiveness of behaviors for a number of ratees. Finally, they must translate this judgment onto a rating scale" (Steiner, Rain, & Smalley, 1993, p. 438). Compound this with rater biases, lack of enthusiasm, and the time period covered by the review. Rater inaccuracies and disagreement among raters evaluating the same individual are not surprising under these circumstances.

The fewest rating errors occur when scale formats include concrete, behavioral descriptions that are understandable, observable, and important to the job. Items that are general, focused on personal characteristics, unclear, judgmental, and/or not critical to the job are likely to result in the most rating errors. Rating scales that are based on job analyses with input from people doing the job are likely to be clearest and most acceptable to the raters and the recipients of the feedback. The items may be phrased as behavioral expectations—that is, what the employee could be expected to do. Or they could be behavioral observations—examples of actual employee behaviors observed by the supervisor. Figure 4.1 provides some examples of rating scales. (For more details about performance appraisal scales, see a good text in human resource management, such as Cascio, 1986).

A "Ratingless," Narrative Appraisal

Some authorities recommend eliminating grading altogether. For instance, Meyer, a former human resource executive at General Electric and later professor of psychology at the University of South Florida, believes that attaching a numerical score or overall adjectival grade (e.g., satisfactory) to the review is demeaning and unnecessary (Meyer, 1991). Any administrative actions, such as a salary increase or a promotion, communicate an overall appraisal better than a grade. To show that this is not far fetched, Table 4.1 includes some commonly asked questions and expert answers about the ratingless appraisal.

Simple Graphic Rating Scale
Circle one response for each performance category:

Quantity of   Outstanding   Above   Average Below Unacceptable
Performance: Average   Average

Quality of   Outstanding   Above   Average Below Unacceptable
Performance: Average   Average

Comments:

Behavioral Observation Rating Scale for a General Manager

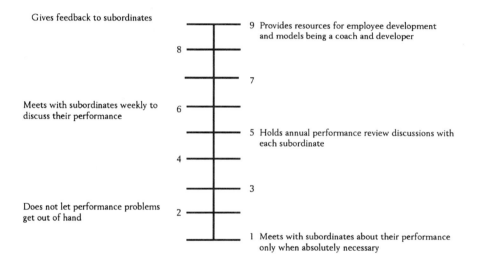

Note. Each item is scaled by an independent group of managers in the firm to fall at these points. The items provide examples of the type of behavior typical of each point on the performance scale. The rater is instructed to indicate the one number that best applies to the ratee. Other scales are constructed for other performance dimensions. A variation is the Behavioral Expectations Scale that words representative items in terms of what the ratee could be expected to do. That way, the rater does not have to have actually observed the behavior during the performance period.

Ranking System
Sometimes used in conjunction with ratings, this system asks the manager to rank order subordinates from highest to lowest. Managers in the same department at the same organizational level may meet to rank all immediate subordinates on one list. They discuss each subordinate and then attempt to agree on a rank order.

FIG. 4.1. Some examples of performance evaluation formats.

TABLE 4.1
Questions and Answers about the Ratingless Appraisal
(adapted from London, 1995b)

1. *How do we make sure poor performers are identified and addressed?*

   The narrative appraisal should be part of a larger system of performance excellence that ties together objective setting, development planning, and periodic performance review and feedback. Marginal performance will have to be identified and dealt with by addressing issues of capability and motivation, giving direct and constructive feedback, setting realistic goals and consequences, and tracking performance. The intention of the performance review is to encourage communication about performance between managers and subordinates, provide documentation, and not let performance problems slide.

2. *Do we eliminate both ratings and rankings?*

   Yes, both should be eliminated. The goal of the new process is to move away from categorizing people toward providing more detailed summaries of performance linked to specific objectives. The ratings (even without forced choice) are a crutch that is highly subjective, likely to be inconsistent across groups (e.g., "exceeding objectives" may mean different things to different managers), and not necessarily backed by solid and well-documented performance information. Encouraging the meaningful review without the rating will focus attention on performance rather than distract attention to an artificial category.

3. *How do we handle compensation under this type of system? How do we differentiate and support the compensation?*

   Compensation decisions should still be made by peer groups of managers discussing their subordinates' accomplishments. Instead of calling these "ranking and rating sessions", they might be called "performance review discussions".

   In these sessions, each manager reviews the material for each subordinate, including (a) the objectives and any changes in objectives during the year, (b) the development plans established jointly with performance objectives, (c) the periodic review and feedback sessions, and (d) the final appraisal. Points a–c can be covered quickly, with most attention given to d. (Having to recount the subordinate's performance in this way will have the side benefit of encouraging managers to carry out the objective setting/appraisal process seriously during the year and write meaningful annual reviews.)

   After all subordinates have been reviewed, the peer managers can determine a fair pay structure based on distinctions between subordinates. Several patterns of results are possible. For example:

   1. All subordinates are equally high performers and should receive the same merit treatment.
   2. The subordinates can be grouped into three or four categories. Demarcations of performance between these categories will determine if the groups should receive substantially different levels of merit pay. (After groups are established, another decision could be to pay people somewhat differently within groups.)
   3. The subordinates can be ranked ordered and a decision made about appropriate pay differentials.

TABLE 4.1 (cont.)

In my experience, the previous scenario is basically what happens anyway. The performance ratings going into the ranking and rating session help get things started, but the discussion often reveals differences in how the managers interpreted the rating categories (perhaps because of differences in standards). The ratings are rarely if ever applied in formula fashion to establish individual merit pay. The aforementioned process focuses attention on goal difficulty and accomplishments.

4. *How do we address movement, especially to an organization that uses ratings? Will our people be treated equitably?*

Given differences in standards and the subjective way that rating categories are commonly used, the ratings are not always helpful for staffing purposes. The narrative appraisals should provide far more useful information in making staffing decisions about people. Managers from departments using more appraisals will still be able to understand and interpret the narratives. If they need to, they can draw their own conclusion about what the rating would be. However, the candidate's strengths and weaknesses should be far more apparent in the narratives than could be conveyed by a single rating and the brief documentation that usually accompanies the rating. The more extensive information about employees should give a selecting manager more confidence in making decisions about them. PR folks may have a better chance in being placed elsewhere because the selecting managers will know more about them and will feel more comfortable with them.

5. *How do we align this system with those used in our extended community (i.e., other parts of the company that use traditional ratings)?*

My comments to the previous question suggest that managers in other departments will have no problem using the narrative appraisals. Indeed, they should find them more valuable than the typical rating procedure.

6. *What about dotted line relationships where there is dual reporting and different compensation systems? How do we address membership on multiple teams? What about the matrix management environment?*

This is a problem anyway. Dual reporting relationships suggest that the employee's managers need to agree on how time will be split. If the work is independent (e.g., totally different projects for each manager), then separate appraisal processes (and commensurate merit treatment) can be carried out independently by each manager. If the work is interdependent, then the managers can agree on how they will work with the employee to set goals, give feedback, and write the final appraisal. The managers may meet with the employee together, or one manager can take the lead, getting input from the other manager all along the way.

7. *How do we make sure that motivation is not negatively impacted? How do we ensure that this system will drive performance in a positive way and move the organization forward?*

A process that encourages frequent communication about objectives, development, and performance should enhance motivation and clarify linkages to company and department goals. The process can highlight any major departmental goals (e.g., customer responsiveness, quality, awareness of corporate objectives, and creativity) to ensure that these are reflected in the objectives.

TABLE 4.1 (cont.)

8. *How do you include customer input? How much should customer input be included?*

   Customer input is important and should be gathered by the manager before writing periodic performance reviews and the final appraisal. In general, input is important from multiple sources, and managers should be encouraged to contact the employee's subordinates, peers, and other departmental supervisors as appropriate to obtain information. The employee can be asked to nominate several people who are familiar with their work.

9. *Can we provide the forms in electronic process?*

   Yes. The form should cover objectives; development; periodic review and feedback; and annual narrative appraisal of performance, task evaluation, and work methods. The form has several columns allowing the manager to write an objective in the left hand column and link performance review and methods of accomplishment in the middle and right hand columns.

10. *Should appraisals be done during each project and when a project is completed? How long should they be as a guideline? What constitutes a project?*

    Frequent feedback should be encouraged, and feedback during and at the completion of the project is certainly desirable. The performance excellence process should require a review and feedback several times during the year at designated, regular intervals (e.g., once every 3 or 4 months).

    The issue of what constitutes a project might best be stated in terms of what constitutes an objective. An objective might be general (e.g., deliver high quality products on time). My feeling is that objectives can be project based but should also include a set of performance standards reflecting how the project will be carried out. So, for instance, a project might be to complete a media package for a particular department, and to do so on time in a manner that demonstrates knowledge of the client's needs.

11. *How do you do appraisals on a team, especially a self–managed team?*

    Separate guidelines for self–managed teams can be established. Generally, the team will be responsible for objective setting and review and for discussing and agreeing to each other's development plans. The team can work in a group to write the appraisals, discussing their performance and giving each other feedback in the process.

    Turning to the issue of managers evaluating team performance, a separate process can be carried out (and form completed) to establish the team's goals and review the team's performance. As usual, input would be obtained from multiple sources. The manager would meet with the team as a whole for periodic goal setting and performance reviews.

    A team appraisal might occur even if there are separate individual appraisals for each subordinate. This would depend on the extent to which subordinates work on team projects. Teams could include employees from more than one department. Team goals are established and a team award can be given as part of the compensation merit review.

12. *How do we ensure there are no surprises at the end of the year? How often should appraisals and feedback sessions be conducted?*

    Periodic feedback should ensure that there are not surprises. Reviews should occur quarterly or every 4 months.

TABLE 4.1 (cont.)

13. *What is the linkage to on-going feedback and on-going development? How do you ensure that managers are held accountable for the development of subordinates? How do we measure the development? How much input should come from the subordinates?*

As evident from responses to earlier questions, I envision a complete process that ties together objectives, development, and on-going feedback. One of the objectives of a manager's job should be developing subordinates. As such, managers should be evaluated on how well they carry out the goal setting and performance review process and how much attention they give to their subordinates' professional growth and development (to do better on their current jobs, prepare for anticipated changes in job requirements, and/or prepare for other jobs in line with their career interests and corporate needs).

14. *How do we communicate the roll out of this program to the employee body?*

Roll out should have several components: announcement from the senior vice president in the form of a memo and/or video message; a memo/brochure describing the process; half-day orientation meetings (i.e., training workshop) to discuss the principles of the programs, policies and procedures, expectations, and examples of constructive meaningful narrative appraisals and poor narratives; the orientation can be delivered by departmental managers (a good developmental experience for managers who are part of a fast track advancement program); and a video of the training can be made for new entrants to the department.

Self-Appraisals

Meyer (1991) pointed out the value of incorporating self-appraisals into the performance appraisal discussion. The subordinate takes the lead in the appraisal process. The supervisor's role is to give the employee recognition and suggest changes in behaviors or activities. He wrote:

> The appraisal feedback interview is a very authoritarian procedure—a parent–child type of exchange. Most modern organizations are moving away from authoritarian management toward an involvement-oriented working environment. A performance review discussion based on the subordinate's self review fits an involvement-oriented climate much better than the traditional top-down performance review discussion. It also has the advantage of forcing the manager into a counseling mode, rather than serving as a judge. Research has shown that performance review discussions based on self-review prove to be more productive and satisfying than traditional manager-initiated appraisal discussions. (Meyer, 1991, p. 68)

Supervisors are likely to need training in how to be a "counselor" and react to problems, such as how to deal with subordinates who have an inflated self-evaluation or, conversely, an unnecessarily self-deprecating view.

Meyer recommended that the conventional, one-way approach to feedback is sometimes appropriate when the subordinate is dependent on the supervisor, as is the case for new employees, trainees, or people in highly structured jobs. Except for these people, self-appraisal is extremely valuable because it increases the subordinate's dignity and self-respect; places the manager in the role of counselor, not judge; engenders the subordinate's commitment to goals and development plans that emerge from the discussion; and avoids employee defensiveness. However, several problems with self-review should not be ignored:

1. It violates traditional mores about the proper relationship between boss and subordinate.
2. Its value may be limited by a self-serving bias that inflates self-appraisals, especially if the appraisal is to be used for administrative purposes rather than solely for development.
3. It increases supervisor leniency because supervisors are sensitive to subordinates' self-judgments and prefer to avoid confrontation that comes from subordinate defensiveness (Blakely, 1993).

MULTISOURCE FEEDBACK

Multisource (sometimes called 360 degree) *feedback* refers to ratings from subordinates, peers, supervisors, internal customers, and external customers or some combination. Ratings are collected by paper-and-pencil questionnaire, computer, or telephone keypunching. The survey may be administered annually or more often. For example, a division of Motorola collects ratings quarterly by computer for automatic averaging of scores and providing feedback reports to managers. Multisource feedback is growing in popularity and importance as a method for evaluating employees and providing them with input for development. All Fortune 500 companies use or are planning to use multisource feedback (London & Smither, 1995). Multisource feedback contributes to individual development by providing information on worthwhile directions for learning and growth. It promotes organizational development by specifying dimensions of managerial behavior that are important to the organization's management. In this way, it clarifies management's performance expectations. It recognizes the complexity of managerial performance—that performance is viewed differently by different constituencies and that managers need input from these different sources for a comprehensive view of their performance (Latham & Wexley, 1981; Tsui & Ohlott, 1988). The supervisor does not have sufficient information or perspective to be the sole reviewer. Supervisors are often reluctant to evaluate subordinates honestly. They want to avoid having to confront the subordinate with negative information (Fried, Tiegs, & Bellamy, 1992). Also, managers may need to behave differently with subordinates, peers, supervisors, and customers. Managers confronting organizational change recognize the importance of being attuned to the changing expectations of multiple constituencies, and they realize that this requires continuous learning.

Multisource feedback highlights the manager's multiple, changing roles. Boss–subordinate relationships are a major part of managing, after all, and may be the primary focus of the manager's job. So, performance information from subordinates can be valuable. Others' perspectives are important for different reasons: Peers' have information about the manager's contribution to teamwork. Customers have information about the manager's responsiveness to the customer's needs.

Use for Management Development

When multisource feedback is used for development alone, the managers who were rated are generally the only ones receiving their results, unless they choose to share the results with others (Cialdini, 1989; Van Velsor & Leslie, 1991). This highlights the importance of managers' using the information for their own development. The organization takes responsibility for a rating process that protects rater confidentiality, a computer generated report of the results, help in interpreting the reports, and opportunities for training and development (Kaplan, 1993). Recipients of the feedback must take responsibility for interpreting their results and using the information to guide their development and performance improvement.

Use for Administrative Decisions

Increasingly, organizations use multisource feedback for administrative purposes, such as merit pay and advancement decisions (London & Smither, 1995). This makes the feedback all the more salient to the individuals receiving it. But the process is likely to feel threatening to managers, especially to those who are worried about the quality of interpersonal relationships they have with their colleagues. Such managers will say that they do not trust the process. Efforts need to be taken to demonstrate the reliability and validity of the ratings in providing meaningful information that cannot easily be undermined by raters who want to get even with, or impress, ratees.

Recommendations for Implementing Multisource Feedback

When starting a multisource feedback process, use the information just for developmental purposes. It may take 2 or 3 time periods for raters and managers to become comfortable with the process. This may take several years if the process is administered annually. After that time, the policy can be changed to incorporate the results into making decisions about the managers rated. Generally, managers tend to be more accepting of multisource feedback when the organization provides training to help managers improve on the performance dimensions rated (Maurer & Tarulli, 1994).

The use of computer or telephone to administer a multisource rating survey is increasingly common. In computer administration, the survey comes on a disk or on-line. Raters complete the questionnaire on the computer and send back the disk or, in the case of on-line, return the data directly via the computer. The telephone can be used to record responses. In this case, the survey comes by mail. Raters dial a given number and they key in their numerical response corresponding to each question. Raters can request a printout of their responses be sent immediately to their printer so they can check their answers. Of course, the questions can actually be delivered on the telephone by a computerized voice. These high tech methods have many advantages over paper-and-pencil surveys. As technology develops, they are becoming increasingly cost effective. Results are computed automatically.

The following tables are a resource for designing and implementing a multisource feedback program. (They summarize the points I made in London, 1995c, chapter 10.) Table 4.2 outlines guidelines for designing and implementing a multisource feedback program. Table 4.3 presents a sample upward

TABLE 4.2
Guidelines for Designing and Implementing a Multisource Feedback Program

Item Content

Performance dimensions rated should be derived from analyses of current jobs or top managers' beliefs about new behaviors they want to develop and reward in the future. Items should be worded in terms of behavioral frequency, expectations, or evaluations. Ratings are likely to be most reliable when the items refer to objective or observable behaviors instead of individual qualities (e.g., trustworthy, responsive).

Involvement of Employees in Program Design

Employees should be involved in writing the items that will be used in the rating process. They can interpret performance dimensions set by top management and write comprehensible items to reflect these dimensions. Also, their involvement will increase their sense of ownership of the process. Furthermore, managers are more likely to accept the results when they know the items reflect performance dimensions that are important to the organization and meaningful to the people making the ratings.

Scale Format

Many scale formats are possible. One format is to have raters simultaneously rate and rank peers and themselves on the same scale. Richard Klimoski and I used a 20–point scale. Work group members listed their own name and each of their peers' names next to a letter and placed the letter corresponding to each name on the appropriate place on the scales (one 20-point scale for each behavior rated, as indicated in the following). Multiple letters could be placed on the same point. The method forced raters to compare themselves to their peers and compare their peers to each other in a deliberate way.

TABLE 4.2 (cont.)

Sample 20-point scale
(Letters stand for names of peers, "a" represents the self-rating.)

```
                                a
                                d
                        b     e f     c
Decisiveness            . . . . . . . . . . . . . . . . . . . . . .
                        low                   high
```

A disadvantage of this method is that it is more difficult to code than other formats, and it may be hard to computerize if the survey uses optically scanned forms, on-line computer ratings, or input on a computer disk that is returned for analysis—although software could be developed for this.

Rater Anonymity

The process should ensure raters' anonymity. This means guarding the ratings, probably by having an outside consultant code and analyze the data and prepare feedback reports. Such reports are usually computer generated, particularly if the survey is on an optically scanned sheet, on a computer disk, or on computer program tied to a local area network server or mainframe. Hand written comments need to be typed to disguise the handwriting. Managers should not receive subordinate ratings if there are too few peers or subordinates (e.g., four or less) because this might suggest the identity of the raters.

Rater Training

Raters and ratees need to understand fully the rating process and use of the results. Instructions should be clear. Employee briefings should be provided to explain the reason for the ratings, how the data will be aggregated, and the nature of the feedback reports. Rater training should make raters aware of rating errors (e.g., leniency, central tendency, and halo—rating all elements of performance alike).

Uses

Use of multisource feedback is likely to affect employees' attitudes about the feedback process and possibly the favorability of the ratings. Respondents are to be different (more or less lenient) if they know the ratings will be used to make decisions about the ratee than if the ratings will be used solely for the ratee's development and no one else will see the results other than the ratee.

TABLE 4.3
Sample Upward Feedback Survey

Instructions: An important aspect of leadership is the management of people. This survey focuses on your satisfaction with the relationship you have with your supervisor. Use the following numeric scale to rate your supervisor. Indicate the number that best describe your rating. Use "N" to indicate you have had insufficient opportunity to accurately gauge your degree of satisfaction.

Your responses will be averaged with those from other subordinates who also report to your supervisor.

TABLE 4.3 (cont.)

Scale:

1 = Very dissatisfied
2 = Dissatisfied
3 = Somewhat dissatisfied
4 = Somewhat satisfied
5 = Satisfied
6 = Very Satisfied
N = No opportunity to observe

_____ 1. Jointly sets performance objectives with you.
_____ 2. Supports you in developing your career plans.
_____ 3. Motivates you to do a good job.
_____ 4. Gives you authority to do your job.
_____ 5. Provides the support necessary to help you do your job (e.g., advice, resources, or information).
_____ 6. Understands the work to be done within your work group.
_____ 7. Is available to you when needed.
_____ 8. Encourages innovation and creativity.
_____ 9. Holds employees accountable for meeting performance objectives.
____ 10. Keeps commitments.
____ 11. Allows adequate training time for you.
____ 12. Provides ongoing performance feedback.
____ 13. Provided a useful performance appraisal within the past year.
____ 14. Conducts productive staff meetings.
____ 15. Demonstrates trust and confidence in you.
____ 16. Treats you with dignity and respect.
____ 17. Informs you about issues affecting you.
____ 18. Balances the work load fairly.
____ 19. Communicates the reasons for his or her actions.
____ 20. Supports and backs you up.
____ 21. Has the subject matter knowledge to do the job.
____ 22. Fairly evaluates your job performance.
____ 23. Represents the group effectively to others (e.g., to clients, to management, or at meetings).
____ 24. Insures that you get credit/recognition for your work.
____ 25. Encourages open, two-way communication.
____ 26. Modifies his or her position based on feedback from you (e.g., ideas, plans, or solutions).
____ 27. Provides opportunities for you to develop new skills.
____ 28. Strives for quality in spite of time pressure.

Note. From London, M., & Wueste, R. A. (1992) and Wohlers, A. J., & London, M. (1989). Adapted with permission.

feedback rating form. A sample feedback report is provided in Table 4.4. Table 4.5 gives excerpts from an interpretation guide to help feedback recipients use their results.

SURVEY FEEDBACK

Another formal method of providing feedback is the employee attitude survey. Known as *survey feedback*, this process reports attitude survey results to managers and employees (London, 1988). Employee attitude surveys may be

TABLE 4.4
Sample Feedback Report

	Self Rating	Mean Subordinate Rating	Range	Number of Subordinates Responding to Item		Norm[1]
				Low	High	
1. Jointly sets performance objectives with you.	5	3	1	4	7	3
2. Supports you in developing your career plans.	4	4	2	4	8	4
3. Motivates you to do a good job.	6	5	3	6	8	4
4. Gives you authority to do your job.	5	4	3	5	8	3
5. Provides the support necessary to help you do your job (e.g., advice, resources, or information).	6	4	2	5	7	4

[1]Norm is the average of subordinate ratings for the item across all managers in the unit.

TABLE 4.5
Results Interpretation Guide

An interpretation guide would ask the manager receiving the report to compare his or her self-ratings to the average subordinate ratings.

The number of responding subordinates is an indication of the representativeness of the results across the work group. Data would not be presented if four or less subordinates responded to an item.

The norm provides a comparison to how managers overall were perceived by their subordinates.

The guide would include information about training and developmental experiences available that would be useful for each category of items.

collected via paper-and-pencil questionnaire, one-on-one interviews, or interviews with groups of employees (termed *focus groups*). This is different from
multisource surveys, such as upward and 360-degree feedback, because the
survey items ask for general attitudes about different facets of the company,
possibly including the supervisor. However, instead of averaging the results
separately for each unit manager and giving the manager an individualized
feedback report, a single report is generated for the entire department or even
the entire company. So, managers must evaluate the extent to which the
overall results apply to them and their work groups.

Employee attitude surveys are less costly than analyzing and preparing
reports for each manager separately, although the results are necessarily less
precise. Nevertheless, survey feedback results can be a useful way to stimulate
discussion in the work group about issues that may be relevant to other parts
of the company as well. Results may be reported to everyone in the organization or department in special bulletins. Supervisors should be encouraged to
meet with their work groups to discuss the meaning of the results for the
organization as a whole and the work group in particular.

The overall corporate survey results become a tracking mechanism to
evaluate the effects of organizational policies on employee satisfaction. Also,
the importance of the satisfaction measures can be determined by examining
the correlations between employee satisfaction and outcome measures such
as employee turnover and absenteeism.

CONCLUSION

This chapter reviewed traditional approaches to performance appraisal—in
particular, supervisor ratings. I described rating formats. However, I suggested
the use of ratingless, narrative appraisals that avoid threatening grades. This is
especially valuable after an organizational downsizing. The survivors may
benefit from detailed, constructive feedback, but not ratings that label people
and may be unnecessarily harsh. I also recommended incorporating a self-appraisal into the performance review process. Then I considered multisource
ratings, such as 360-degree feedback processes that collect ratings from peers,
subordinates, customers, supervisors, and self. This can be a useful supplement
to supervisory ratings, and a valuable tool in helping the employee to plan
development activities. I concluded the chapter with a description of more
general employee attitude surveys as another source of feedback. Less specific
to an individual manager's actions, the attitude survey is a mechanism for
tracking employees' reactions to managerial behaviors and organizational
policies.

To summarize the major points from the chapter:

1. The supervisor is the traditional source of performance appraisal and
   feedback, and the appraisal process usually involves a feedback discus-

sion with the subordinate—thereby mandating explicit feedback if conducted properly.

2. Some organizational policies and cultures support serious attention to feedback and development by making them an important (expected and rewarded) part of the way organizations operates.

3. Rating formats can be designed to accentuate a focus on behaviors (rather than general opinions of personality, for instance). Such rating scales enhance rater accuracy and generate constructive information.

4. Ratingless appraisals can avoid the defensiveness that often accompanies grading and focus the recipient's attention on behaviors and directions for development and performance improvement.

5. Self-appraisals should be incorporated into the performance review process. Beginning a performance review with a self-appraisal increases the recipient's involvement in, and commitment to, the process and diffuses the recipient's defensiveness.

6. Multisource feedback (ratings from subordinates, peers, supervisors, internal customers, and external customers, or some combination thereof) is growing in popularity as a method for evaluating employees and providing them with input for development. It captures information from multiple constituencies and focuses the recipient's attention on his or her role from different perspectives.

7. Feedback of employee attitude survey results is another way to stimulate discussion in the work group of how supervisory behaviors and organizational policies and programs influence employees' motivation and desire to remain in the organization.

The next chapter examines means for obtaining information about employees' abilities. These techniques are used to diagnose development needs and, as such, are valuable sources of feedback.

5

Assessment Centers and Business Simulations

This chapter focuses on methods that give employees information about their skills and capabilities: assessment centers, computerized assessment, and simulations. These offer participants a chance to learn about themselves and try new behaviors. Some organizations use these techniques as part of a development program. Such programs are available in a number of forms to anyone who wants to enroll in them. They may be run by universities, leadership development institutes, and training firms. In other cases, firms have their own programs customized to the needs of their employees and the objectives of the organization.

ASSESSMENT CENTERS

Assessment centers measure employees' skills and abilities. Assessment centers are often used to evaluate job candidates in the employee selection process. But, they are also used to evaluate current employees, especially those being assessed for possible promotion. An assessment center may also be used solely for development purposes. The results provide diagnostic information that will help employees identify directions for development in areas that will be needed in managerial positions at higher organizational levels. Often, managers who have already been determined to have the potential to advance are nominated to attend a developmental assessment center.

The assessment center (which does not refer to a place, but a process) includes such exercises as the in-basket (written material requiring prioritization and responses), an interview, management games, a leaderless group discussion, and a variety of psychological and achievement tests (Munchus & McArthur, 1991; Thornton & Byham, 1982). Assessment centers are expensive to develop and operate, and they cannot be implemented without a good deal of work and investment. They are a way to assess general managerial skills

52

and then consider directions for development. This may cost several thousand dollars per participant.

The goal of an assessment center is to collect and integrate diverse information about an employee. The exercises mirror job requirements and are meant to assess dimensions of behavior important to job performance such as managerial skills for middle management positions. Multiple assessors' evaluations of participants' behaviors in job-like situations produce more reliable and valid results than can be obtained by any one method alone (Cascio & Silbey, 1979).

Steps in designing an assessment center include the following:

1. Identify performance dimensions to be assessed. Examples for general managerial ability are organizing, communication, decision making, and leadership.

2. Identify relevant tests and behavioral exercises to measure the performance dimensions. For instance, a sales assessment includes simulations of sales situations and measure relevant knowledge of marketing. A managerial assessment center includes techniques to evaluate behavior on boss/subordinate relationships.

3. Run the assessment center. Multiple assessors observe participants (ratees) and evaluate them on the performance dimensions.

4. Review the narrative reports and test scores during a group discussion with assessors called an *integration session*. The assessors rate the participant on each dimension and discuss their individual ratings, usually trying to agree within one point on, say, a 5-point scale.

Developmental Assessment Centers

Developmental assessment centers are those used primarily, or solely, for development of the participants rather than as input to decisions about them. The results are reported to the participants by an assessor or a psychologist. During the feedback session with the participant, the assessor reviews the meaning of the results and offers guidance for development. Suggestions for development may recommend building on one's strengths rather than eliminating weaknesses. Some elements of managerial performance cannot be learned easily. Decision making would be an example. Others are learned more easily, such as communication skills.

Developmental assessment centers provide feedback that *encourages* people to engage in activities that make them more eligible for promotion into management. This was demonstrated in a 10-year study of 151 insurance company employees who participated in an assessment center and received formal feedback and recommendations for development (Jones & Whitmore, 1995). They were compared to a group of 167 people who were not assessed. The assessment center consisted of eight exercises completed by six assessees at a time over a 2-day period. The exercises included a background information questionnaire, a standardized interview, a supervisor–subordinate discussion role play (with a trained middle manager playing the subordinate), an in-basket, a writing exercise, a formal presentation, and two group problem-solving discussions. Assessors were upper-level managers who had received 2 days of training on assessment methods. After the assessment, the assessors met with two of the program administrators to discuss each candidate, rate the candidate on seven performance dimensions, and consider specific developmental recommendations on each dimension. For instance, an assessee judged to be low on oral communication skills might receive a recommendation to attend a course on public speaking. Written feedback reports provided dimension-by-dimension evaluations. Assessees reviewed their feedback reports privately and then met with one of the assessment center administrators for a discussion. The assessees were encourage to consider the causes and accuracy of the results and describe their intentions of accepting the information and following the recommendations for development. The assessment manager also met with each assessee's manager to review the results. The goal of this meeting was to gain the manager's support for the assessee's development. Assessees were asked on a follow-up survey to rate their acceptance of the feedback (e.g., to indicate on a 5-point scale from 1 = *strongly disagree* to 5 = *strongly agree*, their responses to 7 items such as, "The feedback I received from the center was accurate", and "The feedback I received adequately captured my performance at the center").

The results showed no differences in career advancement between the assessees and non-assessees over the 10-year follow-up period. However, within the assessee group, those who followed up on the developmental recommendations advanced further. Interestingly, assessors' ratings of the participants' career motivation, rather than performance, predicted subsequent developmental activity and career advancement. Thus, the assessment center information was valuable feedback for those with high career motivation who followed the assessors' recommendations for development. The results suggest that feedback and career motivation lead to developmental activities, and these activities, rather than abilities at the time of assessment, contribute to advancement.

COMPUTERIZED ASSESSMENT

A variant of the assessment center method that is increasingly available and cost effective is computerized assessment. This method uses computers to present items customized to the assessee's ability, measure a variety of responses (e.g., time to respond to different situations), and, if appropriate, provide feedback at various points in time. It uses computer technologies, including the CD-ROM with full-motion video (Drasgow, Olson, Keenan,

Moberg, & Mead, 1993). As such, it presents realistic, clear information; allows people to see how others might react to their behavior and decisions; repeats similar situations across assessees; can vary the difficulty and complexity of the simulations; offers immediate and repeated feedback; and records precise information about the assessee's performance (e.g., it can also determine whether the assessee responds to an issue before viewing other pertinent information). It is most valuable for assessment of skills not easily or inexpensively measured via traditional in-person exercises or paper-and-pencil tests.

BUSINESS GAMES AND SIMULATIONS

Business games and simulations are often incorporated into training programs as a way to communicate changing business strategies and directions and help participants assess their strengths and weaknesses in relation to these strategic directions. These techniques are sometimes referred to as *practice fields* in that they help individuals and the organization as a whole learn and develop. They are valuable because managerial action in the real world may be too slow, ambiguous, and even risky to learn by doing (Drew & Davidson, 1993; Senge, 1990). Feedback from a simulation can be fast and clear. Moreover, a simulation is a safe place where managers may practice decision making and experiment with new styles of management. Managers have a chance to do, think, and feel, and feedback is an important part of the learning (Keys, 1994; Stumpf & Dutton, 1990). Of course, the simulation must be realistic enough to be engaging, but not so complex that it is threatening.

A Computer-Based Simulation

A telecommunications firm engaged consultants to deliver a new leadership training and development program that would communicate a vision for the organization and encourage managers to take more responsibility for leadership as well as increase managers' knowledge and understanding of the industry (Drew & Davidson, 1993). The program was designed for the firm's 350 top managers. About 16 managers attended each 2-and-a-half day session. One-and-a-half of the days were dedicated to a simulation that modeled new global alliances, joint ventures between cable and telephone companies, and linkages with computer network providers and other industries, such as publishing and entertainment.

The computer-based game (which took 18 person-months to develop), had four teams of usually four participants each enter decisions on new products, marketing, salesforce, customer service, and operations. Participants were assigned roles, such as VP Marketing and VP New Product Introduction. Each team could launch up to 12 products. Each team worked in a room with a PC networked to a central file server. Each team established its own strategic plan and goals at the start. Printable screens provided the teams with support data. Each round of the simulation required that the team search for data and decide about such issues as new products, pricing, and budget allocations between departments. Decisions were made about each function performed (e.g., marketing, customer service, operations) which, in turn, had implications for quality and market results. The teams could cooperate by licensing new products to other teams or invest in national advertising.

At the end of each round, key results were summarized and teams were encouraged to compare each other's performance.

Group Simulations: Foodcorp and Globalcorp

A behavioral simulation lasting 6 to 10 hours assigns people to senior manage-ment roles. Two examples are called Foodcorp and Globalcorp (Stumpf, Watson, & Rustogi, 1994). Foodcorp is a fictitious international food manu-facturing organization with three levels of organizational hierarchy, two prod-uct groups, and two subsidiaries. Its products are sold to distributors and retail supermarkets throughout the United States and 60 other countries. Global-corp is a fictitious diversified international financial services conglomerate with $27 billion in assets and a consumer banking sector (comprised of branch banking, credit card operations, and consumer credit) and a commercial banking sector (comprised of investment banking, institutional banking, and transaction services). Whereas Foodcorp has homogeneous lines of business and cross-functional activities, Globalcorp involves active coordination and competition across its lines of business within sectors.

These are especially lifelike simulations in that participants adopt roles in a formal organizational hierarchy, deal with realistic information, serve on committees (with prescheduled committee meetings that can be attended, rescheduled, or ignored), and receive and send mail. Both simulations began with the complex and ambiguous task: "Run the organization as you see fit." After 6 or more hours of operating, the simulation concluded with an address by the president and other key executives to the employees. Postsimulation questionnaires and observer evaluations are used in the feedback process during the debriefing session. Feedback covers how decisions were made, how formal and personal power were used, what climate is created and how it affects participants, and actions taken or not taken.

These simulations were applied by two different firms with different goals for development of their managers (Stumpf et al., 1994). Northern Telecom, a midsized telecommunications equipment manufacturer headquartered in Canada wanted a practice field experience that placed their managers in a matrix organizational structure confronting a competitive, global marketplace with a line of products that had potential for rapid growth. Foodcorp fitted their needs. In contrast, Citicorp, a large, international financial services firm headquartered in the United States, wanted a practice field that reflected a decentralized, multiproduct-line firm that was diverse in its product offerings. It wanted a situation with a large number of profit centers within it parallel to the Citicorp organization. Globalcorp fitted their needs.

The simulations were incorporated into 1-week residence leadership development programs. The programs covered skills related to global issues and a diverse workforce. Lecture-discussions set the stage for the simulation. Both programs used results from multirater feedback ratings from coworkers and subordinates as a start to help the participants recognize their developmental needs. Participation in the program was voluntary, but limited to middle and top managers who were responsible for managing other people and/or to people who had significant responsibility for a line of business or function.

Post-training evaluations indicated that most participants felt the program's objectives were met (a total of 357 people who participated in 48 behavioral simulations gave ratings ranging from 4.2 to 4.7 on a 5-point scale—5 being the most favorable). Postsimulation assessments completed by the participants and observers revealed that most participants used the simulation to practice new behaviors. These efforts were used as the substance for hours of feedback discussion immediately following the simulation as the participants met with observers individually and then as a group. During the feedback discussions, participants identified areas for further development and opportunities to transfer new knowledge and skills to their work.

These simulations are available through Dr. Stephen A. Stumpf at the University of Tampa. The program can be set up on a company's site or at a convenient training center or university.

A Simulation for R&D Managers

Another simulation, called RADMIS, was developed for training research and development managers (Bailey, 1990). Trained observers assess task behaviors and interpersonal styles and feed back this data to the team. Also, the information can be used to help each team member develop more effective managerial behaviors. Players take the role of members of a development group employed by a firm that makes printing plates. It had one primary competitor until recently when that firm began marketing a new printing plate. The new plate could overtake the entire market within 6 months, putting the team's firm out of business. The day-long simulation asks members to develop a product and launch it in the market quickly. The simulation provides participants with ample information about financial data, including marketing costs, environmental concerns, and risk entailed in two possible new products. Team members work up data to support different possibilities, and they negotiate alternative directions. The feedback session focuses on what it is like to work with or for each team member. Each person gets cogent feedback from the other team members. The simulation works well for managers in development work whose primary training has been in technical, as opposed to managerial, areas. More information about the simulation is available from Betty Ann Bailey at the Center for Creative Leadership in Greensboro, North Carolina.

Looking Glass

Perhaps the best known realistic simulation, and the model for others, such as Foodcorp, Globalcorp, and RADMIS, is Looking Glass, Inc. Looking Glass was developed by the Center for Creative Leadership (a nonprofit organization established in 1970 by the Smith Richardson Foundation to study issues of management and leadership) with funding from the Office of Naval Research (Kaplan, 1986). Looking Glass is a fictitious organization in the glass business. The simulation assigns roles to up to 20 managers ranging from president to plant manager. After reading extensive materials on the firm (for instance, an annual report, financial data, job descriptions, and recent memos), the participants interact as they deal with the more than 150 problems embedded in the material. The simulation is used as a part of a week-long leadership development program by the Center for Creative Leadership. Managers can enroll in these programs as individuals or as part of a corporate group.

One Person's Experience in Looking Glass.   Robert Kaplan of the Center for Creative Leadership gave an example of how Looking Glass and subsequent feedback helped one manager improve his self-understanding (Kaplan, 1986). Here is a synopsis:

> Allen Bruce was a successful manager with a bright future in a growing firm. A bachelor in his mid-thirties, he thought of himself as someone who was friendly and good with interpersonal relationships. He was shocked when he learned from an associate that he had a reputation of being "threatening" to work with and that others saw him as an ambitious, somewhat self-serving person with little concern for others. After discussing this discrepancy between how he saw himself and how others seemed to see him, his boss recommended that Allen enroll in the leadership development program run by the firm that incorporated the Looking Glass exercise.
>
> At the start of the workshop, Allen suggested to the other participants that they have a presimulation meeting with other participants. After reviewing the materials, Allen came to the first meeting very-organized with special interest in a memo from the company president that the three divisional directors of sales and marketing, of which Allen was to be one, get together to coordinate solutions to common problems. Allen's goal was to formulate a plan that would bring about dramatic improvement in Looking Glass's operations, and he planned to take the initiative to get things moving.
>
> During the simulation, participants were assigned to office space. Phones rang, people talked, and mail was delivered. Allen began by calling the president as a way of making himself visible "upstairs." He then attended a products division meeting, but did not contribute much because he was preoccupied by his own

plans. He later pigeonholed another participant, Carl, who played the role of Looking Glass's vice president and suggested that all the company's problems were due to inefficiency from lack of coordination, and he wanted to be given the authority to work with the other directors to develop a comprehensive plan to clean things up. Carl agreed, but during a subsequent meeting with the other directors, Allen had trouble convincing them that they really needed sweeping change.

Allen then worked in his office to draft a memo to the president that outlined a reorganization of the firm that would address the principal problem, as Allen saw it. But he received no response. The president had spent the day emphasizing cost containment, and even sent a memo to the staff indicating that all recommendations should address cost cutting. Allen then shared his plan with the vice president, Carl. He suggested that Allen revise his plan to limit it to sales and marketing. This might make it more palatable to the management committee that would be meeting shortly.

Before the meeting, Allen telephoned one of his fellow regional directors, Wendy. She had seen Allen's plan and indicated she did not think there was any support for it in the management committee. In fact, she informed him that the committee members had already ruled out his plan. Allen did not see how Wendy would know that unless she had access to the president. Allen told her it was quite a shock to him to find that someone he trusted was a "back stabber." Allen felt better later when he learned from Carl that his reorganization plan had received some consideration from the management committee and that the sales and marketing areas would be restructured in some way.

Allen later confronted Wendy with his feeling that Wendy and the other regional director took the essence of his plan for their own plan. Wendy was astounded that Allen would think she and others had spent their time plotting against him. Wendy said that she had been working on a little agreement for transfer pricing, and this is what Carl referred to when he implied that parts of Allen's plan would be implemented. Allen was embarrassed and wondered how his imagination could have made him so paranoid.

The simulation ended in midafternoon. During the evening and following day, Allen participated in three debriefing sessions. The first two were general sessions with all the participants to discuss the experience as a whole and the performance of each division as a unit. During the third session, each participant's individual performance was discussed. Four main points emerged with the help of a facilitator and the other participants. Allen realized that he had a tendency to manipulate people. He sometimes invested too much in his own plans at the expense of what others were trying to do. He was a skilled communicator and wanted to cooperate with superiors, but he was less concerned about building rapport with peers and subordinates. Finally, he discovered that he tended to attribute to others the same manipulative motives that he himself had as a way to justify his own actions.

Allen showed resilience in accepting this new self-awareness. He admitted that the messages were not easy to hear, but that they were useful. He felt that he got what he came to learn.

Looking Glass As a Vehicle for Organizational Change.   First Union Corporation, a bank with headquarters in Charlotte, North Carolina, used Looking Glass as a management development tool (Johnston, 1986). The company wanted to increase managers' understanding of the dynamic nature of managerial work, help the managers assess their own strengths and weaknesses, and encourage them to make developmental plans. The firm also wanted to enhance managers' awareness of the importance of training and development and refine the training department's teambuilding and feedback skills. Looking Glass was used as the "catalyst experience" in a 4-day management development program for 20 managers at a time. Although initially the managers questioned the relevance of the simulation's manufacturing environment for bankers, they found that the absence of banking-related issues helped them focus on aspects of their managerial behavior. Participants for each 4-day program were selected from a cross-section of the bank's departments and levels (with management from first line up to senior positions participating).

The program proved to be popular, with frequent requests from past participants to have their subordinates attend. Many participants made important career decisions soon after the program (e.g., deciding to change jobs, pursue further management opportunities, or improve their relationships with coworkers). Participants formed informal networks that continued to be useful to them long after the program. Some participants were later assigned to jobs that have them reporting to each other, and they reported that Looking Glass feedback enhanced their understanding of each other.

ORGANIZATIONAL ANALYSIS

Top managers may seek feedback through an organizational analysis conducted by outside consultants.

Here are two examples:

Management Interviews

In a $28 million company with about 130 employees in the industrial adhesives business, Gerrit Wolf (a fellow faculty member at Stony Brook) and I were called in by the two owners, brothers and sons of the founder. They asked us to assess their nine managers' competence for moving the firm toward its goal of achieving 20% growth in sales per year during the next 3 years. The firm was nowhere near achieving this goal, and would be lucky to achieve 3–5% growth during the first year of the plan. Economic conditions were partly to blame for these results, but also the owners were beginning to feel that they did not have the right management talent to make it happen. They felt their managers were not sufficiently knowledgeable or aggressive to meet the changing demands of the industry and the firm which, for 30 years before, had been a highly profitable and growing enterprise with little need for advanced management tactics. Two years earlier, the brothers decided to hire some new management talent in technology, marketing, sales, and accounting to increase the firm's value. Prior to this, the company had little understanding of the profitability of its various product lines let alone how to formulate a business plan.

The managers viewed our consultancy with trepidation. They felt it was a threat, and they worried about being open and honest with us. However, all of them seemed to be quite above board in providing insight into the operation and leadership of the business. What started out as a management assessment turned into an upward appraisal of the two owners.

We began with a 2-hour interview with each of the nine managers. We asked three basic questions: What are the threats and opportunities facing the company? What does the firm need to do to respond to these threats and opportunities? How do you fit into this picture; that is, what do you need to do to respond to these opportunities and threats? Much of the discussion during each interview centered on the role that the owners played as leaders and visionaries. The results were consistent across the managers.

Tom, the manager in charge of production scheduling and customer services, provided the following example: For the last 6–7 years, the owners' goal has been to ease themselves out of purchasing and hand over the function to Tom, who is nominally the head of it. However, this has not happened. The owners are reluctant to let go. They seem to lack trust in their managers' ability to learn new functions. Also, the owners seem unsure about how to pass on their knowledge.

The owners need to get out of the day-to-day business. They say they want to change, but they do not. Tom rarely gets a direct answer to his questions and concerns. They should give them direction, explain their expectations, then hold the managers accountable. The customer service department is not empowered to do anything. They cannot make pricing decisions on their own. But people will not grow unless they are involved in learning. The owners have imposed too many hurdles. When someone makes a decision, they are likely to berate the decision maker. A memo might come back with the comment, "What the hell is this?" We need feedback on whether we are heading in the right direction. Now the owners are not responsive. They let things ride.

He would like to see more enthusiasm from the owners for the managers' ideas.

Our overall recommendations to the owners included the following:

1. Give each department manager a budget and let them manage it.
2. Get out of the day-to-day minutia and into the field.
3. Improve responsiveness to managers' proposals and give definitive answers.
4. Be better at communicating your expectations and holding the managers accountable.

5. Do not second guess small decisions.
6. Do more to recognize your managers' competence and ability to learn. Provide them with feedback. Reward their accomplishments. Be less combative.

This was tough feedback to hear, but it helped to hear it from outside parties. Although the information was not really a surprise to the owners, it forced them to deal with issues of their own management and leadership style that were necessary to change to move the business forward.

Another Example

In another case, Gerrit Wolf and I conducted interviews with the CEO, the vice president, and department managers in a small firm. The company, with about 30 employees and annual sales in the range of $9 million, manufactures products used in food production. The firm had been a privately held family business for 25 years, until it was sold a year ago to a larger foreign company in the food service industry. The analysis was initiated by the CEO who was transferred from the headquarters of the new owners. He initiated the review because he wanted a better understanding of why managers were not getting along and feedback about what he could do better. We identified the following issues described here in an excerpt from our report to the company:

Conflict Over Corporate Philosophy.   Objectives of the firm have changed with the merger. This used to be a "cheap and cheerful" business—meaning that it was run by the seat of the pants with little technical know how and little understanding of costs and profits of product lines. Today it is far more technical. There is a divergence of opinion about how the business should be guided. The parent company and CEO want a market driven enterprise that develops new product lines (e.g., niche products with proprietary markets). The old guard (principally the sales staff) wants to maintain business based on personal relationships with customers.

Communications Problems.   Attempts to address relationship issues among the executive staff have not been fruitful (referring to last June's peer quality meetings). Partly, this was the fault of how the meetings were structured. Rotating chairs and discussion of operational issues failed to provide continuity and commitment to the process. In general, insufficient time was devoted to the process.

Current Status of the Business.   The company is still experiencing growing pains. The management team (exclusive of the CEO) has little management experience and no corporate management experience. Only the technical staff has had substantial experience in the industry.

The sales and marketing managers do not communicate well, yet they need to talk the most. This is the weakest link in the management team. The purchasing and technical staffs work well together.

The firm is small and the responsibilities blend, making it difficult to maintain distinct lines of authority. Although job descriptions exist, people get involved in others' areas. This leads to friction. Work needs to be done to more clearly delineate job descriptions. For instance, everyone seems to think they have some responsibility for pricing (the finance vp, the sales vp, the marketing manager, and the CEO).

The firm is overcoming a poor image problem. Before the merger, the firm seemed to run with the philosophy of "doing business at any cost." This meant pricing to meet customer needs, reacting to customer requests rather than creating requests. The firm was relegated to trying to be the low bidder in a commodity business with one or two products carrying a season. The goal is to have the firm called in by customers at the inception of jobs. This is beginning to happen. Also, the firm wants to market more general products that can be sold to a variety of customers. However, the firm is still caught between new and old ways of doing business.

Reasons for Recent Sales Problems.   The slow down in sales may be due to many factors:

- The recession.
- Poor decisions about some customers (e.g., not lowering prices despite additional product development).
- Poor pricing decisions.
- Slow production of prototypes in response to customer briefs.
- Low morale in the sales force,
- Insufficient sales coverage (some salespeople responsible for too broad a geographical area).
- Lack of action on marketing strategies.
- Sales manager's inexperience in sales and not spending sufficient time in the field.
- Over-reliance on easy sales of commodity products.

A Frequent Complaint.   There are too many meetings. The meetings that do occur are often a waste of valuable time.

Perceptions of the CEO (Some "Upward" Feedback).   The CEO does not give managers a chance to do the jobs for which they are responsible and should be held accountable. Often the CEO assigns the same project to more than one person. Some see this as a result of the CEO's distrust or lack of confidence in his people. Others see this as a result of the CEO's desire to get things done quickly. When one person does not come through, the CEO goes to someone else. Alternatively, some believe that the CEO does not recognize each manager's specific responsibilities. Whatever the reason for these actions, most of the managers find that this creates confusion and erodes morale. They feel the CEO is undermining their authority and setting up competition among the executive staff. The CEO is giving them mixed signals (giving them responsibility on the one hand and taking it away behind their backs on the other).

Other perceptions of the CEO:

1. He demeans and humiliates people in front of others making it difficult for them to save face.
2. He manages by threat.
3. He micromanages, getting involved in minute details and making others suffer through views of these details (this is alternatively viewed by some as necessary to get people to follow-through and by others as a total waste of time).
4. He undermines agreements made with others.
5. He fails to tell some managers when a decision is made that affects their unit.
6. He is very definite and specific about what he wants done.
7. He does not let others do their jobs.
8. He is not open to input (he may occasionally say he wants to know what others think, but he really does not).
9. He is simply doing what needs to be done to turn the firm around.
10. He does not want to deal with performance problems (firing managers would show corporate that things are out of control).
11. He has covered up interpersonal problems from corporate. Recent attention to management difficulties stems from corporate's recent awareness of issues (having heard difficulties directly from some of the top managers).
12. He avoids confrontations. He is not firm with others. He may dislike an action, but he does not reverse it. He does not face up to others in one-on-one conversation. He prefers to dress down subordinates in public.
13. He is quick to blame others for failures and take credit for successes.
14. He changes priorities in midstream. To some, this is being responsive to customers. To others, it is undermining their authority.
15. He does not have confidence in his management team.
16. He is too controlling. He makes directives and even carries them out himself.
17. He has definite ideas, and he intends to get what he wants.
18. He is not interested in developing the management team (by seeking and using their ideas and letting them carry out their responsibilities).
19. He does not leave it to the managers to determine what is needed.
20. He has faith in his managers and leaves them with things to do.
21. He can be overzealous because he wants things done quickly.

22. He asks whoever is around to solve a problem, not necessarily the individual who has formal responsibility.
23. He does not take sides. He tries to let managers work out their problems.
24. He has the most confidence in the one manager he knows the best.

Open Questions.   Is the CEO behaving this way because he does not trust his people and he believes the people cannot change, or because his management style and cultural background lead him to be authoritarian and controlling? Is there truth to the previously mentioned perceptions of the CEO?

Some Conclusions.   Most managers are insecure about their jobs. They tend to go to the CEO with problems rather than to each other. Most of the managers have strong wills and they will not let go—change their ways for the good of the company and their colleagues. The marketing and sales manager have different views about strategy for the business.

Several managers view the marketing manager as highly political and divisive, yet responsive to the CEO's directives. Also, she appreciates the expanded role she has working in a small business. She can get a fast decision on an idea and act on it tomorrow. She recognizes the need to understand the financial implications of her role. She feels she does everything she is supposed to do, but others do not understand her role. Regarding the sales manager, the marketing manager believes she is expected to influence him when he does not report to her.

The California production vp is relieved to be in a new job where he is in control. The amount of work is the same, but he is away from the daily backstabbing. He sees the problems more clearly now that he is at a distance. He is grateful that the firm had confidence in him.

The finance and production vps and their staffs work well together. They meet every morning to review progress. Also, he works well with the sales vp. They understand and know the customers. They both seem to be of the "old school." He also works well with the production vp in California on purchasing issues.

Consultants' Views of What Is Needed.

1. Get the right people in the right jobs.
2. Make sure each person is clear on expectations.
3. Let people do their jobs. Teamwork will follow naturally from the above.
4. Need for the management team to recognize they are not a peer group. They are at different organizational levels and have different responsibilities.

Alternative strategies:

5. Decide how the business will be run and go to it!

6. Introduce development planning for each manager.
7. Help the CEO understand his management style, communications, and decision process.
8. Design a management development program with role plays to help managers understand different roles and perspectives.

CONCLUSION

This chapter and the last considered different sources of formal feedback. Organization systems can be designed to facilitate appraisal and feedback. They are a way to make feedback a normal part of organizational processes. However, the appraisal process does not do the job alone. Employees are responsible for self-evaluation, asking for feedback, and using it for performance improvement and career development. This way the feedback recipient is committed to paying attention to, and doing something about the feedback. When the recipient cares, the source of feedback will be more conscientious in collecting and communicating performance results. And when the source cares, the recipient will be more conscientious in understanding the results and applying them to their own and the organization's benefit. More specifically:

1. Assessment centers give employees feedback about their performance and suggest directions for their development.

2. Assessment centers that are aimed mainly at providing participants with information to guide their development are most useful to participants who are high in career motivation—that is, they want the feedback and they intend to use it constructively.

3. Computerized assessment offers readily accessible, cost-effective, self-paced methods for self-evaluation.

4. Practice fields are business games and simulations that allow participants to experiment with new behaviors in settings that are realistic and nonthreatening. These simulations are often incorporated into management development programs to provide feedback and stimulate learning.

5. Practice field simulations can be tools for individual and organizational change and development. They can give individuals information about their performance, and they can provide groups with information about how they work together.

6. Individuals can seek programs on their own that use practice field simulations, or organizations can commission the design of customized simulations to be used as an organization development intervention.

7. Another source of feedback is an organizational analysis conducted by outside consultants—particularly useful for small businesses. The consultants interview key personnel and given them feedback about their performance

and potential in relation to organizational objectives. The method also provides valuable upward feedback to the CEO and/or top managers who may use the information to change their management style or redesign the organization's structure and possibly make personnel changes.

Now that I have covered formal sources of feedback, I turn in the next chapter to how people seek feedback informally.

III

GIVING FEEDBACK

6

Becoming a Coach and Developer

This chapter explains what it means to be an effective coach and developer. This is a key element to being a manager. Yet the effective management of people is often given short shrift in evaluating and rewarding managers' performances. Because of this, and because of a general discomfort with, and lack of training in, "people skills," many managers give low priority to their subordinates' performance improvements and career developments. This chapter examines the roles of performance management and being a coach and developer. I show how some corporate cultures encourage these roles, whereas others discourage them. I suggest that organizations that educate and reward managers for performance management and being coaches and developers are prepared to adapt to changes in the business environment and, consequently, are more likely to be profitable and grow. Organizations that are attuned mainly to maximizing current performance with existing human resources are less prepared to adapt to changes and are more likely to miss opportunities.

SELF-ASSESSMENT

A good way for managers to understand their role as coach and developer is to complete the questionnaire in Table 6.1. Try it. The items ask about your relationship with your subordinates—in particular, the extent to which you support their performance improvement. Then across all the items in the questionnaire consider the following: What do you do most frequently? What do you do least frequently? Are these behaviors important to your organization? If you did these behaviors more often, would your unit perform better? What's stopping you?

REASONS FOR SUPPORTING PERFORMANCE MANAGEMENT

Performance management should not be left to chance or the assumption that it will "just happen." It needs to be encouraged and cultivated by supervisors

TABLE 6.1
Manager Self-Assessment

Rate how much *you do the activity now*. Use the following scale for each rating:

1 = very infrequently/never
2 = infrequently
3 = a moderate amount
4 = frequently
5 = very frequently

1. _____ Facilitate and support my employees' efforts in meeting their goals.
2. _____ Provide on-going coaching and counseling on ways to improve each employee's effectiveness.
3. _____ State and demonstrate my commitment to customer satisfaction.
4. _____ Clearly articulate performance expectations to my employees.
5. _____ Set clear performance goals
6. _____ Provide my employees with all relevant information to do their jobs.
7. _____ Create an environment where candid communication is the norm.
8. _____ Create an environment where teamwork and collaboration is the norm.
9. _____ Create an environment where each employee feels valued.
10. _____ Treat all employees equally regardless of their individual characteristics.
11. _____ Be sensitive to the personal needs of my employees.
12. _____ Own up to the commitments I make to my employees.
13. _____ Encourage and value my employees' ideas
14. _____ Provide opportunities for my employees to make decisions on their own.
15. _____ Provide meaningful and timely performance feedback to my employees.
16. _____ Highlight episodes of good performance.
17. _____ Explain areas for performance improvement.
18. _____ Address developmental needs of marginal performers.
19. _____ Explain career opportunities available in the organization
20. _____ Coach employees on what they need to do to achieve their career goals in the company.

(Hillman, Schwandt, & Bartz, 1990). Certainly, there are many good reasons for paying attention to employees' performances.

- It demonstrates a commitment to excellent management.
- It accomplishes your group's objectives.
- It maintains high quality relationships.
- It develops critical job skills.
- It increases employees' satisfaction, competence, and effectiveness.
- It helps employees understand how they can better contribute to the firm's success.
- It improves employees' morale and quality of work life.

Some Common Problems

Although the value of performance management may seem obvious (a "no brainer" as they say), unfortunately it is not done well. Here are some common problems that subordinates cite about their managers:

- Managers do not face up to performance problems.
- Managers need training in how to give negative feedback and make it constructive.
- Compensation is not related to performance.
- Objectives change quickly.
- Managers do not explain the performance rating process. So, employees have little understanding of the system (salary grades, rating procedures, salary treatment, and career opportunities).
- Managers give little attention to helping subordinates with career planning.
- Top management believes that employees are not motivated by money.
- Managers have little discretion about important decisions regarding employees' careers.
- Managers are not rewarded for developing subordinates.
- Managers "micromanage"—they do not leave employees alone to do their jobs.
- Managers do not know what employees want or expect from them.
- Managers lack "people" skills.
- There are no career paths.

These are the kind of negative conditions that can and do occur. They happen because in many organizations, the role of managing people is not given enough attention. This is an important part of the reason why managers do not try to give meaningful performance feedback. Thus, some of what must change for feedback to improve has to do with the culture of the organization.

TOWARD A SUPPORTIVE
CORPORATE CULTURE

Some organizations recognize that being a coach and developer is an important part of the manager's job. Others do not. Consider two types of organizations: One expects employees to do their current jobs as assigned. The supervisor's attention is on the current performance of the department and each individual in the department. Occasionally, people are promoted, but these promotions are limited to young managers in a special program for high potential managers. Even for this select group, there are few opportunities for job movement.

In the second kind of organization—one in the same industry in the same region of the country—the culture is very different. The CEO talks about the importance of development to the organizations. All employees are expected to know their current jobs well and perform their best. Also, they are expected to think ahead and be aware of anticipated changes in the industry and the company that may change their jobs. They are encouraged to take courses, read, and in other ways stay ahead of the curve as much as possible. All employees are expected to understand the changing and emerging technologies affecting their industry, at least in general, conceptual terms, even if they do not know every technical detail. Also, they are expected to be alert to changing market conditions, including elements of globalization, competition, and the economy that affect their business. The company supports this learning in a number of ways. It provides frequent updates through newsletters about the firm's progress and directions. It holds regular information forums with managers, and managers are expected to communicate this information to their work teams. Also, managers are expected to work with individual subordinates to plan their development activities in relation to what they need to know to do their current jobs better now and in the future and in relation to other jobs they might like to have in the firm. Although the company does not have rigid career paths, because department structures and job functions change frequently, it does have logical career paths that serve as guidelines to help employees prepare for career moves. These career paths show how one job can help prepare for one or more other types of jobs. The company encourages job movement for the sake of development. That is, job moves are initiated by managers because they have subordinates who are ready for developmental experiences, not just because there happens to be a vacancy that must be filled. Human resource policies support this philosophy by providing ample training opportunities in competencies important to the organization, by appraisal and pay systems that reward the manager's role as developer, by encouraging managers and subordinates to work together on career planning and development, and by making it easy for managers to help their subordinates move to new positions and, in turn, for managers to find the right people to fill vacancies in their units.

Although both firms are doing well financially now, officials in the second firm believe that their company will be better positioned for new developments in the future. That has proved true in the past as the firm found it easier to adapt to new products, markets, and distribution channels. Although the other company responded to similar conditions by downsizing and restructuring, the latter company was able to respond to changes faster and reorganize with no lay offs. As a result, they have more cash on hand for new ventures. Moreover, although the surviving employees in first company have been traumatized by fear of insecure employment, the employees in the second company feel competitive as individuals and as a firm. They recognize the importance of understanding themselves, the organization, and the environment. They know how to learn, and they look forward to new developmental experiences. They are poised for change.

In the first organization, there are some managers who believe in developing subordinates regardless of an unsupportive corporate policy. They have developed reputations as good managers to work for and, as a result, they are able to attract the best people to their units. Unfortunately, these individuals are not rewarded for their supportive development efforts. In the other organization, some managers are not good at developing subordinates. They feel uncomfortable talking with subordinates about their performance, and they do not like disrupting the daily flow of activity to worry about what might happen in the future. These managers wonder why they are rewarded as well as others who have comparably good bottom lines. Some have been encouraged to take advantage of an early retirement incentive.

Given these differences in managers' approaches to subordinate development, I now consider supervisors' *motives* in providing subordinates with performance feedback.

SUPERVISOR INTENTIONS IN GIVING FEEDBACK

People who give feedback should realize that those who receive it make fine distinctions about why the feedback is given. For instance, they are aware that supervisor intentions may reflect daily swings in work pressure, mood, and prevalent organizational rumors. In one study, business students (full and part-time) and faculty were asked to recall all the "constructive" and "not so constructive" reasons they perceived concerning why supervisors had given them feedback about their performance (Fedor, Buckley, & Eder, 1990). The intentions fell into four major groupings: supervisor dominance, attentiveness to unit expectations, subordinate nurturance, and exhortation to increase subordinate performance. Here are some examples of specific intentions related to each theme:

Supervisor Dominance

- Demonstrate his or her power or authority.
- Bolster his or her own self-image at the subordinate's expense.
- Cover his or her own shortcomings.
- Belittle the subordinate.
- Put the subordinate in his or her place.

Attentiveness to Unit Expectations

- Insure that the subordinate's performance meets departmental standards.
- Explain the standards the subordinate should use to evaluate his or her own performance.
- Provide the subordinate with information on progress toward unit goals.
- Encourage the work group to perform as a team.
- Help the subordinate perform the job more efficiently and with less effort.

Subordinate Nurturance

- Make the subordinate feel more relaxed about work.
- Bolster the subordinate's self-image.
- Insure that the subordinate does not store up feelings of dissatisfaction.

Exhortations to Increase Subordinate Performance

- Have the subordinate work harder.
- Increase productivity level.
- Change the attitude of the subordinate toward work.
- Encourage the subordinate to take the initiative and be creative.

Subordinates may perceive their bosses as having other than the best intentions in giving feedback. This perception is likely to affect their reactions and responses to the feedback (Fedor et al., 1990). Thus, supervisors should consider not just the message they are giving but the intention they are conveying to subordinates. However, supervisors are only partially in control of subordinates' conclusions about their intentions. In part, perceptions of supervisor intentions are in the eye of the beholder. Therefore, supervisors should try to be explicit about their intentions. They should explain to the subordinates the purpose for the feedback. Also, they should consider other organizational occurrences when choosing when and under what conditions to provide feedback. For instance, providing unfavorable feedback when there are rumors of downsizing may be perceived as a warning or a way to build a rationale for laying off the subordinate.

Supervisor Biases

Supervisors' behavior toward subordinates may be biased in favor or against individual employees. Considerable research shows that this bias influences the attention and support employees receive to enhance their performance. The *Pygmalion effect* occurs when managers' expectations are raised about a subordinate's potential. Raising managers' performance expectations can improve their leadership and result in an increase in their subordinates' performance. This is a special case of the self-fulfilling prophecy (Fedor et al., 1990). The *Golem effect* is the Pygmalion effect in reverse: Low manager expectations restrict subordinate achievement, causing either absolute decreases in subordinate performance or smaller gains in performance than could have been achieved otherwise (*Golem* means "oaf" or "dumbbell" in Hebrew slang; Rosenthal, 1991; Rosenthal & Jacobson, 1968).

Interventions to Correct Biases

Interventions can restrict or enhance the effects of these biases. Consider the following:

Reduce the Golem Effect. In a study of the Golem effect, military squads were randomly assigned to an experimental or control condition (Babad, Inbar, & Rosenthal, 1982). In the experimental condition, subordinates who received low test scores on a physical fitness test were targeted for de-Golemization by treating the leader's low expectations toward all low-scoring subordinates in the squad. Squad leaders in the control condition were not treated. The treatment consisted of an explanation to squad leaders that was designed to prevent them from forming low expectations toward their low scorers. They were told that "research on the . . . test, as well as past experience in many . . . units has shown that low scores do not predict performance well" (Oz & Eden, 1994, p. 746). The explanation continued to say that men with low scores often achieve as much or more than those who have scored considerably higher. Several possible reasons were given (e.g., perhaps because the test is unreliable for low scorers, or because low scorers were not motivated to do their best). During biweekly follow-up meetings, squad leaders were asked specifically how things were going with the leader's low scores and how the leader was handling them.

Repeats of the physical fitness test showed that initially low-scoring subordinates in the experimental squads improved more than those in the control squads. Moreover, the initially low-scorers in the experimental groups maintained their improved scores, rated their squad leaders more favorably, and were more satisfied than initially low-scorers in the control group.

Induce Pygmalion.   Earlier experiments showed that interventions could induce the Pygmalion effect—i.e., that managers get the performance they expect (Eden, 1992). Subordinates designated as having high test scores reflecting high–achievement potential scored higher on achievement tests after training. The subordinates designated as high potential had been randomly assigned to this group. The Pygmalion effect works, in part, because managers who expect high performance communicate those expectations to their subordinates and unwittingly treat these high–potential subordinates differently. This is likely to raise the subordinates' own expectations (the Galatea effect). This stems from the expectancy theory of work motivation that predicts that people exert greater effort when they expect to succeed.

Interventions to Increase Feedback

Ways to improve feedback depend on the nature of the relationship between supervisor and subordinate. In chapter 2, I described three types of relationships based on the supervisor's primary need: control-dominated, reward-dominated, and relationship-dominated. Each has implications for improving feedback:

In Control-Dominated Relationships

 • Train people in self-management skills to help them understand the control they have over their own behavior and its effects on others.
 • Train people to understand the importance of building a power base such that the recipient views the source of feedback as expert, attractive, and trustworthy (Hill & Corbett, 1993)—once established, the recipient is likely to react constructively to negative feedback in order to reduce dissonance from receiving such feedback from a trusted source of feedback.
 • Train people in counseling techniques as is true of a counselor, when the source of feedback recognizes, clarifies, and accepts the recipient's expressed feelings, the recipient's feelings will become more positive, the recipient will develop understanding of his or her feelings and will initiate positive coping actions (Hill & Corbett, 1993).
 • Take management actions such as removing the source of feedback from the situation (through transfer or dismissal) and altering the source of feedback's formal control over the recipient (e.g., demoting source of feedback or changing the source of feedback's assignment).

In Reward-Dominated Relationships

 • Learn how to alter the reward structure to link the recipient's performance to outcomes valued by the recipient.

• Change the recipient's job to increase opportunities for achievement and challenge.

• Train the source of feedback (and recipient) in task skills will also enhance performance outcomes.

• Train people in behavioral modeling and reinforcement principles (help the source of feedback to understand the value of clarifying outcomes to the recipient and help the recipient understand how his or her behavior leads to outcomes).

• Raise the value and size of behavioral outcomes or rewards (for instance, combine outcomes, encourage the source of feedback to withdraw from the situation before having a chance to say something destructive, increase the recognition and other rewards from giving constructive feedback, and highlight the long-term negative implications of destructive feedback (Logue, 1995).

• Implement reward structures to increase cue salience, interventions to encourage perceptiveness (e.g., recording and feedback mechanisms).

• Change outcome contingencies (for instance, be sure that the source of feedback does not have a chance to give destructive feedback after withholding it for awhile, encourage the source of feedback to publicly precommit to behavior that precludes destructive feedback, and be sure that the source of feedback is aware of the outcomes that result from destructive and constructive feedback).

In Affiliation-Dominated Relationships

• Train in observations skills (methods are described in the next chapter).

• Train in social-management skills (to help people understand behaviors that influence interpersonal dynamics and help them be more sensitive to these relationships as they evolve).

• Model constructive feedback (managers who receive constructive feedback from others are likely to be constructive when giving feedback to others).

• Offer sensitivity training and various individual and group therapies (to help individuals understand how others react to them and how they react to others).

• Administer multisources of feedback (ratings from subordinates, supervisors, peers, customers, and other constituencies) to help people understand how others see them.

COACHING

Support from coworkers, especially one's supervisor, encourage employees' motivation and resilience in the face of daily job pressures (London, 1995b). Here are eight behavioral dimensions of *caregiving* within organizations (developed by Kahn, 1993):

Accessibility. Remain in the employee's vicinity, allowing time and space for contact and connection.

Inquiry. Ask for information necessary to prove the employee's emotional, physical, and cognitive needs; probe the employee's experiences, thoughts, and feelings.

Attention. Actively attend to the employee's experiences, ideas, self-expressions; show comprehension with verbal and nonverbal gestures.

Validation. Communicate positive regard, respect, and appreciation to employee.

Empathy. Imaginatively put oneself in the employee's place and identify with the employee's experience.

Support. Offer information (about salient issues/ situations), feedback (about employee's strengths/ weaknesses), insights (about caregiving relationship), and protection (from distracting external forces).

Compassion. Show emotional presence by displaying warmth, affection, and kindness.

Consistency. Provide an ongoing, steady stream of resources, compassion, and physical/emotional/cognitive presence for the employee.

Now, consider these three patterns of organizational caregiving: (a) *flow* (caregiving that flows from supervisors to subordinates during role-related interactions), (b) *reverse flow* (subordinates giving unreciprocated care to supervisors), and (c) *barren* (a mutual lack of caregiving between supervisors and subordinates that leads people to emotionally withdraw from one another; Kahn, 1993). The particular pattern that emerges depends on the level of staffing. Having fewer employees than are needed increases workload pressures and leaves little time for caregiving within the organization. The pattern also depends on the executive director who establishes expectations by modeling caregiving and on covert organizational dynamics, for instance, splitting the caregivers off from the rest of the organization leaving them little outlet for painful emotions and anxieties.

Coaching is harder than giving feedback. It is easier to say what is right or wrong with performance than it is to identify ways to correct a performance problem (Hillman et al., 1990). An important managerial skill for effective coaching is problem solving, because coaching is essentially problem solving applied to a performance problem (Stowell, 1988). Here are some steps for effective coaching discussion (adapted from Hillman et al., 1990, p. 26):

1. *State the purpose.* Be direct (e.g., "I want to talk about the report you gave me yesterday.").

2. *State the performance problem.* It helps to have observations or measures. Describe the expected performance, the actual performance, and the effects of the actual performance on the job (e.g., "The Vice President wanted the report to include a time series analysis of the company's financial performance, but you did not do that."). Also, admit that there are multiple perspectives.

This results in greater liking for the information and better memory of it (Langer, 1992).

3. *Get reactions from the subordinate.* Ask for the subordinate's view ("What do you think?," "Do you agree with me?"). Keep the discussion on track. Do not get sidetracked by ancillary issues (e.g, a response such as, "Other reports do not include the information and I recall that their authors were given a chance to present the results in person to the vice president. I hope you'll let me have that chance.").

4. *Analyze why the performance is unsatisfactory.* Explore with the subordinate possible causes of the performance problem. Ask the subordinate to identify factors he or she has control over that may be causing the problem (e.g., "Maybe you don't know enough about the database or software to get what we need here."). Consider external factors that may have caused the performance problem (e.g., "The computer systems were down.").

5. *Seek a collaborative solution if possible.* Ask the subordinate for ideas about how to solve the problem (e.g., "How can we fix this?"). Be patient, and consider all ideas. Offer your own course of action if the staff member is uncertain what to do. Summarize the agreed-to course of action (e.g., "Okay, so we agree. You will ask Bill for help in analyzing the data, and you will revise the report this weekend.").

6. *Provide assistance and follow up.* Establish assistance that the subordinate will need in the future. Determine what each of you will do for follow-up and subsequent performance review (e.g., "Let me have the revised report on Monday morning. I'll read it right away, and we can discuss in right after lunch.").

THE APPRAISAL AND DEVELOPMENT CYCLE

Performance appraisal and feedback should not be merely annual events, nor should attention to development. Rather, they should comprise a "systematic and continuous process of improving employee performance" (Silverman, 1991, p. 128). Moreover, this process should involve the subordinate every step of the way and, as such, establish and reinforce the subordinate's commitment and motivation to improve. The process changes the relationship between supervisor and subordinate by requiring clear communication, collaboration, and follow up on goal accomplishment and performance improvement. Also, the process engenders a climate of support for development and continuous learning in the organization. The process can be viewed as a 5-step cycle (adapted from Silverman, 1991, pp. 129–149). The cycle is repeated as new responsibilities are added. Each step is reviewed in the following:

Step 1: Clarify the Employee's Major Responsibilities. The supervisor and subordinate should have a clear idea, and the same idea, of what is needed.

Vague communications about job requirements and expectations can lead to frustration on the part of the supervisor and subordinate. This does not mean that a rigid, written job description is necessary. Companies such as Computer Associates do not use formal job descriptions because jobs are highly fluid. Assignments and responsibilities change constantly, and job descriptions impose unnecessary limitations and engender a civil service mentality (i.e., employees may decline to do activities that are not clearly part of their job description). But, at Computer Associates, supervisors work with subordinates to generate a common understanding of expected work activities and outputs.

Step 2: Develop Performance Standards.   Expectations are refined further in the process of developing performance standards through goal setting (discussed in the following). Standards might be expressed in terms of behaviors (controllable and observable actions that employees exhibit on the job), or results (accomplishments that are under the employee's control and depend on the employee's actions). AT&T developed a philosophy expressed in performance management guidelines that managers should set goals in terms of outputs not activities (London & Mone, 1987). This did not mean that it did not matter how employees accomplished a task as long as they got the job done. Certainly, they would be held accountable for their actions. However, it meant that goal setting should focus on the end result. Goal setting did not have to specify every action needed to accomplish the goal.

Step 3: Give Periodic Performance Feedback.   Frequent communication between subordinate and manager about performance is vital to the success of the performance management cycle. Once-a-year performance reviews have questionable value unless they are accompanied by on-going discussion about performance.

Step 4: Diagnose and Coach Employee Performance.   When performance improvement is needed, the manager and subordinate need (a) a clear understanding of the discrepancy between current and expected performance, (b) a discussion and common understanding of the causes of the performance discrepancy, and (c) the development of action plans to enhance the employee's performance.

Step 5: Review Overall Performance.   This last step should not be a surprise to the employee if the first four steps were conducted adequately. This requires preparation and follow up, as detailed next in the section on goal setting and feedback, reprinted from London (1995b).

Goal Setting and Feedback

Goals and feedback are mutually supportive. Goals help feedback work, and feedback helps goals work. Goals have little effect when feedback is not given.

Similarly, feedback has little effect if it does not result in goal setting. Moreover, the combination of goal setting and feedback is more effective than either one alone (Locke & Latham, 1990).

To be more specific, goals are one of the key ways that feedback gets translated into action. That is, feedback motivates improved performance by means of goal setting. Research on goal setting and feedback indicates that feedback alone, without goal setting, does little to change performance. Similarly, when feedback is given for multiple aspects of performance, those areas that later improve are those for which goals have been set. Also, goals regulate performance more reliably when feedback is present than when it is absent. (See Locke & Latham, 1990, chapter 8, for an extensive review of feedback and goal setting.) Goals focus attention on information that is significant, and they direct subsequent action. Further, goal setting and feedback are important because they have positive and negative consequences. That is, they are followed by reward or recognition.

Internal and External Cues. Goal setting and feedback are not necessarily explicit. Even when goals are not assigned or employees are not asked to set goals following feedback, they may do so anyway. Also, even if feedback is not provided explicitly, employees may use a variety of cues to get an idea about how well they are doing. They may use internal cues, such as how fast they are working or how hard they are trying. Although these cues may be inaccurate, they still play a role in the employee's cognitions about performance judgments.

Steps in the Cognitive Process. Consider the steps an employee follows in evaluating his or her performance and setting subsequent goals (adapted from Locke & Latham, 1990, p. 175).

1. An employee's performance leads to feedback, probably from multiple sources.

2. The employee detects, understands, and appraises (judges the accuracy and implications of) the feedback. The importance and value of the feedback is evaluated (whether it indicates good or poor performance; whether the performance level is significant or not). The employee has an emotional response to the feedback and these judgments.

3. If the employee believes the feedback is inaccurate, he or she may ignore it or seek more information. If the employee judges the feedback as unimportant, he or she is likely to simply ignore it. If the employee believes the information is important and suggestive of favorable performance, he or she will set a goal to maintain or increase the level of performance (or, if satisfied with the performance, may switch activities).

4. If the employee believes the feedback is important, but is dissatisfied with the level of performance, he or she will set a goal to improve, especially if the individual is committed to doing well and believes that he or she has the

potential to do better. If the employee believes he or she cannot do better and/or is not committed to the task, the employee may lower the goal or give up altogether. If the employee cares about the task but is unsure about his or her potential to do better, the employee may try performing the task in a new way.

Locke and Latham, noted researchers of the goal-setting process, summarized the relationship between feedback and goal setting as follows:

> Feedback tells people what is; goals tell them what is desirable. Feedback involves information; goals involve evaluation. Goals inform individuals as to what type or level of performance is to be attained so that they can direct and evaluate their actions and efforts accordingly. Feedback allows them to set reasonable goals and track their performance in relation to their goals, so that adjustments in effort, direction, and even strategy can be made as needed. . . . What gets measured in relation to goals gets done. (Locke & Latham, 1990, p. 197)

Learning How to Be a Coach and Developer

Some firms offer explicit training in each step, with videos to demonstrate points and activities. Although very helpful, this is not necessary. Managers can incorporate the steps in their appraisal process even when the company provides little support and expects much less from the performance review. Managers can still show their personal concern and commitment to performance management and employee development. Even if managers are not rewarded directly for coaching subordinates, coaching should enhance the department's performance, increase employees' motivation, and attract the best people into the department.

Training and Practice.   The appraisal/development cycle and performance review steps require practice. Supervisors should consider each step in the cycle. Think about characteristics of effective and ineffective performance. Understand major responsibilities and performance standards. Observe and document employee performance. Consider what is required to diagnose and coach employees on their performance. Review elements of the employee's performance that you want to discuss during the review.

Some Corporate Examples

The performance management cycle may be implemented differently depending on the organization's needs and preferences. Consider two firms: Sovran Financial Corporation and Metro Information Services, Inc. (These cases were described by McAfee & Champagne, 1993.) Sovran is a financial holding company with major offices in Maryland, Washington DC, Virginia, and

Tennessee. It has more than 15,000 employees and assets exceeding $50 billion. Metro provides computer consulting and information services implementation to clients through the Southeast. It has more than 450 people with sales exceeding $25 million.

Impetus.   The need for the program at Sovran came from one regional manager in a retail division who wanted a new performance appraisal form. A consultant hired for the project suggested that the form, per se, was not the answer. So the regional manager worked with the company's head of training and organization development to create a new system. The training and system was implemented one region at a time. Metro's program emerged from a similar need. The company hired a team of three consultants to design a performance management workshop and introduce the process. The workshop reviewed each program area (performance planning, managing performance, and reviewing performance) with a lecture, cases, and role plays.

Performance Planning.   Sovran managers are asked to meet each employee annually to develop jointly a development plan, performance goals, and standards along with expected completion dates. A competence-rating form is used as a basis for discussion of the employees' competencies in such areas as decision making, planning and organizing, and teamwork skills. The system is integrated into the company's overall strategic planning program in that each employee's goals and development plan are established after reviewing the firm's overall goals, business plans, and department direction.

Metro's approach is a bit different. Annually, managers complete a personal assessment development form that requests two strengths and two areas for development and suggested actions. Employees complete the same form for themselves. Supervisors and subordinates meet to discuss their evaluations and arrive at an agreement for development in areas of technical skills, professional competence, and/or management abilities.

Managing Performance.   At Sovran, managers are expected to follow four key steps: (a) observe and document performance, (b) provide periodic feedback, (c) offer coaching and counseling, and (d) revise goals/developmental plans if needed based on changing business or economic conditions. Metro does much the same thing. The company trains managers to write specific and behavioral statements of performance accomplishments with sufficient details to determine the extent to which the employee was accountable for the results (versus events beyond the employee's control).

Reviewing Performance.   Sovran employees are encouraged to complete a self-evaluation and come to the feedback discussion prepared to review it. Managers prepare their evaluation by considering what was expected, how much was done, when it was done, and how it was done in reference to each performance goal. During the discussion, the employee explains his or her self-assessment and then the manager makes his or her presentation. Areas of disagreement, if unresolved, are noted on an "Employee Comments" section of the appraisal form. A separate meeting is set to establish a new set of goals and development plans. The process is similar at Metro except that the firm expects that 80% of the performance discussion will focus on "where do we go from here." This is because both the employee and manager should already know what has and has not been accomplished by the time they review annual performance, if they have had an ongoing series of performance reviews.

Implementation. When these cases were reported, Sovran's program had been in operation for 6 years and Metro's for 4 (McAfee & Champagne, 1993). Metro used the program in all its offices. At Sovran, managers using the program reported few problems, and most viewed it positively. Some indicated it is more time-consuming than the more traditional appraisal system that preceded it. Some employees expressed frustration with developing a specific list of goals that later need to be revised or changed completely as a consequence of organizational changes. The company's director of training and organization development argued that just telling employees what is or is not important results in major performance improvement.

Components of a Systematic Program Evaluation

Metro and Sovran did not conduct a systematic review of the success of their performance management programs—at least, such a review was not reported. Indicators that might be used for such a systematic evaluation range from determining whether the program was used and collecting perceptions of the program's use, to measuring changes in performance that resulted from the programs. Here are some of the possible indicators:

• Reported use of the program.
• An examination of copies of forms maintained in a central human resource office. Such forms may be copies of actual reviews or merely certification by each supervisor/subordinate pair that the process was completed for the performance period.
• Attitude survey questions that ask specifically for satisfaction with different elements of the program.
• Upward feedback ratings that ask employees to rate the extent to which their supervisor complies with elements of the program. Comparison of managers' self-ratings to their subordinates' ratings to determine any gaps in perceptions about how the program is being implemented. Such measures can be used to hold managers accountable for their implementation of the program.
• Reports of unsolicited complaints or reactions to the program.
• Examination of performance over time (perhaps comparing units with the program and those not using it while accounting for other factors that might contribute to any performance differences).

CONCLUSION

This chapter explained what it means to be an effective coach and developer. It outlined reasons for supporting performance management and why managers do not face up to performance problems in their units. I argued for a supportive corporate culture that trains and rewards managers to be coaches and developers of their subordinates. Supervisors' intentions and biases were considered along with how to encourage managers to have high expectations for their people. Ways to be an effective coach were described. Finally, I reviewed elements of an effective appraisal and development cycle.

Here is a review of the chapter's central points:

1. Learn to be an effective coach and developer by starting with self-assessment. Review your style of management, including how you support your subordinates' career planning and development.

2. Unfortunately, managers often fail to face up to performance problems. Performance management needs to be encouraged and cultivated. Doing so demonstrates your commitment to excellent management, your desire to accomplish your group's objectives, and enhance employees' satisfaction, competence, and effectiveness.

3. People who receive feedback try to evaluate the source's intentions, and this influences their reactions to the feedback. Supervisors want to communicate their desire to seriously consider the best interests of their subordinates and the organization. In general, supervisors who have positive expectations for subordinates' performance provide more support to encourage the subordinates' success. Conversely, low manager expectations restrict subordinates' achievement.

4. Managers can learn to give more constructive feedback. How they give feedback should depend on the nature of the relationship they have with each subordinate. For instance, in control-dominated relationships, managers should learn self-management skills to help them understand the control they have over their own behavior and its effects on others. In reward-dominated relationships, managers should learn how to alter the reward structure to link the subordinate's performance to valued outcomes. In affiliation-dominated relationships, managers should improve their observation and social-management skills. A manager who has different relationships with different subordinates may have to learn all three approaches.

5. Coaching involves encouraging employees' motivation and resilience in the face of daily job pressures. This entails understanding how to be accessible and attend actively to subordinates' experiences, ideas, and efforts at self-expression.

6. The appraisal and development cycle is a continuous process of improving employee performance that involves the subordinate. It rests on a foundation of clear communication, collaboration, goal setting, follow up on goal

accomplishment, and performance improvement. It involves (a) clarifying the employee's major responsibilities, (b) developing performance standards, (c) giving periodic performance feedback, (d) diagnosing performance problems and coaching in ways to improve, and (e) reviewing overall performance.

7. Consider the kind of manager you want to become and establish a plan for learning how to be a developer and coach and track your success.

Now answer the questions in Table 6.1 again, this time indicating the type of behavior you want to exhibit in the future. What do you have to do to make this a reality? Develop a plan for yourself to become a better coach and developer. Then, read the next two chapters on how to be more accurate in evaluating others' performance and how to conduct effective performance review discussions.

7

Toward More Accurate Performance Appraisals and Meaningful Performance Reviews

Here I continue the discussion of what managers need to learn to make feedback constructive. Although people shy away from giving feedback, they can learn to make giving feedback a natural part of their management style. They can improve their observation skills, become more accurate raters, be more supportive and constructive in giving feedback, and manage marginal performers. I begin by considering how supervisors can become more accurate evaluators and raters of job performance.

TOWARD MORE MEANINGFUL APPRAISALS

We know from the second chapter that information is likely to be perceived more accurately and be accepted when it...

1. It comes soon after the behavior.
2. It is positive.
3. It is frequent.
4. It is specific.
5. It comes from a source who the recipients view as having expertise, familiarity with the task, trustworthiness, and power (control over valued outcomes).
6. It covers behaviors the recipient has the competence and power in the organization to control.
7. It tells the recipient what behavior leads to improved performance.

Table 7.1 includes these and other important points that should be followed in giving feedback. Use it as a checklist to give feedback at any time, not just once a year.

Here are some reasons why managers do not like to give feedback, regardless of whether it is positive or negative (Hillman et al., 1990). Managers do not believe that feedback is useful or necessary. (They believe that "no news is good news.") Managers believe that they are not competent to judge others. Managers fear that their subordinates will react negatively to the feedback. Or, they fear that feedback may be used against them (as when subordinates defend themselves by blaming the manager).

Common Rating Errors

Managers' judgments of others' performance may be affected by a variety of perceptual errors. These common biases are often evident in performance ratings, although they may pervade narrative descriptions of performance even when ratings are not made. They include the following:

TABLE 7.1
Checklist for Preparing and Giving Feedback

Feedback should . . .

_____ Be given as soon as possible following the behavior.

_____ Require ample time for discussion.

_____ Be conducted in a private setting.

_____ Not be given when the supervisor or subordinate are frustrated, angry, or tired.

_____ Encourage self-evaluation by the subordinate.

_____ Be derived from factual information.

_____ Initially be descriptive rather than evaluative.

_____ Be specific.

_____ Focus on behaviors, not personality.

_____ Be related to an expected task.

_____ Show that you are interested in, and concerned for, the subordinate.

_____ Show that you respect the subordinate's dignity and opinions.

_____ Exhibit a trusting climate.

_____ Demonstrate that the supervisor prepared for the review.

_____ Reflect adequate collection of information.

_____ Ensure that the supervisor and subordinate understand what has been discussed.

_____ Encourage input from the subordinate.

_____ Address both effective performance and areas needing improvement.

_____ Review the consequences of not effectively addressing a performance problem.

_____ Use effective verbal and nonverbal communication skills.

Note. Adapted from Hillman, Schwandt, and Bartz (1990).

Leniency. The tendency to give overly favorable ratings on all performance dimensions regardless of actual performance.

Severity. The tendency to give overly negative ratings on all performance dimensions regardless of actual performance.

Halo. The tendency to allow perceptions of one performance dimension influence ratings of other, unrelated performance dimensions.

Similarity. The tendency to give overly favorable ratings to ratees who are similar to the rater on characteristics that are unrelated to performance (e.g., age, race, or gender).

Central tendency. The tendency to give mid-range ratings on all performance dimensions regardless of actual performance (e.g., ratings of 3 on 1–5 scales).

First impression. The tendency to allow one's first impression of the ratee to influence ratings. (This is especially relevant to the employment interviews, but also applies to ratings of subordinates when a manager develops an immediate impression of a new subordinate, and this impression colors the raters subsequent judgments of the subordinate's performance.)

Recency effect. The tendency to allow a recent incident to influence judgments of performance dimensions for the entire performance period.

Such errors suggest the need for training to reduce managers' errors of judgment and increase their rating accuracy.

RATER TRAINING

One approach to performance appraisal training is to alert managers to common errors of judgment so they can spot them in how they evaluate others and guard against them. Other approaches change the evaluation method rather than the rater. Appraisal methods that have clear performance dimensions expressed in behavioral terms are likely to reduce rating errors. In general, the more ambiguous the performance dimensions and the less likely they relate to observable job behavior, the more raters' biases affect the ratings. Other approaches try to make managers better observers of performance assuming that if they have clear recollection of job behaviors and they have a clear understanding of performance standards that their judgments will be relatively bias free.

Observation Skills Training

Here are some ways to improve observation skills: (a) give observers prior experience in judging the topic and object of interest, (b) use good actors as models, (c) make the discriminations as discrete and defined with familiar terminology as possible, (d) select judges of at least normal intelligence and median age, (e) allow judges to see all of a subject including the context that may have provoked his or her actions, and (f) allow observers sufficient time to observe (Boice, 1983).

Training methods to increase insight might include:

- Train people to observe cues.
- Encourage self-disclosure and feedback.
- Train people to search for disconfirming evidence.
- Train people to ignore biases, such as *confirmation bias* (leaning toward one perspective and seeking support for our initial view and avoiding disconfirming evidence) and *hindsight bias* (believing that the world is more predictable than it really is because what happened often seems more likely afterwards than it did before hand; Russo & Schoemaker, 1992).
- Train people in ways to conceptualize and process perceptions so they learn to think about how they think (Perkins, 1981).

Frame-of-Reference Training

Another training approach entails giving raters a frame of reference to evaluate the accuracy of their ratings as part of the training in addition to lecture and discussion of job behaviors and rating dimensions. One study compared frame-of-reference and rater-error training with a control condition called *structure of training* that presented examples of typical job behaviors and rating dimensions, practice ratings, and discussions about ratings (Stamoulis & Hauenstein, 1993). This control condition produced results that were similar to the frame-of-reference training. Raters may still improve dimensional accuracy from training that is limited to lecture and discussion of job behaviors and rating dimensions and rating practice. Also, they suggested that frame of reference and rater-error training should be used together to (a) increase the correspondence between the variability in observed ratings and the variability in actual ratee performance and (b) provide practice in differentiating among ratees (rather than focus on rating errors). This may be accomplished by lecture and discussion of job behaviors and rating dimensions, general performance examples, rating practice, and general rating feedback.

Behavior Modeling

Behavior modeling encompasses four steps: explaining principles, demonstrating principles, providing a chance for trainees to try the new behaviors and receive feedback about their performance, and transfer to the job (Goldstein & Sorcher, 1974). Here's how the four steps apply to learning how to give constructive feedback:

1. *Learning the value of feedback*. Constructive feedback is defined, and its potential value is described (as reviewed in chap. 2).

2. *Observing*. Trainees are shown a video tape (or in-person role plays by the trainers) with several scenarios acted out—examples of constructive, benign but worthless feedback, and destructive feedback. The scenarios are interspersed with opportunities for discussion during which the trainers ensure that the trainees understand the differences between the desired and undesired behaviors.

3. *Practicing giving feedback and receiving feedback on feedback behavior*. Trainees are given several role-playing exercises. For instance, one person may take the role of the subordinate and another the supervisor giving feedback. Each would receive a paragraph describing their point of view. Trainers or fellow trainees observe the role play and give the "actors" feedback. Each trainee should have several opportunities to play different roles and receive feedback.

4. *Applying new behaviors on the job*. Trainees are expected to apply their newly learned behavior on the job. They may return to the training center at some later time for a follow-up description and postmortem of their behavior and effectiveness. Another way to give feedback for on-the-job behavior is to be sure that higher level supervisors are trained in the same behavioral principles, and know how to evaluate behaviors and give feedback. Still another way is to ask those receiving feedback to describe the feedback process. The limitation here, of course, is that the recipient's views may be biased by the favorability of the feedback. Nevertheless, the extent to which they viewed the feedback as constructive is likely to be indicative of how the feedback was presented. Still, another evaluation technique is to examine changes in behavior of those receiving feedback. Positive changes in behavior would be expected from constructive feedback (although, admittedly, short-term improvements in performance can occur from coercive or destructive feedback). Consequently, a multipronged approach should be taken by gathering a variety of evidence for how feedback is being given, and using that as a basis for "feedback on feedback."

TOWARD MORE CONSTRUCTIVE
FEEDBACK REVIEWS

This section considers what managers should do to give more comprehensible information to their coworkers—feedback that will be accepted and used. It also covers how to conduct an effective feedback discussion, a topic I deal with in more depth in the next chapter. Here, I show how to incorporate self-appraisals in the performance interview, link feedback to goal setting, eliminate or reduce the threat of performance grades, and separate the discussion of salary and career development.

Some General Guidelines

First, consider the following guidelines:

Conduct Annual Performance Reviews and Give Frequent Informal Feedback

- Focus on the most significant areas of performance.
- Give feedback soon after the incident.
- Be specific and concrete. Focus on behavior.
- Reinforce good performance and discuss areas that require change.
- Agree on performance objectives.
- Schedule development activities.

Give Positive Feedback

- Review accomplishments.
- Do not use generalities.
- Be specific. Cite the outcome and explain why you liked it.

Give Negative Feedback

- Do not use generalities.
- Be specific.
- Set specific objectives for improvements.
- Do not get off track. This will be easier if the employee has had an opportunity to give you input prior to the performance review discussion.

Now, here are some steps to follow in conducting a constructive, nonthreatening performance review discussion.

Diffuse defensiveness by requesting input from subordinate at the start of the discussion. Give the subordinate a chance to prepare answers to your questions. You prepare as well. However, do not begin the discussion by handing the subordinate an already completed written performance review. Rather, prepare and review notes and other documentation about the subordinate's performance. Have key pieces of information (e.g., sales results, or reports that represent the subordinate's work). You may want to refer to these during the performance review discussion. But let the subordinate do the talking. Meanwhile, take notes. If issues do not arise that you feel should be raised, bring them up. Remember that your verbal and nonverbal behaviors are important signals of your confidence and comfort. Look the subordinate in the eye. Use strong voice inflections that communicate certainty. For instance, try asking the following:

"In your view, what have your major accomplishments been during the performance period?" Discuss why these were important to the department. Discuss what went right and whether there were any surprises or limitations.

"What disappointments did you have? Why? What could have been done to avoid them?"

"Overall, how well do you think you did during the performance period? What can you do to improve?"

For issues that did not come up during the discussion, do not avoid mentioning them. This is a good time. For instance, ask, "How do you think you did about . . . (e.g., developing new customers)?"

Ask the subordinate to identify areas and ways for development. Jointly design a development plan, including training or special assignments, for the next performance period. Also, agree on goals for performance improvement in light of expected development. Be realistic. Be sure to record the development plans and performance goals.

Write up your notes and ask the subordinate to revise them. This becomes the formal appraisal and development plan. Review your appraisal with the subordinate, fine tune the report, and both sign it. Usually, the signature refers to your attesting to the contents of the appraisal and the subordinate's attesting to having reviewed the appraisal, not necessarily agreeing with it. If you cannot reach agreement, the subordinate can add a personal addendum.

Linking pay increases to performance is important, of course, because it establishes consequences for performance results and improvement. Sometime after the formal appraisal is completed, a separate discussion should be held with the subordinate to explain pay treatment (any merit bonus and/or increment in base salary). You should explain how the amount of money is related to the subordinate's performance as reflected in the appraisal. You may also need to provide comparative information. For instance, the subordinate may have shown considerable improvement, and may receive a certain amount of additional pay for that, but may still not be rewarded as highly as others whose performance is superior. You may indicate how well the individual performed relative to other people in the same or similar jobs and organizational level as the subordinate (e.g., "You were in the lower third," or "You were in the top ten") and explain how this related to pay treatment.

The subordinate might want some assurances of future pay treatment if goals for the next performance period are met. Be careful here, because the amount of money available for salary increments may depend on the financial performance of the department or firm as a whole on dimensions that go beyond the subordinate's and your control. Also, you do not know how well others will do. You can promise that you will work with the subordinate to evaluate his or her performance fairly, and you will factor in comparisons with others at the time.

The organization should have a policy about pay for development. Presumably, if an employee attends training, the employee's performance will improve. However, there may be a delay. The employee may appreciate knowing that he or she will benefit financially to some degree by devoting time and energy to professional development during the next performance period, even if it may take one or more additional performance periods to show appreciable increases in performance. This will foster a spirit of appreciation for continuous learning in the organization. Indeed, everyone can benefit from development, and development objectives should be part of every employee's performance plan, even if the development does not have a direct and immediate effect on performance.

MANAGING MARGINAL PERFORMERS

Marginal performers are employees who lack the ability and/or motivation needed to perform well (London & Mone, 1993). Doing marginal work means the person has failed. Rather, the person is doing the minimum necessary to get by. The potential for marginal performance has increased due to pressures on organizations to reduce costs and improve efficiency. Consider different types of marginal performance: *underutilization* (high ability and low effort), *misdirected effort* (low ability and high effort), and a combination of the two (low ability and low effort). Underutilization stems from inadequate goal setting, misunderstanding subordinate skills, oversupervision, and/or poor boss–subordinate communication. Misdirected effort may occur because of a poor job match or changing job requirements. People who lack both motivation and capability are likely to withdraw from work as they do not live up to increasing standards.

Ways to address marginal performance problems depend on whether the problem is motivational and/or ability related. Here are some ways to improve marginal performance.

Underutilization

Employees with high ability but low effort may benefit from the following:

• *Performance feedback*. Give honest and direct feedback about the subordinate's marginal performance.
• *Training*. Offer in-house or external training programs that help the employee acquire needed knowledge or skills.
• *Rewards*. Clarify what needs to be done to accomplish goals and highlighting the value of goal accomplishment.
• *Highlighting role models*. Publicly reward people considered to be role models.
• *Team building and conflict resolution*. Improve interpersonal relationships through communications skills assessment and training, group meetings for sharing perceptions, and problem solving sessions.
• *Counseling*. Help employees achieve better insight into their skills and interests in relation to the current job and available opportunities in the organization.

• *Burn-out prevention and management*. Encourage that the work get done during regularly scheduled hours and recognize employees for meeting performance goals rather than reward them for working overtime; recognize burn-out when it occurs and deal with it by reducing work load or providing some extra time off.

Misdirected Effort

Employees with low ability who try hard may benefit from the following:

• *Goal setting*. Set and clarify goals in relation to the subordinates' capabilities and organizational requirements and subordinates' insight into the job requirements and expectations.
• *Coaching*. Provide suggestions for behavior change; provide frequent performance feedback and reinforcement for desired behaviors.
• *Delegation*. Help managers structure the work, delegate clear tasks, and coordinate the work to reduce the manager's work load and increase the department's productivity.
• *Temporary assignments for skill development*. Transfer the subordinate to a less demanding job or to a job in a related department.
• *Restructure the job assignment*. Recognize that the marginal performer's strengths lie in other directions, and (when possible) restructure the job to rely on those strengths.

In addition, training may resolve misdirected effort just as it may help underutilization.

Low Ability and Low Effort

Employees in this category may be helped by more drastic steps:

• *Withhold merit pay and cost of living pay adjustments*. Do not provide financial rewards to marginal performers just to avoid the issue.
• *Transfer or demotion*. Identify other jobs that would be more suitable for the marginal performer.
• *Outplacement*. Invite a voluntary decision to leave the organization, possibly with generous severance pay and assistance in finding employment elsewhere.
• *Firing*. Remove the marginal performer from the organization based on proper documentation of marginal performance over time (e.g., performance appraisals during the last 3 years).

CONCLUSION

This chapter explored conditions for enhancing feedback acceptance and examined reasons why managers resist giving feedback. I reviewed common rating errors, and then outlined training methods to improve observation skills and rating accuracy. The chapter concluded with some general guidelines to enhance performance reviews followed by ways to manage marginal performers.

Here are points to remember:

1. Information is likely to be perceived more accurately and be accepted when it follows a number of conditions: For instance, it comes from a source who the recipient views as knowledgeable and trustworthy, it comes soon after the behavior, and it is positive, frequent, and specific.

2. Managers should be alert to common errors in evaluating others' performances, such as leniency, halo, central tendency, similarity, and recency. Be alert to these common rating errors to guard against them.

3. Appraisal methods that have clear performance dimensions expressed in behavioral terms are likely to reduce rating errors.

4. Observation skills can be improved by communicating performance standards, giving raters feedback on the accuracy of their ratings, and giving them a chance to practice observing, integrating, recalling, and evaluating behaviors.

5. Incorporate self-appraisals in the performance interview, link feedback to goal setting, eliminate or reduce the threat of performance grades, and separate the discussion of salary and career development.

6. Conduct annual performance reviews *and* give frequent informal feedback.

7. Reverse marginal performance by improving ability (through skills and knowledge training) and enhancing motivation (through rewards and recognition).

In the next chapter, I turn to the performance review discussion—a vital component of an effective performance management process.

8

Fine Tuning the Performance Review Discussion

This chapter focuses on a central ingredient to the performance management process—the review discussion. Feedback is not information alone. It must be communicated and digested. In the last chapter, I described the components of a meaningful performance review. Here I offer more detailed steps and guidelines for a review that produces results. The steps and guidelines apply to conducting a formal review annually or semi-annually, or to holding an informal performance discussion. I begin with some general guidelines for managers including how to respond constructively when a subordinate is defensive. I outline specific steps for conducting the review and then discuss some recommendations. Then I consider ways feedback is given in groups—to individual group members and to the group as a whole.

PERFORMANCE REVIEW GUIDELINES

Consider how you feel when your manager gives you feedback. How would you respond to the following statements (adapted from Fedor, Buckley, & Eder, 1990)?

When my supervisor gives me feedback about my performance . . .
I am often confused as to where my supervisor is coming from.
I am not certain as to what it means in terms of our working relationship.
I am usually confused by the feedback.
I am not immediately sure what it requires me to do.
I still really do not know how well I am doing.
I am not certain how best to respond to it.
I am not sure about his or her motives.
I am not sure what will result from the feedback.

How do you think your subordinates feel when you give them feedback? Do they feel the way you do when you receive feedback?

Now, here are some guidelines for conducting a formal performance review discussion (from Silverman [1991]. Copyright © Human Resource Decisions, Inc., 1988. Adapted with permission):

• *Avoid sweeping statements.* Words such as *always* and *never* only make people angry and defensive. It is too easy for them to say, "That's not true. I don't *always* . . . !"

• *Focus on major responsibilities and performance standards.* People want to know what is expected of them, not how they compare unfavorably to others.

• *Have employees identify causes for poor performance.* Self-evaluation avoids defensiveness and gives the manager an alternative viewpoint to consider. (See the following discussion about the value of incorporating self-evaluation into the performance review discussion.)

• *Provide feedback frequently.* As noted already, performance feedback should not be saved up and dumped on the employee once a year.

• *Discuss behavior or results, not the person.* Focusing on traits (e.g., "You are too passive") is likely to be seen as personal attacks. Supervisors should focus on the employee's observed behaviors or results.

• *Specify what needs to be done.* Do not just tell employees what they did wrong. Help them establish a direction for improvement.

• *Use both positive and negative feedback.* Positive feedback provides encouragement and enhances motivation. Provide negative feedback in a way that *informs* the subordinate rather than attacks the subordinate's self-esteem.

• *Coach rather than judge.* A tenet of this book, the manager should help the subordinate develop.

• *Fit feedback to the individual.* As stated earlier, providing information enhances a person's insight into himself or herself and organizational expectations. Some people need more feedback than others, perhaps because of their experience or their ability to discern their effectiveness in the organization. Some employees may not realize what is important in the department, perhaps because it was never discussed openly. Or, they may not realize the effect that certain behaviors have on coworkers' or the unit's performance.

• *Prepare for the review.* Employees should receive at least 2 weeks' notice of the impending performance review. During this time, the employee should conduct a self-assessment and the supervisor should review documentation on the employee's performance (Cascio, 1986, p. 312).

• *Develop a structure for the review discussion.* The supervisor should have a definite set of points, which focus on the subordinates' behaviors and results, to cover.

• *Agree on responsibilities and performance standards.* After the review, the employee and supervisor should review both the employee's major responsibilities and his or her performance standards. The cycle then starts again.

Here is a way to *start*:

"I would like you to start the discussion. What do you think are the three most important things you accomplished during the last 6 months? [later] What are the areas in which you wish you had done better? What do you think needs improvement? What do you need to help you improve?"

Be prepared for *defensive reactions*—denying the problem, changing the subject, focusing on something else, or attributing external blame. Here are some possibilities:

"That's not the way I see it at all! I tried my best, but there was nothing more I could have done. It was out of my control."

"I do not know where you are getting your information, but that's not what happened."

"Several people in the group just do not like me. But I worked as hard as anyone."

"I am doing my best. I did everything you wanted me to."

"It is unfair to be telling me now you wanted something else. I would have been happy to change if you had only told me."

"I have had plenty of experience, and I know how things work around here. This is the way we have always done it, and I see no reason to change now."

"I agree with you that things did not turn out as well as they could have. If we only had . . . better information, a new computer system, more cooperation from other departments, etc. Something should be done about this. Maybe I can work on it now that we all recognize the problem."

Avoid *destructive comments in response to defensiveness*: Do not argue, debate, deny, insist, cite others as the source of the evaluation, generalize and personalize. For example, do not say . . .

"You are just going to have to see it my way. You really have no choice."

"You better think it over."

"It does not matter what you think."

"This is not the way I feel. I am just passing on what our boss thinks, and you better come to terms with that."

"How could that be?"

"Face it, you are not cut out for this job."

Here are some *constructive responses to defensiveness*: Recognize and diffuse the problem up front. Agree and move on. Be repetitive. Focus on facts (behaviors or outcomes) rather than personal characteristics. Suggest directions for improvement. For instance:

"I know you do not agree with me. I am just asking you to hear me out."

"This is how I see it, and you need to know that. Now here is what I recommend."

"Here are some things you could do differently next time."

"Rather than debate the issue, let's work on what you can do differently next time."

These statements may have to be repeated several times before the employee hears.

Steps for Conducting the Performance Review

Here is a 12-step structure to follow when conducting the performance review (from Silverman, 1991, pp. 142–143; also in Fletcher, 1986, pp. 5–6):

1. Explain the purpose of the review meeting.
2. Ask the employee to summarize accomplishments and developmental needs related to the most important responsibility.
3. Summarize accomplishments and development needs from the supervisor's perspective.
4. Reach agreement on what developmental steps should be taken.
5. If there is a gap between current and expected performance on the most important responsibility, diagnose the causes of the discrepancy (whether the outside environment, the organization, the manager, and/or the employee).
6. Develop action plans to improve performance on the major responsibility.
7. Do the same for remaining major responsibilities.
8. Summarize overall performance in relation to each major responsibility and review action plans.
9. Compliment the employee on accomplishments.
10. Set a time and date to discuss any needed changes in responsibilities and performance standards for the next performance review period.
11. Have other sources of feedback available (e.g., from peer ratings or customers). This reduces defensiveness and should mean less need for feedback, per se, and more willingness to discuss the results.
12. Practice frequent communication about performance feedback. Managers who have the most frequent communication with their subordinates the rest of the year have the most productive appraisal interviews.

Table 8.1 summarizes the steps in the performance review process.

Feedback and Goal Setting

Use the review session to initiate goal setting. Goals for performance improvement and development should be initiated during the appraisal review session, but this should be only the beginning of goal setting and reviews of progress.

TABLE 8.1
The Performance Review In Brief

The purpose of the performance review is to evaluate the extent to which the employee has met the department's and company's expectations for excellence.

1. You and the employee write a performance review.
2. Hold a performance discussion. Have the employee begin as a way to encourage the employee to be as accurate as possible and less defensive.
3. Focus on outputs (objectives) separately from methods/activities for accomplishing the objectives. In discussing activities, you may want to address a variety of "soft" performance dimensions, such as cooperation, job skills and knowledge, customer relationships, customer development, communications, organizing work, and quality of work. Give behavioral examples.
4. In the 6-month review, determine if changes should be made in the objectives.
5. In giving feedback, be sure the employee understands the difference between performance, potential for movement (lateral and upward), and competitiveness for merit increases and job movement.
6. Conclude the annual review by asking the employee to prepare objectives for the goal-setting discussion to occur at a later time.

Throughout these processes, recognize differences between experienced and inexperienced managers in their abilities and career concerns. Some people need more direction than others. All employees should want to know how their jobs help the company accomplish its objectives. Also, remember that in addition to formal goal setting and performance review discussions, you should discuss performance frequently—at least weekly. Be specific and focus on behaviors and critical incidents.

The Goal Setting Process

- Outline your view of the employee's job.
- Specify clearly what you want done.
- Describe your vision of the desired outcomes.
- Explain why the job, project or action is important to you and the company.
- Clarify any limitations employed with the job you are delegating.
- Recognize what is and is not likely to be under the employee's control.
- Encourage and reinforce the employee by indicating confidence in him or her.
- Consider excellence criteria relevant to different aspects of the job.

Characteristics of Excellence Criteria

- They spell out the meaning of excellence.
- They are not minimum standards.
- They reflect different points of view.

TABLE 8.1 (cont.)

- They may not be measures, per se, but they describe qualities that can be discussed.
- They may be qualitative (e.g., satisfies customer) as well as quantitative (e.g., achieves x% more sales).
- They stress results. They emphasize what must be produced.
- They emphasize communication and negotiation between the manager and the employee.
- They are clear and brief.
- They are revised when necessary.

Examples of Excellence Criteria

Customer:	Solve customer problems.
	Be available and approachable.
Design:	Use available technology.
Sales Management:	Develop a sales strategy
	Focus on key accounts.
	Increased orders.
Senior Management:	Margin results.
	Increased volume

Conducting a Performance Review

1. Write a 6-month or annual review.
2. Seek employee's input prior to developing the performance review.
3. Be sure employee knows that his or her input is an integral part of the evaluation process and not just a courtesy.
4. Recognize roadblocks that can adversely influence the performance evaluation—for example, defensiveness.
5. Use multiple performance dimensions:
- Cooperation
- Job skills and knowledge of work
- Sense of responsibility
- Customer development
- Quality of work

6. Avoid common evaluation errors.

Goal setting is a continuous process with several meetings needed to suggest, negotiate, and agree on goals. Also, review sessions on goal progress should be held throughout the year—quarterly, monthly, or even weekly, depending on the job and employee's experience (Meyer, 1991).

Some Goal Setting Principles. Here are some principles for goal setting (adapted from Latham & Wexley, 1981, p. 126).

- Outlining specific goals leads employees to higher performance than telling them to do their best.
- When employees participate in goal setting, they tend to set higher goals than when the supervisor assigns them without the employee's input.
- As long as an employee perceives a goal as reasonable and achievable, the higher the goal, the better the employee performs.
- Employees must receive ongoing feedback on how they are doing in reaching their goals.
- The employee must have control over the factors essential to attaining the goals.

Separate Salary and Development Discussions

As suggested in chapter 7, separate the salary discussion from the discussion of motivation and development. The roles of judge and counselor are incompatible, and linking development to administrative action is likely to be counterproductive. Also, administrative decisions are usually made by more people than the immediate supervisor (Maier, 1958).

During the subsequent meeting about pay, remind the employee about the evaluation and explain that pay treatment is commensurate with the evaluation. State it as fact. If possible, for next time, establish a pay-for-performance contingency. Let the employee know how subsequent goal accomplishment or performance improvement will be related to pay treatment. Also, remind the employee that corporate and unit performance will determine the actual amount of money available for salary merit increases.

Use Self-Appraisals

Self-appraisals should be incorporated into the performance appraisal discussion. The subordinate takes the lead in the appraisal process. The supervisor's role is to give the employee recognition and suggest changes in behavior or activities. To repeat what I said in chapter 4, Meyer (1991) wrote the following:

> The appraisal feedback interview is a very authoritarian procedure—a parent–child type of exchange. Most modern organizations are moving away from authoritarian management toward an involvement-oriented working environment. A performance review discussion based on the subordinate's self review fits an involvement-oriented climate much better than the traditional top-down performance review discussion. It also has the advantage of forcing the manager into a counseling mode, rather than serving as a judge. Research has shown that

performance review discussions based on self-review prove to be more productive and satisfying than traditional manager-initiated appraisal discussions. (p. 68)

Supervisors are likely to need training in how to be a "counselor" and deal with problems, such as how to deal with an inflated self-evaluation, an unnecessarily self-deprecating appraisal, an important issue not raised by the subordinate, etc.

Meyer recommended that the conventional approach to feedback is sometimes appropriate when the subordinate is dependent on the supervisor, as is the case for new employees, trainees, or people in highly structured jobs. Except for these, self-appraisal is extremely valuable for the following reasons:

1. It increases the subordinate's dignity and self-respect.
2. It places the manager in the role of counselor, not judge.
3. It is more likely to engender the subordinate's commitment to goals and development plans that emerge from the discussion.
4. It avoids defensiveness.

However, there are some possible problems with self-review (Meyer, 1991):

1. It violates traditional mores about the proper relationship between boss and subordinate.
2. Employees have a self-serving bias that inflates self-appraisals. However, this "leniency error" can be minimized by orienting the self-appraisal toward development rather than appraisal for administrative purposes.
3. Supervisors are influenced by subordinates' self-judgments because supervisors prefer to avoid confrontation that comes from subordinate defensiveness (Blakely, 1993).

So, supervisors tend to be lenient when they know the subordinates see themselves positively.

Eliminate Grading

Another recommendation is to eliminate *grading*—the practice of attaching a numerical score or overall adjectival grade (e.g., satisfactory) to the review (Meyer, 1991). I introduced this idea in the description of ratingless appraisals in chapter 4. Grading is demeaning, and any administrative actions, such as a salary increase or a promotion, communicate an overall appraisal better than a grade.

So far, this chapter has considered how to conduct a meaningful performance review discussion with an individual subordinate. However, what if the feedback is to an entire group, or to an individual with the group present? These situations are discussed next.

GROUP FEEDBACK AND REWARDS

Similar processes can be followed in giving feedback to groups. Group feedback is a potentially threatening experience for the supervisor or facilitator responsible for giving the feedback and for the group members. After all, the source of the feedback has to look all the group members in the eye. The group members hear the same thing and will later compare their views of the feedback. As such, the supervisor is publicly on the spot. Here, the supervisor should focus on providing information about group performance, not each individual member's performance. This works well when there is group level information—for instance, total number of units produced by the group, or projects completed. It also works well when the group members are interdependent and the group's output is a function of a team effort.

The group setting is also a good time to establish group goals for the next performance period. The group should discuss potential goals, and the supervisor should facilitate the goal setting in relation to organization-wide objectives. The goals should be challenging—neither impossible nor too easy. The group's committing to the goals in public is a way to enhance team members' commitment to the goals. They will all feel a stake in accomplishing them.

If group goals are set and group performance is reviewed, it stands to reason that there should be a group reward. As with individual performance review, the group award should be discussed and distributed some time after (preferably soon after) the group performance review. The tie between performance achieved as a group and the reward should be explicit. Also, a policy should be established for how to distribute the group reward.

Some supervisors agree at the time group goals are established to split a monetary award equally among all group members. Other supervisors may say they will split the group award according to each team member's contribution. Team members may be asked to rate each other's contribution as a basis for the distribution. Such a policy has the potential for destroying group unity; an equal distribution is probably most equitable. Keep in mind that group performance review and reward should be coupled with individual performance review and reward. As such, the supervisor can recognize outstanding individual performance and reward it accordingly after appropriate review. Such review may include collecting information from coworkers (e.g., as part of a multisource rating system, as discussed in chapter 4).

Individual Feedback in Groups

The group setting can also be valuable for giving feedback to individuals (actually giving the feedback in front of others). This is common after business simulations in management development programs (as described in chapter

5). Here is an example of an appraisal session that stems from a team building process and feeds back peer ratings on a behavioral observation scale (this process was outlined by Locke & Latham, 1990).

Job analyses are conducted and behavioral observation scales constructed, hence, the behaviors rated reflect specific job behaviors and requirements. Also, the scales are developed *by* employees *for* employees, so the raters and ratees understand the items as critical job behaviors. Another advantage of the process is that the behavioral scales reminded raters about what behaviors are important to think about in providing their ratings. Open-ended questions asked what the ratee should continue doing on the job and what the person should start doing, stop doing, or do differently.

1. Employees meet as a group.
2. Each person's appraisal is given in a 1- to 2-hour time period.
3. A psychologist or a person skilled in group process facilitates the feedback by first asking the individual if he or she has any questions regarding his or her colleagues' evaluations.
4. Colleagues are requested to offer comments regarding the evaluations.
5. Peers are coached by the facilitator on how to emphasize what the person is to do differently in the future.
6. The person assessed is then asked to summarize what was "heard" and to set specific goals as to what he or she will do differently as a result of this feedback.
7. Subsequent discussion focuses on another individual in the group until every person has received feedback and has set goals.

CONCLUSION

This chapter offers guidelines and steps for conducting an effective performance review discussion with a subordinate. It also discusses ways to deliver feedback to groups and to individuals in groups.

Major learning points are:

1. Guidelines for conducting a formal performance review discussion include focusing on major responsibilities and performance standards, and identifying causes for poor performance. Steps to follow include explaining the purpose of the review meeting, asking the employee to summarize accomplishments and developmental needs, summarizing accomplishments and development needs from the supervisor's perspective, reaching agreement on what developmental steps should be taken, and initiating goal setting.

2. Principles for goal setting include encouraging employee participation and agreeing on specific goals. Employees do best when they perceive their goals as challenging, under their control, and achievable.

3. As noted in the last chapter, discussions of performance, salary, and development should be separated.

4. As first noted in chapter 4, self-appraisals should be incorporated into the review process. This is a way to increase subordinates' self-respect and places the manager in the role of counselor, not judge. Employees' self-serving biases can be minimized by orienting the self-appraisal toward development rather than evaluation.

5. Also as noted in chapter 4, overall ratings or grading of subordinates' performance should be avoided.

6. Group feedback and rewards are valuable in informing group members about the performance of the group as a whole. This is appropriate when there is information about the group's performance and group members are interdependent. Group goals should be established during group discussion.

7. With sufficient care, the group setting can be useful for giving feedback to individuals. This works well during developmental programs where group members in a nonthreatening environment can give each other constructive feedback.

In the next two chapters, I consider ways to help people seek and use feedback effectively.

IV

USING FEEDBACK

9

Seeking Feedback and Managing Impressions

As I pointed out throughout this book, there are many sources of feedback. Sometimes feedback comes without asking. Other times, it must be sought. Yet, people shy away from feedback. When they do ask how they are doing, they may have an ulterior motive—for instance, to get someone to say something nice about them. They may wonder how asking for feedback will affect what the source will think and say. They may wonder whether their asking will highlight behaviors that may otherwise have gone unnoticed. They may ask in a way they hope will make a favorable impression on the source. This chapter considers informal sources of feedback. I explore the process of feedback seeking and its relationship to managing (or trying to manage) others' impressions. This leads me to a discussion of ways to ask for and receive constructive and meaningful feedback.

HOW PEOPLE REACT TO FEEDBACK

In general, the recipient's cognitive and behavioral responses to feedback depend on characteristics of the message (such as its favorability, specificity, and timing), individual differences, and source credibility (Ilgen, Fisher, & Taylor, 1979). Source credibility includes characteristics such as perceived expertise, reliability, dynamism (energy and boldness), personal attraction, and intention. Reactions to feedback depend on whether the feedback is constructive or destructive. Table 9.1 presents likely reactions to constructive and destructive feedback organized by the three types of role-dominated relationships introduced in chapter 2.

Control-dominated behavior that is constructive increases the recipient's sense of independence, empowerment, and self-control. The recipient understands what behaviors lead to what rewards. Also, the recipient gains *negotiation lattitude*—the freedom to make decisions and act as the recipient deems necessary without being constantly monitored and checked (Graen & Scan-

TABLE 9.1
Reactions to Feedback

| | Feedback Reactions | |
	Constructive	Destructive
Control-Dominated Relationships	Independence generating	Entrapped
	Empowered	Disabled
	Self-control	Disenfranchised
	Clear reward contingencies	Managed
	Negotiation latitude	Dependence
		Anxiety
		Threat
Reward-Dominated Relationships	Goal clarity	Goal ambiguity
	Increased challenge	Loss
	Self-confidence	Manipulated
	Gain	
	Pride	
Affiliation-Dominated Relationships	Trust	Disharmony & dislike
	Confidence	Unfair treatment
	Fairness/Equity treatment	Distrust
	Friendship	Differences emphasized
	Commonalities emphasized	Lonesome
	Team	Outcast
Overall	Expanding cycle of growth and development	Constricting cycle of behavior

dura, 1987). Control-dominated behavior that is destructive leads to feelings of entrapment and disability. Moreover, the recipient feels managed and dependent. The recipient's anxiety increases along with feelings of being threatened (e.g., "You will do this or else!").

Reward-dominated behavior that is constructive increases goal clarity. The recipient is challenged to do better or overcome disabilities or barriers on their own. The recipient feels increasingly self-confident and proud. He or she gains materially and psychologically. Reward-dominated behavior that is destructive increases goal ambiguity. The recipient feels manipulated and a sense of loss. Note that recipients of negative feedback, even feedback that is intended to be constructive, are unlikely to try harder to overcome the negative feedback (Eden & Kinnar, 1991; Hurley, 1993).

Affiliation-dominated behavior that is constructive leads to reactions from both the recipient and source of feedback. Their feelings of mutual trust and confidence increase. The recipient feels that he or she has been treated fairly. The source and recipient have a sense of deeper friendship. They recognize their commonalities and feel that they are "in this together" and "on the same team." Affiliation-dominated behavior that is destructive creates disharmony and dislike. The recipient recognizes that he or she has been treated unfairly. The source and recipient increasingly distrust one another and recognize their differences. The recipient is likely to feel like a lonesome outcast.

The recipient's behavior reinforces the source. As was previously implied, destructive feedback is likely to result in immediate reinforcement. The recipient reacts negatively, and the source's stress is relieved in the short-run. The outcomes of constructive feedback are likely to be delayed, but they also positively reinforce the source and encourage the continuance of constructive feedback. Although the outcomes may be long-term (e.g., the recipient's development and advancement and/or positive task outcomes), the source may gain intermittent satisfaction in seeing meaningful progress and anticipating a positive result.

Overall, constructive feedback contributes to an expanding cycle of growth and development. Feedback, reactions, and subsequent behavior reinforce a positive cycle of comfort and support. On the other hand, destructive feedback contributes to a constricting cycle of dysfunctional behavior that, in the extreme, leads to the breakdown or dissolution of the relationship. A slow-moving, yet ever-constricting, cycle is incrementally dysfunctional, preventing the development of eventual productive behavior and happiness of both parties in the relationship.

INFORMAL FEEDBACK

Informal performance feedback comes from numerous sources as we interact with others—our supervisors, peers, subordinates, customers, and suppliers. Indeed, feedback is just about continuous in that we observe and react to others as they interact with us. This assumes one is in a work environment where there are people with whom to discuss performance issues or at least observe reactions to one's performance. Hence, people who spend considerable time working alone (e.g., telecommuters) may need to make special efforts to seek meaningful feedback. Similarly, their supervisors may need to make special efforts to keep open lines of communication about performance.

One-on-one Feedback

In one-on-one situations, people convey information about each other to each other. (This section is adapted from chapter 6 of London, 1995c, where I provide a more detailed explanation of interpersonal insight in one-on-one situations.) In the process, they express and fulfill their needs and expectations. We learn from others when they say or do the following:

Direct statements:
"I do not understand what you mean."
"You need to work on that."

Questions from others:
"Why were you so rough on him?"
"Why didn't you let her get a word in edgewise?"

Reactions to your behavior:
Looks of puzzlement, surprise, confusion, etc.
Being ignored or excluded from events or conversations.

Such feedback occurs spontaneously in any interaction. We pay attention to how others acted toward us, to informal, unsolicited feedback, and to casual remarks others make about us (Ashford & Tsui, 1991). Other cues are more indirect. For instance, we observe how quickly they return our phone calls, how often they come to us for advice, and how long we are kept waiting when we have an appointment. The danger is that we misunderstand or draw erroneous conclusions. This depends on our insight into interpersonal relationships in general, and the closeness of the specific relationship.

Insight into interpersonal relationships requires understanding the expectations we have for each other. People expect to hear about task achievement and competence from their coworkers, whereas they expect to hear about personal feelings and social relationships from their friends—some of whom may also be work associates (Gabarro, 1990). Over time as a relationship develops, people disclose more about themselves to others and they feel more comfortable giving others feedback. The relationship becomes closer and more direct as people deal with problems and dilemmas (Altman & Taylor, 1973). Self-disclosure, exploration, testing, and negotiation deepen over time. A well-developed relationship is characterized by spontaneity of exchange, efficient communication, and mutual investment.

Mutual exchange relationships occur when both parties give and receive something of value. According to social exchange theory, the development of interpersonal relationships depends on the expectation that continued interaction and commitment will be more rewarding than weakening or discontinuing the relationship (Organ, 1988). At work, relationships between two people evolve as they develop expectations about what the task is, what the outcomes of the joint endeavor should be, and how they should work with each other. Social exchange is based on implicit obligations and trust (Blau, 1964). The value of the exchange may depend on the identities and status of the two parties relative to each other. Such a social exchange occurs between a supervisor and subordinate, with the supervisor providing the subordinate with choice assignments or opportunities for career development.

Developing the social exchange relationship requires knowing something about the other party—what the other party needs and values and the social processes the party can benefit from and enjoy. So, for instance, individuals may value information, influence, favors, or just friendship. Each party has expectations about how he or she can benefit and what must be rendered in return. However, these expectations and the timing of their delivery are not specified. Neither party knows the extent of the other's expectations and whether they have been fulfilled.

Norms of reciprocity guide the social exchange by imposing implicit standards about when and how the receiver of benefits must repay the donor in some way (Gouldner, 1960). People want to reciprocate those who benefit them (Bateman & Organ, 1983). People who feel they are benefiting from a relationship will try to provide something in return, and this fosters the relationship (Greenberg, 1990). The fairness of the exchange can affect its continuation and growth.

Interpersonal feedback can be an important part of mutual exchange and development of a close relationship. Close acquaintances and friends establish ways of providing each other with clear feedback that is accepted as constructive. However, relationships are fragile. Those that are not fully developed can easily unravel when explicit negative feedback takes the recipient off-guard, causes embarrassment, or suggests mistrust. Even in close relationships, a tactless comment can be insulting and undermine the relationship. Situational norms also influence appropriate comments. People who have worked together for years may feel comfortable discussing performance issues, but not personal behaviors, such as personal appearance. Next, consider how feedback occurs in situations involving more than one other person—in particular, group and negotiation situations.

Feedback in Groups

In organizations, groups may be task forces, quality circles, and quality improvement teams. Such groups occur with increasing frequency in organizations (Hackman, 1990; Saavedra, Earley, & Van Dyne, 1993). Group development occurs when members are comfortable enough to share their feelings with each other (Luft, 1970). The group becomes more productive as the members begin sharing information about themselves and others. Therefore, it is important to consider the effects of self- and interpersonal insight on group interaction processes and performance. (For more information on this topic, see London, 1995c, chap. 7).

Group task demands and interaction patterns among group members mean that members must respond to stimuli from multiple sources. People generally have a common understanding about appropriate group behavior (Gersick, 1988, 1989). This is a basis for the development of habitual behavior patterns. In fact, different groups have similar patterns of behavior. Groups develop these interaction patterns early in their "lives," and they maintain this pattern even after the situation changes. For example, one study found that groups that assigned a tight time deadline early in their limited existence maintained a fast rate, but with low quality and with an interaction pattern that was highly task-focused (Kelly & McGrath, 1985). The pattern continued on later trials even though they no longer had the tight time deadline. Conversely, groups that began working against a less stringent time deadline worked at a slower rate but with higher quality and with an interaction pattern that was more interpersonally focused. This pattern continued on later trials despite shorter time deadlines. Under task conditions for which early trials yielded an experience of qualitative difficulty, groups tended to slow down on later trials and may thereby have increased the quality of their work.

Group members give each other feedback that helps them understand the emerging behavioral patterns. Also, newcomers to the group receive feedback quickly. This helps them understand how to be an effective group member in relation to other members' roles and abilities. Explicitly or implicitly, group members convey their expectations for the new member.

Performance Dynamics in Groups.   Feedback can be important to group process and performance, just as it is to individuals. Groups that receive feedback that their task and/or interpersonal behaviors do not match an ideal are likely to change their behaviors accordingly, whereas groups that do not receive feedback are not likely to change (McLeod, Liker, & Lobel, 1992). Process feedback focuses on elements of how the group members interact with each other. Consider three of the major elements of group process based on interaction process analysis (Bales, 1950, 1988):

1. *Dominancy.* The amount of group members' talkativeness, leadership, and influence, at one extreme, and submissiveness, quietness, and obedience, at the other. Large differences between the most and least dominant people in groups should be detrimental to group process and task performance (McLeod et al., 1992).

2. *Friendliness.* The amount of cooperation and loyalty at one extreme, and withdrawal and antagonism at the other. Behaviors should be primarily group-oriented and friendly, as opposed to individually oriented and unfriendly.

3. *Expressiveness.* The amount of joking, nurturing, and affection at one end of the continuum, and emotional control, task-orientedness, and attention to rules at the other end. Groups should have a reasonable balance of task-oriented and socioemotional behaviors, though task-oriented behaviors should dominate.

One study had teams of observers make systematic ratings of each group member's behavior on these three dimensions (McLeod et al., 1992). The groups received the observers' ratings of group process along each dimension with a set of norms against which to compare their results (e.g., for dominance: "Group discussions should not be dominated by one or two people. There should not be more than an 8-point difference between the most dominant and the most submissive group members"). Each group member knew his or her own score on each dimension. After the feedback, the groups had time to discuss their process feedback and determine how they could improve during a subsequent task. The researchers found that small behavior changes could be manipulated using the feedback and information about ideal ratings on process dimensions compared to groups receiving only task performance feedback followed by an unstructured discussion.

Reacting to this study, other researchers suggested that stronger effects might occur by concentrating on each members' personal goals (Locke & Latham, 1992). Specific goals should be assigned, rather than merely given ideal ranges. Groups assigned difficult goals perform better than those assigned moderate or general ("do your best") goals (Whitney, 1994). Each member's goals, and commitment to these goals, could actually be measured to be sure the goals were internalized prior to group performance. Group members' perceptions of the group's ability to do the task (induced by providing the group with norms of excellent performance prior to doing the task) also enhances performance. Furthermore, group feedback may be differentially relevant to group members depending on their results. For instance, only members at the extremes on dominance would need to act differently in order to change the distribution of dominance behavior in the group. However, the group process discussion about dominance differences gives everyone a chance to participate and influence the most and least dominant members.

Thus, attention should be given to how process feedback is used. Members should be asked whether they found feedback to be valuable (Wells, 1992). The interplay between the effects of feedback to individuals and to the group should be considered. Positive feedback to an individual may paradoxically disrupt group identity, for example. Such a paradoxical effect may explain why group members planned to change their behavior regarding dominant expressions in the group but seemed to reject feedback that increased their range of emotional expressiveness, maybe because the group members did not see emotional expression as consistent with their image of how managers should act.

Types of Groups.   Now, consider interpersonal feedback in different types of work groups (these work categories were distinguished by Sundstrom, De Meuse, & Futrell, 1990).

1. Teams that give advice or provide an avenue for employee involvement (e.g., committees, review panels, and quality circles).
2. Teams that produce a product or service (e.g., assembly teams, flight attendant crews).
3. Teams that work on a project (e.g., research groups, planning teams).
4. Teams that engage in action or negotiation (e.g., sports teams, entertainment groups, expeditions, negotiation teams, surgery teams, and cockpit crews).

The first three teams benefit from fluidity and loose coupling, action and negotiation teams act as tightly coupled systems most of the time. Another name for these groups is *ensembles*. Ensembles are groups that produce a particular effect or product (London & London, 1996). The members of ensembles are highly interdependent. Therefore, mutual feedback from the ensemble's leaders to its members and vice versa and between the ensemble's members is particularly important to the development of the ensemble as a tightly coupled system (Gersick & Hackman, 1990). The product of the ensemble has a distinctive quality beyond any one of the individual members. Having highly expert ensemble members does not mean that the ensemble's performance will necessarily be excellent. The members have to work at achieving a tightly coupled system.

The Role of Feedback in Negotiation Processes

The goal in groups is to cooperate in a way that will generate an effective product. Consider another type of interaction where individuals (or groups) are attempting to resolve conflict (this section was adapted from London, 1995c, chap. 8). Negotiation or bargaining sessions are good examples. During negotiation sessions, opposing parties gather information to test the acceptability of their own positions. Therefore, feedback becomes a mechanism for making good decisions in negotiations (Neale & Bazerman, 1991). Negotiators use feedback to adjust their behavior and offers. But this feedback is not likely to be straightforward. More likely, it is biased or ambiguous. Opposing parties do not readily reveal their strategies and reactions to offers. They may even try to mislead the opposing negotiator. Also, negotiators are likely to be biased in how they perceive the opposing party's reactions. Even experienced negotiators may misjudge cues from the opposing party.

Feedback is important to avoiding faulty judgments in interpersonal conflict and negotiation situations (Thompson & Hastie, 1990). Negotiators often fail to exchange information about their interests during the negotiation process (Thompson, 1991). Feedback has a self-correcting function that allows negotiators to compare their present strategy to a more favorable ideal (Thompson & DeHarpport, 1994). Outcome feedback is knowledge of the results of a decision, whereas cognitive feedback is information about relations in the environment, such as information about the task and one's own and others' thought processes (e.g., weights people give to different dimensions of possible outcomes; Balzer, Doherty, & O'Connor, 1989). Reaching a win–win settlement requires understanding one's opponent's interests. Feedback may come from experience, however, it may help to have information about the opponent. To test this, a study compared negotiators who were given information about their opponents with those who did not have this information (Thompson & DeHarpport, 1994). After an initial negotiation, the negotiators in the cognitive feedback condition were given information about their oppo-

nent's payoff schedule for different possible outcomes, whereas other negotiators were given only information about the payoff resulting from the
negotiation. Negotiators who received the cognitive and outcome feedback
made more accurate judgments about their opponent's interests and subsequently negotiate outcomes that are better for both parties. The feedback
allowed negotiators to develop an effective strategic conceptualization of the
negotiations. This suggests the value of building such feedback into on-going
negotiations, such that both parties are briefed about each others' emerging
interests, perhaps by an independent mediator or by consultants who are hired
separately by each side.

Before negotiation, members of each party's bargaining team often consult
each other about effective strategies. After a bargaining session, they are likely
to give each other feedback, processing their perceptions of the opposing
team's reactions (Ury, Brett, & Goldberg, 1988). They may also discuss the
negotiation process with the opposing team. These discussions may raise points
of misunderstanding and clarify points of difference between opposing parties.
Establish a regular forum for discussion so that the opposing parties can
consider issues that arise in disputes that cut across other aspects of relationships between the parties. An example would be the union and management
representatives meeting together regularly in "common interest forums"
(London, 1988).

Now that I have reviewed how feedback occurs in natural situations such
as one-on-one relationships, groups, and negotiations, let us think about what
makes someone seek feedback.

MECHANISMS FOR SELF-REGULATION

Consider first how people regulate their activities in relation to their perceptions of the world. Some people are more sensitive to others' behavior and
feelings. Others are internally focused and try to elicit reactions that confirm
their self-opinion. Others try to protect themselves against unfavorable information about themselves even at the expense of never learning about their
strengths. Still others try to create situations that verify a negative self-image
and prevent them from being successful.

Conscientiousness

Some people are generally more organized, efficient, goal-oriented, and per-
sistent. These characteristics describe conscientiousness, a stable personality
characteristic that is positively related to job performance (Barrick & Mount,
1991). People who are high in conscientiousness are likely to take on difficult,
unattractive, but necessary tasks (Stewart, Carson, & Cardy, 1996). Moreover,
they are highly motivated and think constructively about what they can
accomplish. Such individuals are likely to seek feedback to regulate their own
behavior.

Self-Monitoring

Some people are more sensitive to feedback and willing to respond to it constructively than others. These people are called *self-monitors*. (For more information on self-monitoring, see Anderson, 1990; Snyder, 1987; and Snyder & Gangestad, 1986). Self-monitors are attuned to what the external environment requires and expects of them. They vary their behavior to meet the needs of the situation. Low self-monitors are influenced primarily by their attitudes, values, and related personality traits. Consequently, their behavior remains fairly stable from one situation to another (Reilly, Warech, & Reilly, 1993). High self-monitors are responsive to group norms, roles, and other features of the social situation and, as such, they display a variety of behaviors depending on the situation. They constantly compare and adjust their behavior to an external standard (the expectations or reactions of other people) or internal standard (one's own concerns and values). As such, they are alert to feedback, attuned to sources' motivation and expertise in providing the feedback, and ready to change their behavior when the feedback is valid. High self-monitors respond positively to the following items (from the self-monitoring scale developed by Snyder, 1974):

- I can make impromptu speeches even on topics about which I have almost no information.
- I guess I put on a show to impress or entertain others.
- In different situations and with different people, I often act like very different persons.
- I may deceive people by being friendly when I really dislike them.

Low self-monitors respond negatively to the previously mentioned items but respond positively to the following:

- I find it hard to imitate the behavior of other people.
- In a group of people I am rarely the center of attention.
- I am particularly good at making other people like me.

Self-Esteem

Another individual characteristic, separate from self-monitoring, is *self-esteem*. Self-esteem enhances a person's adaptability and resilience in the face of barriers. Low self-esteem makes an individual vulnerable—that is, emotionally reactive, sensitive, and intolerant of barriers.

People high in self-esteem respond positively to the following statements (from Fedor, Rensvold, & Adams, 1992; and Rosenberg, 1965):

- I feel that I am a person of worth, at least on an equal basis with others.
- I feel that I have a number of good qualities.
- I am able to co things as well as most other people.

- I take a positive attitude toward myself.
- On the whole, I am satisfied with myself.

People low in self-esteem respond positively to the following:

- All in all, I am inclined to feel that I am a failure.
- I feel I do not have much to be proud of.
- I wish I could have more respect for myself.
- I certainly feel useless at times.
- At times I think I am no good at all.

I expect that self-esteem moderates the high self-monitor's reactions to feedback. High self-monitors who are high in self-esteem are likely to respond to feedback most constructively. Positive feedback bolsters their self-esteem, and negative feedback motivates them to change their behavior to match expectations (or at least try to do so). On the other hand, high self-monitors with low self-esteem are likely to be threatened by negative feedback and hence engage in self-protection mechanisms that limit the likelihood that they will receive such feedback (e.g., they do not seek feedback). Also, they tend to discount or ignore positive feedback. So, they are unlikely to benefit from feedback and may suffer from fear of it. Low self-monitors, regardless of self-esteem, are likely to be impervious to feedback (whether negative or positive, constructive or destructive).

Self-Affirmation

People seek self-affirming information as a way to maintain the image they have of themselves (Steele, Spencer, & Lynch, 1993). This may be initiated by an event that threatens the image in some way—for instance, receiving negative feedback in an area the individual believed was a strong point. Self-affirmation is a rationalization and self-justification process that happens through continuous interpretation of one's experiences until the self-image is restored. People with high self-esteem have more ways to maintain or restore their self-image than people with low self-esteem.

Self-Protection Mechanisms

Self-protection mechanisms are ways people affirm their self-image (Wohlers & London, 1989). For instance, they may implicitly ask for distorted information, as when they request praise ("Did I do okay?") or compel others to say good things about them. People who use self-protection mechanisms receive less accurate information about themselves and, as a result, have less understanding of their abilities. Wohlers and I defined four types of self-protection mechanisms: *denial, giving up, self-promotion,* and *fear of failure*. Table 9.2 describes how these mechanisms are manifest in behavior.

TABLE 9.2
Self-Protection Mechanisms

Denial
- Reacts negatively to feedback
- Blames others for failure
- Never admits mistakes
- Inhibits others' performance
- Accurately perceives one's own performance (inverse)
- Frequently asks for feedback (inverse)
- Gives credit where it is due (inverse)
- Accurately perceives other's performance (inverse)
- Accurately describes events (inverse)

Giving up
- Abandons difficult tasks
- Avoids being compared with better performers
- Tunes out others who perform better
- Would leave a job because coworkers perform better
- Negative feedback lowers performance
- Dislikes better performers
- Tries hard on difficult tasks (inverse)
- Sticks to tasks until succeeds (inverse)

Self-promotion
- Makes sure others know about successes
- Asks for praise
- Concerned about status symbols
- Talks about own good performance
- Makes others feel compelled to say good things about his/her performance
- Does not admit one's own contribution to a group's success (inverse)

Fear of failure
- *Points out own strengths when criticized*
- *Afraid of failure*
- *Gets upset by own poor performance*
- *Tries to prevent others from doing well*
- *Tries to convince others they are wrong*
- *Tries to raise others' opinions of self*
- *Downplays own weaknesses*
- Concerned about making the "right" career moves

Note. From Wohlers, A. J., & London, M. (1989). Adapted with permission.

Self-Handicapping

Self-handicapping strategies are another way people protect their self-image. People rationalize events in a way that is flattering to them. This allows them to increase their pride when they succeed and avoid shame when they fail. Self-handicapping is a way to ensure that they will be able to interpret the outcome of their behavior in the most flattering way (Jones & Berglas, 1978). For instance, they avoid information about their own abilities. They prefer not to know how they did, so they avoid feedback or avoid situations that will make it clear to themselves and others that they were responsible for a particular outcome. People who have low self-esteem are most likely to engage in self-handicapping (Tice & Baumeister, 1990). These individuals are unsure of themselves and would prefer not to know the truth about their abilities. This is especially likely when they doubt their ability to do something well or they believe the evaluator is likely to be highly critical of their behavior.

Self-regulation affects the degree to which we open ourselves to new achievements. Although self-regulation helps us protect our self-mage, it prevents us from realizing our full potential. Having an accurate self-assessment is likely to help us recognize what we can do well and what we cannot do well and, therefore, helps us direct our goals and behavior in ways we can be successful. The next section discusses how people use feedback to develop an accurate self-assessment.

ACCURACY OF SELF-ASSESSMENT

In chapter 4, I recommended incorporating self-assessment into the appraisal process as a way of diffusing denial and making people more receptive to the feedback. However, I also noted that self-appraisals tend to be lenient. Moreover, some people describe themselves differently depending on the impression they want to create in a given situation (Schmit & Ryan, 1993). Also, even if self-appraisals are not used directly to make administrative decisions, supervisors may be lenient just because they think their subordinates will have a somewhat exaggerated view of themselves. This section, adapted from London (1995c, chapter 3), considers variables that influence the agreement between self-perceptions and others' evaluations.

Ashford identified three types of agreement: (a) agreement between self-ratings and individuals' beliefs about how others perceive their behavior; (b) agreement between self-ratings and other's ratings; and (c) agreement between perceptions of others' assessments and others' actual assessments (Ashford, 1989). The elements of the first type of agreement, individuals' perceptions of themselves and the way they assume others see them, tend to be highly correlated. There is less agreement between actual ratings by others and self-ratings—the second type of agreement. The way people believe others see them and the way they actually do see them, the third type, tends to be modestly related. In general, people overestimate the similarity between their self-perceptions and the way they think others see them than is truly the case (Mabe & West, 1982). As a result, we would not want to use self-appraisals as a substitute for ratings from others.

ASKING FOR FEEDBACK

As I previously suggested, the extent to which people seek feedback, and how they seek it, depends on their self-image and mechanisms they use to maintain their self-image (Ashford & Tsui, 1991). Feedback seeking can be a way to gather accurate information about ourselves. It can also be used as an impression management technique—i.e., to control what others think of us. In addition, feedback seeking can be used to protect our ego (Morrison & Bies, 1991). We consider the costs and benefits of asking for feedback. We consider the source's expertise, accessibility, quality of the relationship with the individual, and ability to affect positive and negative outcomes (Morrison & Vancouver, 1993). People with high need for achievement and self-esteem choose sources high in expertise and relationship quality. Those with high performance expectations choose sources high in reward power. Also, those who need to improve their performance the most are least likely to seek feedback (Karl & Kopf, 1993).

Motivation to Seek Feedback

There are a number of reasons why people seek feedback (as reviewed in the chap. 2). These stem from the potential value of feedback for reducing uncertainty (by determining whether one's behavior is accurate and how it is evaluated), signaling the relative importance of various goals, creating the feeling of competence and control, allowing calibration of self-evaluations, and giving the employee a chance to defend his or her ego.

The motivation to seek feedback is not entirely straightforward. Feedback may be useful for correcting errors and reducing uncertainty, but it may be dysfunctional if it threatens self-esteem. Also, low performers who need feedback most may be the most reluctant to seek it.

Many people actively seek feedback (Ashford & Cummings, 1983). The feedback may be obtained by *monitoring* the environment or by active *inquiry*. However, people worry about the effects of asking for feedback. Consider how you would respond to the following statements about the cost of requesting feedback (adapted from Fedor, Rensvold, & Adams, 1992):

If I asked my supervisor to evaluate my performance, he or she would become more critical of me.

I would look incompetent if I asked my supervisor for additional infomation about my performance.

I get embarrassed asking my supervisor for performance information.

It takes too much effort to get my supervisor to talk to me about my performance.

My coworkers do not tell each other how they are doing, even though they may talk about others' performance behind their backs.

Consider how often you directly ask others, "How am I doing?" How often do you talk to your supervisor about your performance or ask for *more* performance information than you are given? People worry about the costs of asking for feedback in terms of the effort required, the possibility of losing face, and the amount and type of inferences required.

Acceptance of Feedback

When employees receive feedback, they evaluate its accuracy. They make an attribution about whether the feedback applies to them or whether it is due to other factors (e.g., the source's motivation to hurt or praise the recipient, or situational conditions that were beyond the recipient's control). When people accept the feedback and attribute the cause to themselves, they are likely to set meaningful, realistic goals that have the potential of improving their performance (Taylor, Fisher, & Ilgen, 1984).

Several personality variables influence employees' feedback seeking and reactions to feedback. People who are low in self-confidence are likely to be apprehensive of being evaluated. These individuals engage in ego protection mechanisms (discussed earlier in this chapter). They tend to deny or avoid negative feedback and, in general, try to control the feedback they receive. Employees who are high in self-confidence are likely to welcome feedback. These individuals tend to engage in self-assessment and self-regulation.

People who are high in self-esteem rate themselves high, especially when the appraisal is done on ambiguous performance dimensions (Harris & Schaubroeck, 1988). Those with a self-serving bias take credit for success and attribute blame to external causes (Levy, 1991). People who are high in internal control make more accurate attributions about their role in causing events and are willing to attribute negative events to themselves and positive events to others when appropriate. Those low in internal control are more likely to rate themselves leniently and protect themselves from criticism (Levy, 1991). (People high in internal control recognize that they can affect positive outcomes; those high in external control believe that they have little control over outcomes.)

Overall, people who are courageous enough to seek unfavorable feedback are able to increase the accuracy of their self-understanding. They are likely to accurately recognize how others view their work (Ashford & Tsui, 1991).

IMPRESSION MANAGEMENT

Impression management refers to ways people try to influence others' perceptions of them. Consider the extent to which you do the following *job-focused* tactics (adapted from Ferris, Judge, Rowland, & Ritzgibbons, 1994):

Play up the value of a positive event that for which you have taken credit.
Try to make a positive event that you are responsible for appear greater than it actually is.
Try to take responsibility for positive events, even when you are not solely responsible.
Try to let your supervisor think that you are responsible for positive events that occur in your work group.
Arrive at work early in order to look good in front of your supervisor.

Now, consider the extent to which you do the following *supervisor-focused* tactics:

Take an interest in your immediate supervisor's personal life.
Praise your immediate supervisor on his or her accomplishments.
Do personal favors for your supervisor.
Volunteer to help your immediate supervisor on a task.
Compliment your immediate supervisor on his or her dress or appearance.
Agree with your supervisor's major ideas.

People try to influence others' impressions of them in a variety of ways. They may try it directly through such assertive behaviors as ingratiation, intimidation, or self-promotion. Or they may act defensively through such behaviors as apologies, restitution, and disclaimers (Kumar & Beyerlein, 1991). Another way to manage others' impressions, or at least try, is associating or disassociating oneself with an event (e.g., boasting in a way that links you to a favorable event or disclaiming a link to an unfavorable event; Gardner, 1992).

When people seek feedback, they are often concerned about how asking for feedback affects what the source of the information thinks of them. Seeking unfavorable feedback can enhance the source's opinions of the employee's performance. However, seeking favorable feedback can decrease the source's opinions (Morrison & Bies, 1991). Recognizing that the seeking of feedback affects others' impressions of them, people may ask for feedback in a way that will enhance what others think of them (Ashford & Northcraft, 1992). They consider whether it is better to ask for feedback sooner after a favorable event than an unfavorable event, and when the source is in a good mood. They consider whom to ask. Good performers ask sources who have high reward power, and poor performers ask sources who have low reward power. They also consider how to ask. They may try to ask for feedback in a way that calls attention to favorable aspects of the performance. People are especially attuned to what others think of them when these others control rewards, and when the feedback is given publicly (e.g., during a staff meeting) or a formal performance evaluation is imminent.

People tend to avoid seeking feedback when others are watching (Gardner, 1992). Having an audience increases the anxiety and nervousness from being evaluated, especially for people who are "publicly conscious"—i.e., sensitive to how others react to them. They are hesitant because they perceive impression-management costs from asking how they are doing. They fear that seeking feedback will be perceived as a sign of insecurity, uncertainty, lack of self-confidence, or incompetence. Obviously, employees are concerned about what their bosses think of them because their bosses control pay, promotions, job assignments, and other valued job outcomes. So they try to create a favorable impression by, for example, setting higher public goals and providing excuses and apologies for poor performance. If the organization's norms make feedback a frequent occurrence and it is okay to request feedback, then employees will be more likely to seek feedback.

Learning About Impression Management

Gardner (1992) offered the following recommendations for using impression management in reacting to feedback:

- Be aware of your impression management behavior and the image you project.
- Size up your audience and the situation (how the people with whom you interact may influence your performance).
- Recognize the dangers of the strategy you have chosen.
- Do a good job. Impression management is not a substitute for high performance—indeed, demonstrating excellence is the surest way to make a good impression.
- Be yourself. Do not try to be something you are not because people will see through the facade.

Further, Gardner offered the following recommendations for those on the receiving end of impression management (i.e., the supervisor, coworker, or customer) in observing others:

- Be aware of your personal characteristics and the situational features that make certain types of impression management strategies more likely (for instance, status differences).
- Minimize personal, situational, and organizational features that foster undesirable performance (e.g., situations in which people are scarce or performance requirements or standards are ambiguous).

- Look for ulterior motives and avoid being overly influenced by dramatic behavior.

Consider the difference between the *ability* to manage impressions and the *motivation* to manage impressions. This distinction can be understood by two 8-item scales listed in Table 9.3. (These scales were developed by Reilly, Warech, & Reilly, 1993, based on a factor analysis of a larger set of items from Leary, 1983, and Gangestad & Snyder, 1985.) They suggest ways that people manage others' impressions.

TABLE 9.3
Items Reflecting Motivation and Ability to Manage Impressions

Motivation to Manage Impressions
1. I am highly motivated to control how others see me.
2. I feel there are many good reasons to control how others see me.
3. Controlling others' impressions of me is not important to me. [inverse]
4. In social situations, one of my goals is to get others to form a certain kind of impression of me.
5. I never try to lead others to form particular impressions of me. [inverse]
6. I do not try to control the impression others perceive of me when I first meet them. [inverse]
7. I try to affect others' impressions of me most of the time.
8. At parties and social gatherings, I do not attempt to say or do things that others will like. [inverse]

Ability to Manage Impressions
1. When I feel that the image I am portraying is not working, I can readily change it to something that does.
2. Even when it might be to my advantage, I have difficulty putting up a good front. [inverse]
3. I am not particularly good at making other people like me. [inverse]
4. In social situations, I have the ability to alter my behavior if I feel that something else is called for.
5. I feel a bit awkward in company and do not show up quite so well as I should. [inverse]
6. I have trouble changing my behavior to suit different people and different situations. [inverse]
7. Once I know what the situation calls for, it is easy for me to regulate my actions accordingly.
8. I have found that I can adjust my behavior to meet the requirements of any situation I find myself in.

Note. From Reilly, R. R., Warech, M. A., & Reilly, S. (1993). Reprinted with permission.

CHAPTER NINE

CONCLUSION

People seek feedback from a variety of informal sources during their everyday interactions at work. These include one-on-one relationships, groups, and negotiations. Mechanisms for self-regulation, such as the desire to enhance and protect one's self-image, affect a person's receptivity to feedback. In this chapter, I discussed variables that affect motivation to seek feedback and the likelihood that feedback will be accepted and used (e.g., a person's self-monitoring tendency). I also made the point that people should understand how they use feedback seeking as an impression management tool.

The chapter suggests the following conclusions:

1. Informal feedback comes from numerous sources as we interact with others. We can view feedback within the context of one-on-one relationships, group dynamics, and negotiations.

2. Norms guide the social exchange by imposing implicit standards about when and how the receiver of information must repay the source. Interpersonal feedback can be an important part of the mutual exchange and the development of a close relationship.

3. Feedback in groups is important because of an organization's heavy reliance on teams to conduct business. Group development occurs when members are comfortable enough to share their feelings with each other.

4. Feedback is important to making good decisions in negotiations during which opposing parties gather information to test the acceptability of their own positions and make judgments about the opposing party's reactions and anticipated reactions.

5. People regulate their activities in relation to their perceptions. People vary in their sensitivity to others' behavior and feelings, desire to confirm their self-opinion, need to protect themselves against unfavorable information, and the tendency to create situations that verify a negative self-image and prevent them from being successful.

6. The way and extent to which people seek feedback depends on their self-image and mechanisms they use to maintain that self-image. Feedback seeking can be used to gather accurate information about oneself and/or as a technique to control what others think of you.

7. Impression management techniques include such assertive behaviors as ingratiation, intimidation, or self-promotion and defensive behaviors such as apologies, restitution, and disclaimers. In general, people should be alert to their impression management behavior and the image they project.

Now that I have explored sources of feedback and what affects a person's desire to receive feedback, I consider in the next chapter how people learn to be better *users* of feedback.

10

Making the Most of Feedback

Just as managers do not like to give feedback, people generally do not like receiving it. People will avoid feedback even when it is intended for development purposes alone and has no implications for personnel decisions. Feedback threatens people's self-esteem, and they prefer not to risk receiving unfavorable information, even when some or most of the information is likely to be positive. This chapter considers how people react to feedback and ways to create an organizational culture that encourages receiving and using feedback. In chapter 4, I recommended incorporating self-assessment into the appraisal process. Here I discuss the value of self-assessment as a way of comparing and understanding feedback, including ways to enhance self-assessment accuracy.

HELPING EMPLOYEES FACE FEEDBACK

Employees may need help digesting performance feedback. They have to learn how to interpret the information (see the outline for interpreting multisource feedback in Table 4.5, chap. 4, this volume). They have to be ready to consider the validity of the feedback without being defensive. People are most receptive to feedback when it is given in a nonthreatening environment. But, they need to be guided through the feedback, essentially forced to digest the information and use it as a basis for development planning.

For instance, consider how results of a multisource feedback survey are typically used during the first part of an off-site management development program. Several weeks before attending a week-long leadership development program, the participants are asked to have their coworkers, subordinates, supervisors, and some key customers complete a survey about their behavior. The respondents return the surveys directly to the firm providing the training. The surveys are scored and a computer-generated report is prepared. Before receiving the report, the participants take part in one or more managerial simulations or business games. Members of the training staff observe the participants' performance and prepare feedback reports. The training session then focuses on important dimensions of managerial performance. Later, the participants meet one-on-one with a trainer to review the multisource feedback and their performance report from the behavioral exercises. The trainer helps the participants compare behaviors that reflect the important dimensions of managerial performance. The participants identify areas for development and have a chance to practice them during the remaining days of the training session. At the conclusion of the week, the participants review the initial performance results and their progress during training. They use this as the basis for setting goals for development and self-monitoring back on the job.

Natural Reactions to Feedback

Not surprisingly, unfavorable feedback makes people defensive. Our natural tendency when faced with a threat to our self-esteem is self-protection (see the description of self-protection mechanisms including denial, giving up, self-promotion, and fear of failure in chap. 9, this volume). Other defense reactions include the following (based on London & Mone, 1993):

Attributing Blame to Others or to External Events.   You recognize the problem but do not view it as a consistent pattern. You have a logical excuse or reason for the unfavorable feedback that blames factors beyond your control.

Recognizing Poor Performance in Others but Denying the Problem in Oneself. A form of external attribution or *projection*, you recognize performance problems in others but not in yourself. You may blame others for your own low performance. You may be correct, or you may be projecting your own poor output on others (e.g., saying that one of your subordinates cannot do the job). You may be projecting your own failings on others when it is not deserved.

Creating the Opposite Impression.   You may try to disguise your low motivation and/or low ability by creating the opposite impression (this is termed *reaction formation* by clinical psychologists). For instance, you may appear extremely busy, coming in early or walking around quickly so that you appear to be working hard. You may even create emergencies or treat what could be minor issues as serious problems.

Substituting One Goal for Another.   You may deny or belittle the importance of doing well on the job while working hard at something at which you can succeed—maybe a voluntary activity off the job.

Creating Nonwork Problems.   You may take out your frustration or displace it on family members and friends, rather than at work where it is not acceptable to show your anger. Family problems may become an excuse for poor work performance. Substance abuse is another way to displace work frustrations.

Feedback is likely to be more palatable, or at least attended to, when it is an expected part of the way managers manage. Next, consider how to establish an organizational environment that recognizes individual learning styles and encourages continuous learning.

CREATING A LEARNING ORGANIZATION

Some organizations work hard to continually develop employees' performance capabilities. These "learning organizations" (Senge, 1990) emphasize *generative learning*—"an emphasis on continuous experimentation and feedback in an ongoing examination of the very way organizations go about defining and solving problems" (McGill, Slocum, & Lei, 1992, p. 5).

Learning Styles

Adaptive learners make incremental changes to improve their performance. *Generative* learners transform themselves through major shifts in behavior after self-study. Adaptive learning works well when the environment is fairly stable. When this is not the case, adaptive learning can be dysfunctional by perpetuating behaviors that are no longer effective. Generative learners know how to learn. As a result, they can be extremely valuable when the organization needs to make a transformation change, perhaps entering new markets or establishing a dramatically new approach to management, such as continuous quality improvement. Generative learners suspend any need for control and are open to different values, backgrounds, and experiences.

Resilience

Resilience is the ability to adapt to changing circumstances and overcome performance barriers. I view resilience as one of three major components of *career motivation* (London, 1983, 1985). The other two components are *insight* (stemming from performance feedback and information about career opportunities) and *identity* (the direction of one's career goals). Resilience consists of several subcomponents: belief in oneself, need for achievement, and willingness to take risks (experimenting with new behaviors). People who are high in resilience are self-confident, desire to achieve higher goals, and are innovative. Resilience is the foundation for using performance feedback and information about career opportunities to gain insight and select a meaningful identity. People who are low in resilience are not likely to gain from performance feedback. Instead of overcoming performance barriers, they deny or ignore them. Although resilience is hard to establish, it can be strengthened by an environment that rewards achievement and encourages and rewards trying new behaviors.

Self-Denying Prophecies

Subordinates can shift their behavior to avoid a negative prophecy (Hurley, 1993). Unfavorable feedback is likely to lower motivation, particularly for people who are low in self-esteem and ready to believe negative prophecies about themselves (Brockner, Derr, & Laing, 1987). The self-denying prophecy happens when a person sets a goal to void a negative expectation.

Performance Enhancement Spirals.   A positive, cyclic relationship between beliefs about one's effectiveness and one's performance can build on itself (Lindsley, Brass, & Thomas, 1995). Coaches and athletes are aware of the cognitive aspects of physical performance. A positive frame of mind can have a similar effect on business performance. Three types of spirals are possible:

1. A self-correcting spiral occurs when a decrease in performance and self-efficacy is followed by an increase in performance. The person adjusts future efforts, reversing the prior decrease in performance.
2. An upward spiral occurs when positive changes in efficacy and perform-ance build on each other creating confirmation of ability and performance that is reflected in subsequent effort.
3. A down spiral occurs when negative changes in efficacy and performance build on each other, limiting subsequent effort, thereby reinforcing the negative trend.

The *Galatea effect* (how expecting to achieve higher goals enhances moti-vation—see chap. 6, this volume) has been induced experimentally by simply explaining to a trainee that test scores indicate he or she has high potential for success (Eden & Ravid, 1982). Thus, using feedback to raise self-expectations can build on subordinates' capacity to mobilize their own resources to perform better (Eden, 1992).

Eden and Aviram showed that building self-esteem was important to improve re-employment prospects of unemployed workers (Eden & Aviram, 1993). As part of an 8-day workshop that met every other work day for 2½ weeks, a behavior modeling process was used to increase job search skills. The process started with short videos demonstrating successful job search behavior followed by a brief discussion of the behavior and then by role playing in small groups. This latter step allowed each participant to practice the behavior and receive feedback from the others. The treatment resulted in increased general self-esteem and job search behavior. Reemployment increased more for those people who were initially low in self-esteem.

Rational-Emotive Thinking.   A method is available for helping employees to organize their thinking and establish new, more positive emotions and more useful behaviors. People uncertain about their job performance express negative feelings including worry, anxiety, and hostility. These feelings can contribute to dysfunctional behavior patterns, such as immobilization, avoidance, and aggression. One type of intervention, rational-emotive therapy, attempts to help people turn an uncertain, stressful situation into a successful career experience. Employees are encouraged to challenge their thinking through positive thoughts and self-questioning. They are guided to validate such statements as:

"I recognize that work demands are not always predictable."

"Many changes and expectations coming at once are uncomfortable and confusing yet I will try to organize life and deal with the most important problems first . . . "

"I will handle this job to the best of my ability . . . "

"It is not too late for me to manage my job in a different way."

Called rational-emotive therapy, the technique suggests that employees examine their strengths, capabilities, and areas for development (Klarreich, 1993). Working with a consultant or one's supervisor, the object is to design a performance management strategy that leads to improvement and tracks outcomes.

Instead of automatically ignoring, denying, or rationalizing unfavorable feedback (see the discussion of categorization in how we process information, chap. 3, this volume), the rational-emotive approach calls for letting go of the old image we had of ourselves and the situation. For instance, "This is no longer the old company that protected me and guaranteed my job security. I have to work harder and smarter. I am being evaluated by higher standards." Next might be an exploration phase during which the person considers areas of weakness that can be corrected to perform better. This might entail a search for development experiences or training programs. It might also suggest the need to look for other assignments that are more suited to the person's strengths and interests. The individual must develop competencies and skills that give value to the firm and help him or her regain a sense of personal control. In doing so, the individual accepts the personal responsibility for managing his or her own development and performance within the context of the support available in the organization. Hopefully, this will lead to a sense of invigoration by the changes in his or her abilities and the organization's expanded performance expectations.

A *New York Times* article vividly described this process for people who survived organizational downsizings but worried about their future job security (Kirk, 1995). Cadorette, an executive development manager who had worked for BellSouth for 14 years, realized the need for a changed outlook when five of her mentors took early retirement during several layoffs. The downsizing caused her to evaluate her competencies and interests in relation to the shifting organizational opportunities and demands:

> First, she let go of her old image of the company and what it represented. "This was no longer a secure employer situation where I joined, stayed my 30 years and got my gold watch," she said.

> Second, she entered an exploration phase, in which she focused "not only on what my interests were, but tried to decide if there were other career options inside or outside the company."

> Third, if this was no longer a "job for life, I had to accept personal responsibility for managing my own career. I had to develop competencies and skills that not only gave value to the company but helped me regain some sense of control," she said. (Kirk, 1995, F11).

Cadorette left BellSouth in 1992 to join the outplacement company Drake Beam Morin.

Another BellSouth survivor, Hodges, explained the need to be resilient. He has been with the firm for 19 years:

> I ache for my friends who have been in positions for 20 years and are struggling with what to do for the rest of their lives. But I am invigorated by the changes going on in our industry. If one will analyze their gifts, understand what they do well and what they don't want to do, and then charge forward and market themselves, they will find more opportunity, not less. I approach downsizing not only without trepidation, but with excitement (Kirk, 1995, F11).

Similar rational-emotive techniques have been used to provide social support and job search skills to unemployed workers (Caplan, Vinokur, Price, & van Ryn, 1989; Vinokur, van Ryn, Gramlich, & Price, 1991). These processes "inoculate" the participants from common setbacks that are part of the job-seeking process by letting them know what to expect and what it will feel like. Participants are inoculated against setbacks by anticipating possible barriers and preparing solutions to overcome them. Trainers offer participants unconditional positive regard and specific positive feedback. Also, the trainers provide support by expressing empathy for the participants' feelings.

In general, people feel better about themselves when they are successful, they realize they can emulate others who have been successful, and they receive positive feedback from others who are in a position to know and evaluate their capabilities (Bandura, 1986). Leaders lead best when they expect success and communicate their expectations (Eden, 1992).

Self-Leadership Training. Positive thinking is one thing. Learning self-observation and self-reinforcement skills is another. Some people seem to learn these skills on their own. As children they became generally conscientious, and this carries over to their approach to the job. Self-leadership training tries to help people learn these skills as adults (Stewart, Carson, & Cardy, 1996). In one application of this training, hotel/resort employees were given a series of self-directed workbooks that focus on (a) skills for addressing difficult, unattractive, but necessary tasks, (b) skills for building motivation into work, and (c) skills for developing constructive thinking patterns. The booklets guide the learners through a set of exercises about the different skills. In one application of this training, the workbooks were introduced during an orientation session. Participants were expected to complete the workbooks on their own during the next 5 weeks. A follow-up training session was then conducted to answer questions and facilitate transfer of training. The employees were paid for the time they spent completing the books and were allowed to work at their own pace away from the work site. Supervisors attended a meeting during which they learned about the training's purpose and the methods. They received information about the possible benefits of self-leadership and were taught how to help employees develop self-regulation skills. However, supervisors were not told who among their subordinates attended training. The training increased performance for employees who were initially low in conscientiousness. Performance remained steady for those who were already highly conscientious, presumably because they were already using self-leadership behaviors.

The Role Feedback on Creating Positive Performance Cycles

Feedback is the key to self-correcting adjustment in effort and performance and avoiding downward spirals (Lindsley, Brass, & Thomas, 1995). Knowing whether you succeeded or failed is not enough. Feedback must provide accurate, timely, and specific information about how your behavior led to performance improvement. Inaccurate or delayed feedback may cause you to use inappropriate performance strategies in the future. That is, the person must understand the cause–effect relationship between his or her behavior and subsequent performance. This is why negative feedback should be provided without threatening the person's self-image. Similarly, positive feedback should be given in a way that fosters attention to the effort-behavior-performance linkages, rather than general flattery. Breaking tasks into small components can be an effective way to obtain manageable information and experiment with new behaviors without undue risk. Small losses can be analyzed carefully and new behaviors tried. Small wins can be repeated and be followed by incrementally more complex actions.

LEARNING TO USE FEEDBACK

Negative feedback alone will not necessarily lead to a constructive response. Instead, it may lead people to be defensive or merely ignore the information. Negative feedback will not have much effect on people who are low in

self-awareness. These individuals are likely to tune out unfavorable information about their performance. However, people who have low performance
who are guided through the feedback in a way that makes them pay attention
to, and reflect on, the performance data, are likely to avoid the same mistakes
later (Heatherton, Polivy, Herman, & Baumeister, 1993). When confronted
with unfavorable feedback, subordinates are likely to be defensive, deny the
problem, or blame situational factors beyond their control, including the
supervisor's unrealistic expectations and demands (Meyer, 1991). Interventions can encourage people to consider feedback more carefully.

Why Self-Assessment?

Consider the following reasons for self-assessment (adapted from Ashford,
1989, p. 135):

1. Self-assessment recognizes the self as a source of feedback.
2. Self-assessment is important to self-regulation and goal achievement.
3. Self-assessment is important in increasingly turbulent organization environments that require employees to sort out supervisory and peer
   preferences and evaluative criteria.
4. Self-assessment may have important strong effects. For instance, self
   assessments have been related to depression, efficacy expectations,
   aspiration levels, persistence, effort, and performance.
5. Self-assessments help reduce ambiguity in the environment (e.g., about
   performance expectations and one's capability to meet these expectations).

Comparing Self-Perceptions to Others' Views.   People form perceptions of
themselves based on direct or indirect feedback from others, objective performance standards or explicit performance expectations, and observations of
how others behave and are evaluated (Wofford, 1994). Thus, feedback provides comparative information to calibrate one's own behavior and feelings.

The Value of Self-Ratings.   Self-assessment questions are both measurements and cues. The self-assessment items tell the rater what elements of
behavior are important to the organization.

Developing Self-Assessment Procedures.   Three recommendations for designing a process for people to assess their strengths and weaknesses are the
following:

1. Present information about the organization to indicate why the self-assessment is important.
2. Provide guidance on how to interpret the self-assessment results.

3. Embed self-assessment methods within the context of a career development program and/or a performance improvement program.

Enhancing Self-Assessment Accuracy

Self-assessments are more likely to be accurate when they are based on objective, easily measured performance dimensions (e.g., number of units produced or communications ability) than on subjective and ambiguous dimensions (e.g., one's organization sensitivity). Also, when self-ratings are compared to ratings by others, overestimation is more common than underestimation. There are a number of good reasons for encouraging accurate self-perceptions (based on Ashford, 1989): Accurate self-assessment can increase the match between self- and other assessment making it easier for employees to understand and use feedback. Accurate self-assessments allow employees to tell the extent to which they are meeting their supervisor's expectations or the performance standards for the job. Accurate assessments can help set a realistic level of aspiration for future achievements. Employees can develop accurate beliefs about their ability to achieve more difficult goals, which in turn can increase their motivation, desire to devote energy to the task, and willingness to persist in goal accomplishment. However, these outcomes will not occur if employees fail to assess their progress on relevant behaviors or if they focus on irrelevant behaviors.

These possible outcomes suggest several challenges to accurate self-assessment (Ashford, 1989). Employees must gather information while dealing with randomness, conflicting cues, and ambiguity. They must obtain information while protecting their self-image as an autonomous and self-assured person.

Importance of Information Quality.   People easily distort feedback. They tend to overestimate their abilities and performance (Ashford, 1989). Also, they are quick to recognize any flaws in the reliability or validity of information about their performance, particularly if the information is unfavorable. However, feedback is hard to deny or ignore when it is objective, easily measured, and understood. An employee will think less of a supervisor's personal judgments of the employees' sensitivity to organizational politics than the supervisor's written descriptions of specific behavioral incidents.

Anticipated Reactions to Feedback.   As indicated previously, people decide whether to seek feedback and the source of feedback. Individuals' feelings about their own likely reactions to feedback may guide these decisions. For instance, they may anticipate that unfavorable feedback will make them feel bad, and so they hesitate to seek the feedback unless they are relatively certain it will not be negative (Ashford, 1986). Casey, Chatterjee, and I examined how people think they will react to consistent and inconsistent feedback from two sources (Casey, London, & Chatterjee, 1995). The student subjects thought that managers would be happier with equal feedback as long as it was the same as or higher than their self-assessment. However, they felt managers receiving inconsistent feedback would increase their post-feedback self-assessment. When feedback is inconsistent, people's fear of negative information may outweigh their satisfaction with the positive information. However, when re-evaluating their self-assessment, the ambiguity in the inconsistent feedback provides justification for self-enhancement. So, receiving consistent information, or at least information that suggests agreement among raters, is important to avoiding biases that may affect reactions to the feedback and later revision of self-image.

Combinations of Self–Other Agreement.   As noted in chapter 2 of this volume, people protect their egos by selectively attending to and/or interpreting information in a way that allows them to maintain a positive self-image. The extent to which self-protection is necessary will depend on the agreement between self- and others' evaluations. Consider several possibilities (identified by Ashford, 1989):

1. Both self- and others' evaluations are positive. This leads to favorable feelings and self-affirmation.
2. Both self- and others' assessments are negative. Although self-affirming, this may lead to discouragement, procrastination, or lack of action.
3. Self-assessment is positive and others' assessment is negative. This is not unusual (Harris & Schaubroeck, 1988). Maintaining a favorable self-assessment in this case is self-delusionary unless the person receiving the feedback has a good justification for denying the data or attributing the unfavorable feedback to a cause other than him or herself. If the unfavorable evaluation is justified and ignored, the dysfunctional behavior is likely to continue to the individual's detriment.
4. Self-assessment is negative and others' assessment is positive. This is less common, of course, but when it does occur, it can be highly dysfunctional. Individuals in this situation are likely to set lower standards for themselves than they are capable of achieving, and they do not try as hard as they should.

Ways to Improve Self–Other Agreement.   Changing an individual's self-image is not easy, particularly if the individual has been conditioned to think of him or herself in negative terms. Over or underestimation of self-performance may be avoided by giving specific and frequent performance information. An effort should be made to ensure that formal evaluations that occur annually or semi-annually be used as a basis for making important personnel decisions (e.g., pay raises and job assignments). This puts teeth into the performance feedback, making the evaluations salient and meaningful to the raters and recipients.

Cultural Differences in Self-Evaluations.   Although leniency in self-ratings is common, it is not universal. However, this may stem from a bias in favor of individualism in Western culture and in other societies. For instance, a study of Taiwanese workers found a "modesty bias" in self-ratings such that self-ratings were lower than ratings obtained from supervisors (Farh, Dobbins, & Cheng, 1991). This may be due to a collectivism bias coupled with high deference to authority in the Taiwanese culture. However, a study of blue collar workers in Nanjing, China (The People's Republic) found a leniency bias in self-ratings compared to peer and supervisor ratings (Yu & Murphy, 1993). This suggests that culture is not homogeneous and may be differentiated by many factors (country, industry, mode of operations and organization, and so forth). The findings suggest that self-other differences in perceptions may be influenced by cultural factors and such factors should be examined and taken into account when interpreting results. This is especially important given the increasing diversity of employees' backgrounds within global and domestic organizations.

DIGESTING MULTISOURCE FEEDBACK

In chapter 4, I discussed the value of feedback from multiple sources and showed how a rating procedure can be developed to collect information from subordinates, peers, supervisors, and customers. The process of developing and administering multisource ratings is one thing, making it effective is another. The content of the ratings, how the feedback is delivered, and support for its use in goal setting for development and behavior change are all critical to making multisource feedback worthwhile. This is especially the case because multisource feedback can be difficult to interpret and may open the door to distorting or ignoring the information.

This section emphasizes the importance of having specific information, considers defensive reactions to multisource feedback, outlines alternative modes of delivering multisource feedback, reviews psychological processes that encourage constructive use of multisource feedback, and suggests ways to make multisource feedback a part of the organization's culture.

Specificity of Information

The more specific the information, the more difficult it is to deny or ignore as long as it corresponds to the way the recipient thinks about the task (Kluger & DeNisi, 1996). In some rating systems, each rater makes ratings on the same set of performance items regardless of the source (whether peer, subordinate, customer, or supervisor). In other cases, different information may be collected from different sources, and there may be a set of general performance items rated by all sources. This is a way to provide comparative information while also collecting information about which a given source has specific observations not available to other sources. So, for instance, subordinates may rate their immediate supervisor on items specific to boss–subordinate relationships that they would know more about than raters from other sources. Customers may rate the manager on delivery of products or services. Peers may rate the manager on collegial relationships. All sources may rate the manager on organization and communication skills.

This individualized feedback may be accompanied by normative information—the average score for each item across all managers rated. This provides a basis of comparison of the individual ratings. For example, knowing that I received an average of 3.89 (on a 5-point scale ranging from 1 = *low* to 5 = *high*) from my subordinates on giving feedback would have different meaning if I know that the mean rating received by supervisors in my organization (across, say, 50+ supervisors) was 2.75 or was 4.66. I would know I was doing better or worse than average.

Another possibility is that employees provide general ratings of supervision, peer, and customer relationships. Everyone receives a summary of the average ratings across the department or the entire organization, but they do not receive specific information about how they were rated. This is known as *survey feedback* (Nadler, 1977). Thus, these employees receive only normative information. Such information may be a helpful and nonthreatening guide to managers in considering issues in their own departments. It can be valuable as an ice breaker in a team meeting aimed at discussing ways to improve interpersonal relationships by asking the team to consider the extent to which the results apply to them. However, it lacks specificity, and it is easy to rationalize unfavorable results by arguing that they apply to others, not to our department.

Of course, feedback may also be informal, coming from others directly (through statements of others' opinions about your performance) or indirectly (through hearsay or other evidence of how others evaluate your performance). Such information may be welcome and even sought, or it may be unwelcome. However, as covered in the last chapter, people may seek feedback for the purposes of creating an impression in others rather than learning how others feel about them. Moreover, informal feedback may be ambiguous. Or, it may focus on personal qualities (you learn that you are "hard to get along with"), rather than behaviors or actions (you "do not listen to others' ideas"). The more ambiguous and general the information, the less valuable it will be.

Toward an Impartial and Dispassionate Reaction

The most constructive ways to use feedback suggest the following guidelines:

- Review all the information thoroughly and objectively.
- Examine each piece of information; consider overall strengths and enumerate the most serious weaknesses.

- For each source of 360-degree feedback, list the 5 highest and 5 lowest ratings, compare the list between sources, and identify the strengths that should be enhanced and the weaknesses that should be reversed.
- Diagnose whether the areas for improvement are *motivational* (need to devote more time and energy to the area; need to overcome discomfort or dislike of the behavior; need for incentives to reward the behavior) or *ability* (need to learn how to do the behavior).
- Set goals for learning (training courses, special job assignments).
- Make commitments for changing behaviors.
- Review the feedback and refine the performance improvement goals with one's supervisor.
- The supervisor should incorporate the multisource results in the formal appraisal.
- The supervisor should follow up by evaluating the subordinate periodically on whether the goals for learning and behavior have been met (e.g., training courses attended, critical behaviors changed).
- Compare feedback from the next rating period to the previous rating period to determine whether the changed behavior has had an effect on the ratings.
- Evaluate changes in unit performance to determine their links to development, behaviors, and rating changes.

These guidelines are easier said than done, given people's tendency to be defensive.

Diversity of Opinion and Defensive Reactions

It is easy to put up a defense against multisource feedback. In informal feedback, recipients can ask only sources they know will be favorable. The recipient of 360-degree ratings can focus on the highest ratings regardless of source and performance dimension. If the feedback report includes the range (lowest and highest ratings) as well as the average for each source, then it is easy to focus on the top of the range. External attributions can be made for the lowest ratings (e.g., "There will always be some people who are unhappy," or "Low performers cannot be expected to be honest."). Alternatively, the recipient can concentrate on the source or performance dimensions providing the highest ratings, rationalizing that these sources/dimensions are the most important.

Modes of Delivery

The way multisource feedback is delivered will affect how much attention the recipient gives to it and the likelihood of defensive reactions. Consider the following possibilities:

One-on-one Delivery of Results From a Consultant. The consultant, an expert in performance improvement (perhaps an industrial/organizational psychologist or a human resource specialist), ideally from outside the company, reviews the results with the individual. This minimizes threat and forces the recipient to consider all the results. The consultant may also help the recipient use the feedback to set goals for performance improvement.

One-on-one Delivery of Results From the Immediate Supervisor. Knowing that your supervisor not only sees your ratings but also reviews them with you makes them highly salient. This enhances the threat and increases chances for defensiveness. However, if the supervisor knows how to review the feedback objectively and constructively, by tying the results to directions for improvement, the outcome can be beneficial. If the supervisor attributes blame and merely demands improvement, then the subordinate may be particularly defensive.

Desk-Drop. The feedback may come in the form of a computer printout or an on-line report. Written guidelines for using the feedback may be provided. However, whether the recipient reviews and uses the information is totally up to the recipient. When the feedback is meant solely for the recipient's development and no one else in the organization will see it, the only incentive for reviewing the information is performance improvement. However, the easiest defense is not to look at the information at all. If recipients know that their supervisor will also see the results, however, there is more incentive to at least know what they are in case the supervisor brings them up.

Group Session With General Discussion on Use. The recipients convene in a group to receive their individual results, usually delivered in a sealed envelope, and hear from a consultant or human resource specialist about ways to interpret and use the results. Recipients then have a chance to examine their individual results and ask general questions for clarification (e.g., "What does it mean if I rated myself lower than my peers and subordinates did?").

Group Session With General Discussion and Targeted Discussion About Each Individual. Here, the previously mentioned procedure is followed except that each person is given everyone else's ratings as well as his or her own. This may occur after a leadership development simulation as part of a course when the participants are all from different organizations. The simulation is followed by a chance for the trainers to rate the participants and for the participants to rate each other. The results are shared as a means of starting a discussion about each individual. Fellow participants share their reactions as a way to help each other. This information is hard to deny at the time it is given, but easy to forget after the course.

Attention to, and acceptance of, multisource feedback can be enhanced by building in reinforcement mechanisms. These rest in several well-understood psychological processes.

Psychological Processes

Information Processing.   The questions asked (items rated) communicate what performance dimensions are important in the organization.

Reward Mechanisms (Expectancy That Behavior Change Leads to Valued Outcomes).   People pay attention to behaviors and outcomes on which they are measured and reinforced.

Impression Management.   People want others to think well of them. Knowing that others will be evaluating them explicitly drives attention to the behaviors evaluated.

Social Comparison.   People want to know their performance in comparison to others. The availability of comparative data (i.e., how others did on average) makes the results more salient.

Goal Setting.   Goals and feedback are mutually supportive. Goals help feedback work, and feedback helps goals work. Using the feedback to set goals translates the feedback into action.

Frequent Feedback.   Some firms, such as Motorola, use 360-degree feedback quarterly, collecting the data and generating reports via computer.

Social Learning.   People model others' behavior when they see it is valued and rewarded. When top managers seek and use feedback, others will too.

Commitment Mechanisms.   People develop commitment to new behaviors when they are "do-able" (i.e., the individual sees the behaviors as possible and realistic), when rewards and valued outcomes can be anticipated, and also, because of anticipated rewards and valued outcomes (a process known as *prospective rationality*). The rewards might be social and self-administered (e.g., a stronger sense of belonging), or material and visible to others (a salary bonus, an awards dinner). Also, people develop commitment to behaviors for which they are making a substantial investment of time and money to develop (a process known as *retrospective rationality*; Salancik & Pfeffer, 1978). For instance, they express commitment to goals that they agree to in public (e.g., during a team meeting). To deny the commitment would be inconsistent with their self-image as an effective, rational person.

Making Multisource Ratings a Part of the Organization's Culture

Organizations need to support the use of multisource feedback for development. One study examined the extent to which multisource feedback led to development responses, such as participating in self-development activities, meeting with raters, targeting skills for improvement, and preparing a written development plan (Holt, Noe, & Cavanaugh, 1995). Managers' were more likely to engage in such development responses following feedback when development planning was required, development plans were complete, and the organization has a total quality management program that promoted continuous improvement. Sharing information publicly decreased the likelihood that managers targeted specific skills for self-improvement.

The organization should strive to make collection and use of performance information a constructive, normal part of doing business—part of the organization's culture. This will happen as 360-degree feedback or upward feedback ratings are . . .

- Collected at regular intervals (perhaps only annually).
- Used to evaluate individuals and make personnel decisions about them (the results are incorporated into the supervisor's appraisal).
- Fed back with organization-wide data for comparison purposes, establishing organizational standards, and tracking the accomplishment of these standards.
- Integrated into a human resource system that selects, develops, sets goals, appraises, and rewards the same set of performance dimensions—elements of performance that have been determined through job analyses to be critical to the organization's performance.

CONCLUSION

This chapter concentrated on helping employees cope with and absorb feedback. I considered how to make people receptive to feedback. A supportive environment certainly helps. Such an environment recognizes different ways people learn and induces them to achieve to their fullest potential. I presented ways to increase self-assessment accuracy as a vehicle for acceptance and use of feedback.

Here are some important conclusions:

1. Employees need help evaluating performance feedback, interpreting the information, and avoiding defensiveness.
2. Defensive reactions to feedback include blaming others for failure, trying to create the opposite impression, and trying to focus attention on other achievements.

3. Some organizations have evolved a corporate culture that supports employees' continuous learning and development. The CEO and top managers pave the way for this culture by modeling and reinforcing continuous experimentation, giving feedback, seeking feedback, and changing behavior in response to feedback.

4. People's reactions to, and use of, feedback depend on their learning styles. Adaptive learners make incremental changes to improve their performance. Generative learners transform themselves through major shifts in behavior after self-study.

5. People who have high expectations for their performance are also motivated to achieve. However, sometimes predictions of failure motivate employees to prove the predictions wrong.

6. Negative feedback alone is likely to be destructive or, at least, lead to defensiveness or the ignoring of the feedback altogether. However, low performers who are guided through the feedback in a way that makes them pay attention to, and reflect on, information are likely to improve. Self-assessments are important in the use of feedback because they prompt self-regulation, track goal achievement, and reduce environmental ambiguity.

7. Multisource feedback processes are more palatable and constructive when they build on psychological processes that model, reinforce, and integrate feedback in employee development and performance improvement.

Now that I have considered the value of feedback, ways to deliver more constructive feedback, and methods for using feedback to improve performance, I turn in the next chapter to holding people accountable for giving and using feedback.

V

CONCLUSION

11

Holding Managers Accountable for Giving and Using Feedback

We assume that people treat performance feedback seriously, learn from it, and change their behavior to improve their performance. Much of the literature on feedback has focused on how to collect information and deliver it to employees. For instance, the literature on multisource (360-degree and upward) feedback has concentrated on the methods and process for collecting survey feedback and providing participants with the results (Tornow, 1993). Here I argue that attention should be paid to how employees apply the feedback and interventions that encourage its effective use. This chapter is adapted from London, Smither, & Adsit (1997). Increasing rater and ratee accountability will improve the value of the performance feedback, increase the ratee's sensitivity to the information, and increase the likelihood that the feedback will improve performance. I describe forces and mechanisms that increase managers' accountability for giving feedback and using feedback. This leads to suggestions for how to enhance accountability.

ACCOUNTABILITY PROCESSES

In performance appraisal, raters are often not held accountable for the accuracy of their judgments. Also, ratees are often not accountable for using the feedback. Yet, accountability is critical to the effective use of feedback. For instance, raters try to be more accurate when their identity is known by the recipient of the feedback (Antonioni, 1994). Revealing the raters' identity is one way to hold them accountable for their ratings. Also, ratees say that they value the feedback more when they know the names of the raters. Although the identity of the rater is generally known in traditional performance appraisal (because the supervisor makes the ratings), this is not the case in multisource feedback processes that usually emphasize to raters that they will remain anonymous. Raters fear retribution from the supervisors and coworkers, and not protecting the raters' identity may destroy the integrity of the process. So, other methods are needed to increase rater accountability in multisource feedback programs.

Now, consider the ratee's viewpoint when receiving multisource rating results. When the ratings are collected solely for ratees' development, they can take the results or leave them unless they are encouraged through some means to use the information. When the ratings are collected to make decisions about the ratees (for instance, how much merit raise they should receive), then ratees may feel compelled to pay attention to the results. However, this does not mean that they will. Ratees may not value the feedback because they know that the raters were not accountable for providing as accurate judgments as possible.

Raters may be held accountable for their ratings by creating the chance that they may have to explain their judgments. In performance appraisal, supervisors rating subordinates are often called on by higher level managers to justify their evaluations. Groups of managers may meet to review and explain how they evaluated their subordinates. Similarly, in upward rating programs, top managers may hold one-on-one skip level meetings with lower level subordinates to review how the subordinates evaluated their supervisor. A difficulty with these ways to increase accountability is that raters may be more lenient so that they do not have to explain a negative evaluation. In addition, they may use their ratings as an attempt to influence how top managers or their peers view them. For instance, some raters may want to show that they are tough. Others may want to give an evaluation they think the top manager wants to hear—or one that they believe conforms to the top manager's opinions (Klimoski & Inks, 1990; Tetlock, 1983).

Definition of Accountability

Accountability may be defined generally as accepting and meeting one's personal responsibilities, being and/or feeling obligated to someone else or oneself, or having to justify one's actions to others about whom we care. Pressures to make people accountable come from law, conscience, or society. We assume that the person who is accountable for an action or decision is usually the one taking the action or making the decision. Or the accountable individual may be someone who supervises the person who takes the action of making the decision. Who is accountable in a given situation and what the person is accountable for should be specified by the person who holds the individual accountable. Moreover there should be some way to track, evaluate, and impose consequences for the person who is accountable for the action or decision. In performance appraisal, we can talk about the accountability of the rater (or, more generally, the source of the information) and ratee (the receiver of the information).

Finding ways to hold raters accountable makes them more sensitive to others' perceptions and feelings (Mitchell & Klimoski, 1984). For example, raters who anticipate having to give negative feedback in-person to a subordinate tend to be more lenient than raters who stay anonymous (Fisher, 1979; Ilgen & Knowlton, 1980). However, having to provide feedback directly to the ratee increases the importance of the rating task (Klimoski & Inks, 1990). Raters who have to give negative feedback often delay the performance review discussion. When they hold the discussion, they are very specific about what they say and provide clear justification for their views. However, sometimes raters who have to give negative feedback simply distort the information so that it is less threatening. If the rater knows that the ratee thinks highly of him or herself, the rater may actually distort the information to conform to what the rater thinks the ratee wants to hear (Larson, 1984).

In general, rating processes are likely to be more complex and the ratings more accurate when the raters are accountable for the outcomes (Tetlock & Kim, 1992). Even if the rater does not have to provide direct feedback to the ratee, having to justify the rating to someone who cares about the quality of the evaluation (perhaps a top manager or a group of peers) also enhances accountability (Beach & Mitchell, 1978). Having to justify ratings to others can influence the judgment process and the ratings themselves (Tetlock, 1985a, 1985b). Raters who know that they may have to justify their ratings think longer and more carefully about their evaluations (Ford & Weldon, 1981). They mentally prepare a justification that matches the other party's expectations. This is called *preemptive self-criticism* (Tetlock, 1983). Raters in this situation criticize their own judgment processes and the favorability of the ratings in light of what they think others expect.

Consider how people cope with accountability. This applies to raters who are held accountable for their ratings and ratees who are held accountable for using the feedback results (Tetlock, Skitka, & Boettger, 1989). People who know what others (those who hold them accountable) expect are likely to conform to these expectations (a phenomenon called *social attitude shift*). People who do not know what others expect and have no prior commitment to conform to others' expectations are likely to think hard, generate high-quality evaluations, and take justifiable actions. They use more complex judgment processes, are more certain of their cognitive processes, and are more careful about basing their evaluations and actions on available information (Mero & Motowidlo, 1995). (This is the phenomenon of *preemptive self-criticism* previously mentioned.) People who already have committed themselves to a particular viewpoint make judgments and take actions that conform to their viewpoints and develop rationalizations for their judgments and actions (this phenomenon is called *defensive bolstering*).

Accountability works because people want to be seen favorably (Baumeister, 1982; Blau, 1964; Carnevale, 1985; Deutch & Gerard, 1955; Jones, 1964; Simonson & Nye, 1992). They are concerned about having to justify their views or actions because they are concerned about how others will evaluate them. They want to appear competent—to make a good impression. Also, they want others' approval. Evaluation apprehension focuses attention on the task.

This helps performance of easy tasks but makes more difficult tasks harder (a process called *social facilitation*; for an in-depth review of these social phenomena, see Geen, 1991).

The purpose of an appraisal affects how raters find and process performance information (Williams, DeNisi, Blencoe, & Cafferty, 1985). If raters know their ratings will have real consequences, they are more observant and evaluate performance behaviors more carefully (Murphy, Balzer, Kellam, & Armstrong, 1984). Also, they know they have to justify the ratings (and, as a result, the rating process has personal consequences for the raters), then the purpose of the ratings is even more salient (Mero & Motowidlo, 1995). So, creating an appraisal situation that uses the ratings to make decisions about people and requires that raters justify their evaluations both increase accountability and improve the quality of the ratings. "Requiring justification essentially makes raters accountable and should cause them to wonder how they might be affected by the ratings they make. This is the point at which feelings of accountability and cues from the motivational context merge to influence performance ratings" (Mero & Motowidlo, 1995, p. 518).

In a study of rater accountability in upward feedback (subordinates rating their supervisor), raters were required to put their names on the upward appraisal questionnaires (Antonioni, 1994). Managers who received feedback from named raters felt more positively about the upward feedback process than did managers who received results from anonymous raters. When raters were identified, the managers receiving the results felt that subordinate raters were more objective. However, the subordinate raters felt less comfortable and were more lenient when they were identified than when they were anonymous. In other research on upward feedback, I found a similar result: Employees would rather be anonymous, and they report they would feel compelled to give more favorable ratings if they were identified (London, Wohlers, & Gallagher, 1990). People usually do not like to give negative ratings, particularly if they know the ratees know who they are (Fusilier, 1980).

In multisource feedback programs, there are three key constituencies: the manager who is rated, the raters (peers, subordinates, boss), and top managers. Each of these constituencies do not want to be accountable themselves, but they want the other constituencies to be accountable. The managers who are rated want confidential feedback (low accountability). Also, they prefer that the 360-degree feedback not be used to make decisions about them. Raters do not want to be identified. They are more lenient when they anticipate giving feedback in person or when they have to identify themselves on the rating form. Top managers expect the feedback recipients to use the results to change their behavior and improve their performance. However, management may not provide the support needed to help ratees interpret and use the results. So, what does the organization communicate when raters are guaranteed anonymity and ratees are guaranteed confidentiality? Such a situation suggests that the organization does not trust ratees to receive feedback from identified sources. The organization may fear that the ratees will punish raters who gave unfavorable ratings. Further, the organization may be concerned that negative performance results will be used against ratees when the purpose of the feedback is to help the ratees improve. Also, an upward or 360-degree rating process may make raters feel that there is no need for honest and direct communication about performance issues. Thus, not holding raters and ratees accountable may be symptomatic of a distrustful environment.

Accountability is enhanced when top managers devote resources to support employee development and assess changes in performance that result from the feedback. Simply dropping feedback reports on managers' desks is insufficient for multisource ratings to be taken seriously. Think about the different levels of accountability depending on how a multisource feedback program is implemented. In traditional employee attitude surveys, managers may be able to choose to receive a special report based on analyses of only employees in their department. However, the managers have no obligation to use the information, and there is no follow up to see if they did. In many applications of upward and 360-degree feedback, managers receive a feedback report. The raters are anonymous and feedback is confidential. Management provides no support or resources for using the feedback. In other cases, multisource feedback is accompanied by guidelines on how to use it. The organization may also provide some resources that managers can use to improve their performance when feedback is negative on some dimensions. The resources may include books to read, training programs to attend, or tips on how to improve specific skills. In all these cases, rater and ratee accountability is low, and so is top managers' accountability.

When multisource feedback results are used in formal appraisal, ratees are held accountable for using the information to improve. If they do not achieve a certain level of performance, or do not compare favorably to their peers, they fail to receive a merit increase in pay or a promotion. However, the feedback report is still dropped on the managers in the hope that they will do something with it. Top management may or may not provide resources to support personal development. Raters are anonymous and not accountable for the quality of their ratings.

Sometimes multisource feedback is incorporated in a training program. Before attending the training, managers are asked to distribute questionnaires to their subordinates, peers, customers, and supervisor. These raters provide anonymous feedback. The managers receive confidential feedback during a 1-week training program that focuses on the skills being rated (e.g., Monday deals with training in conflict management, so on Monday morning participants receive their upward feedback about conflict management). Ratees are encouraged to share their development plan with the boss. Whereas rater accountability is still low, ratee accountability to use the feedback is increased. Top management's accountability is high in that the company is providing a developmental resource to go along with the rating program.

Perhaps the highest levels of rater, ratee, and management accountability occur when the multisource feedback report is supported by a facilitator or counselor who guides the manager through the process. Raters provide anonymous feedback. The feedback results are sent to a facilitator who reviews the feedback and presents it to the target manager. Together, they formulate some initial reactions and plans. They set up a meeting attended by the facilitator, target manager, and raters. The target manager shares initial reactions and plans. Raters offer additional guidance and specific, constructive suggestions. The facilitator meets with the target manager 1 month, 3 months, 6 months, and 9 months after the target manager receives feedback (to help formulate goals and action plans, share approaches others are using, direct the target manager to appropriate resources).

TOWARD A THEORY OF ACCOUNTABILITY

Figure 11.1 outlines how accountability works. It depicts how forces of accountability drive being accountable and feeling accountable. The term *actor* in the figure refers to either the rater or ratee.

Components of the Model

The components are:

1. *Constituencies* of accountability (e.g., coworkers, the boss, organizational policies, or the actor himself or herself).
2. The *objective* (what the actor is being held accountable for).
3. Internal or external accountability *forces* used by the constituencies to affect the actor's feelings of accountability (e.g., internal forces such as the desire to gain recognition or avoid embarrassment, and external forces such as positive or negative financial outcomes).
4. Accountability *mechanisms* (ways the constituencies activate the forces—that is, ways to hold someone—or oneself—accountable).
5. *Characteristics of the actor* that determine what forces can be activated.
6. The *actor's reactions*.

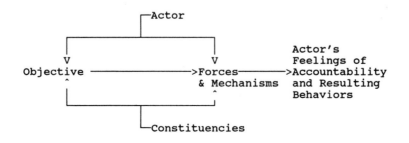

FIG. 11.1. A model of accountability processes.

The model works as follows: The objective determines the forces and mechanisms used to enforce the obligation. This, in turn, affects behaviors and reactions. The nature of the obligation and the accountability forces and mechanisms are influenced by characteristics of the people involved. The following description of the components should make the model clearer.

Constituencies.   Accountability stems from oneself (in that people often hold themselves accountable for decisions and actions), others (e.g., one's boss), the social situation and norms, organizational policies, and/or task demands. The constituencies initiate, monitor, and enforce accountability. They influence the actor's feelings of obligation, and they impart implicit or explicit (behavioral or material) consequences.

Accountability Forces.   These are the reasons (essentially the power behind) why people feel accountable. Some forces are internal, such as feelings of morality, efficacy, and self-control; the desire to gain approval and recognition (or avoid embarrassment); and the goal of meeting an obligation. Other forces are external, such as a valued outcome (e.g., money or job security).

Accountability Mechanisms.   These are the ways people are held accountable—the "switches and circuits" that activate and transmit the accountability forces. Examples are giving feedback; asking for, listening to, and accepting justification; having goals that are known to others; clear attribution for behavior (and not being able to diffuse responsibility or blame others); facing clear measurements and consequences; and having to deal with few intervening variables or factors beyond one's control. Just as these are ways to hold people accountable, other mechanisms avoid accountability. Examples are scapegoating, procrastinating, and passing the buck.

Actor Characteristics.   A variety of individual difference characteristics may influence the extent to which accountability forces successfully induce feelings of accountability. These may include achievement motivation, need for power or control, and need for affiliation or acceptance (McClelland, 1965). These needs increase the extent to which people are susceptible to holding themselves accountable or being held accountable by others.

The Actor's Reactions.   These are outcomes that result from accountability. Example are accuracy, persistence, effort, vigilance, conformity, mindful cognitive processing, and self-satisfaction. Negative outcomes may include the opposites, such as bias, opposition, confrontation, automatic cognitive processing, and depression.

Applying the Model

Now, here are some examples that show how the model can be applied to multisource feedback. First, consider the ratee as the actor. In one organization, the boss could be a constituency of accountability, and the ratee's desire for improved performance and financial rewards could be the accountability force. The accountability mechanisms may be requiring the ratee to share his or her development plan with the boss. Another might be an agreement with the boss to measure the extent of performance improvement by comparing the results from two consecutive administrations of multisource feedback 6 months apart. The behaviors and reactions may include the ratee's participation in a training program and persistence over time toward achieving performance goals.

Next, consider the rater as the actor. A constituency and associated mechanism of accountability could be coworkers' expectations that raters will provide candid, unbiased feedback. An internal accountability force may be the rater's desire to do what's right (i.e., provide fair ratings). An external accountability force may be negative outcomes controlled by the constituency (e.g., the work group does not respect raters whose face-to-face feedback to a ratee is different from anonymous feedback). An accountability mechanism may be the requirement or expectation that each rater will provide constructive comments during facilitated feedback sessions. The consequence of these accountability constituencies, forces, and mechanisms would be raters who provide candid, unbiased, fair, and accurate ratings and constructive feedback in person.

Theoretical Rationale for the Model

Some basic theoretical concepts explain accountability processes in performance appraisal. Rather than reviewing the basic theory, per se, here are some general theory-derived conclusions about raters and ratees. (The footnotes provide references to the relevant theories.)

1. Raters' and ratees' perceptions of the fairness of the rating process and the ratings themselves may affect the accuracy of their ratings and reactions to feedback (Greenberg, 1990).
2. Raters' and ratees' tendency to attribute good things to oneself and bad things to others may influence rating accuracy and acceptance of negative feedback (Festinger, 1954).
3. Ratees may be more likely to use feedback when they recognize their responsibility to others and their ability to make positive things happen.
4. People try harder the higher the probability of meeting performance standards and obtaining desired outcomes.

5. People want to conform to others' opinions, especially opinions of others' whom they like and respect (Tetlock, 1983).
6. People tend to compare themselves to standards or goals and seek to minimize discrepancy between their behavior and these standards (Nelson, 1993).
7. People want to be liked and be evaluated positively by others (Baumeister, 1982; Dobbins & Russell, 1986).

Forces, Mechanisms, and Ways to Facilitate Accountability

Next, consider some of the types of accountability constituencies and the forces, mechanisms, and interventions associated with them. First I will consider accountability processes in general, and then focus on accountability processes in multisource feedback.

First, consider *internal constituencies* for accountability. These may be the desire for feedback (knowledge of results) and the desire for positive outcomes brought on by the forces of self-regulation and need for achievement and regulation by internal self-control mechanisms. Facilitating factors include social norms that suggest the importance of others' views and meeting others' expectations.

Second, *society* may be a constituency for accountability. People feel accountable to society. Norms and peer pressure are the social forces that encourage and reward feeling accountable to society. This feeling may be increased when comparative information is available about others' actions and when there are strong, clear expectations for appropriate behavior.

Third, the *task* itself can be a constituency for accountability. Task requirements specify standards for evaluating oneself and others and setting goals for improvement. A moderately difficult task can create in an individual the sense of challenge and achievement for task fulfillment. This can be enhanced by specific measurements and a clear link between the individual's contribution and the task performance.

Fourth, *interpersonal constituencies* generate accountability. People want to be seen positively by others, and they are susceptible to others' views. People want to avoid embarrassment and maintain their pride. So face-to-face meetings, public displays of behavior, and announcements of outcomes are mechanisms that promote interpersonal accountability. These can be enhanced by task characteristics, referred to previously, that strengthen the relationships between individual behavior and task performance.

Fifth, the *organization* can be a constituency of accountability in that people feel accountable to their employer. Forces include organizational rewards and punishments (e.g., employment security, pay increases) through the consistent application of performance appraisals and their implications for valued outcomes. This is encouraged when goals are clear, performance measures are objective and, again, there are strong links between behavior and valued outcomes.

Now, turning specifically to multisource feedback, people manage their own accountability through motivation for high performance, sensitivity to self and others' views, and wanting to conform to others' wishes. Self-ratings along with feedback from others allows self-other comparisons and tracking improvement. Facilitating factors include requiring that each person explain his or her own feedback to someone else (the supervisor or a counselor) and make commitments for improvement. Knowing that the survey is repeated over time also makes the results more pointed because there will be a chance to show improvement. Being confronted by data about their self-monitoring tendencies and sensitivity to others' views may influence ratees' receptivity to feedback.

Supervisors, subordinates, peers, and customers are interpersonal constituencies of accountability associated with multisource feedback. Supervisors enforce accountability through reward power and their ability or desire to control their work group members. Friendship may also motivate an employee's sense of accountability to the supervisor. Ways to increase the extent to which the performance results are used include giving the supervisor access to the feedback results and the discretion to use them as a basis for salary bonuses and nonfinancial rewards. Another mechanism for accountability may occur when supervisors intentionally or unintentionally establish a tightly knit in-group of subordinates on whom they rely and have confidence. Such mechanisms of accountability can be facilitated by requiring that supervisors conduct performance review discussions with subordinates during which the multisource feedback is examined jointly. Having comparative data about how others did may make the discussion more meaningful. This makes it more difficult for the parties to deny poor performance relative to others and, conversely, easier for them to recognize better-than-average performance. Training should be available to help supervisors to conduct meaningful performance reviews. Also, organizational policies should evaluate and reward supervisors for developing subordinates.

Subordinates are a relevant constituency. Their ratings suggest the manager's obligation to the work group as a whole and to individual subordinates. Managers' obligations to their subordinates are based on mutual dependence and the desire for positive interpersonal relationships. These forces operate as subordinates cooperate with each other and with their supervisor to accomplish work group goals. This occurs through such mechanisms as subordinates' responsiveness to instructions and task demands, their effort and, ultimately their good performance. Also, subordinates can foster the manager's reputation as an excellent supervisor. Facilitating mechanisms include encouraging or requiring that the supervisor hold a group discussion with subordinates to review the results of upward or multisource feedback. In addition, the importance of subordinate ratings may be highlighted to the manager when the subordinates have a chance to participate in the development of the survey items. In this way, the items reflect what is important to subordinates. This is reinforced by top management's willingness to include these items in the survey.

Peers can be another constituency of obligation and, hence, a valuable source of feedback. Employees value their friendship and viewpoints as role models and bases for comparison. Employees' obligations to their peers operate through mutual liking and engagement in social activities. Employees feel a greater sense of obligation to their peers when the peers show them respect and seek out their expertise. These mechanisms can be enhanced by the availability of normative multisource survey results (i.e., showing how other employees were rated on average). Teambuilding initiatives, such as joint participation in leadership development or conflict resolution workshops, may promote mutual support among peers, emphasize their obligation to each other, and increase the value of peer ratings.

Employees are also obligated to their internal and external customers (those who use the product of their efforts). Employees are dependent on customers for business, rewarded by them, and may develop friendships with them. This occurs through repeat business, an enhanced reputation for quality products or services, and involvement in social activities. Obligation to customers and the value of customer ratings can be enhanced when customers are involved in writing multisource feedback items and when customers receive a report of the feedback results. In this way, customers become a direct part in the evaluation process, and knowledge of their opinions can foster improved customer relationships.

A multisource feedback program may be started by top management, the human resource department, or the members of the work group. In encouraging the process, the organization promotes a climate that supports development and continuous improvement. Thus, the process itself encourages an obligation for the raters to provide accurate ratings and the raters to apply the feedback. This is enhanced when the results are used for evaluative and administrative purposes (i.e., as criteria for promotion and pay decisions) and when the organization offers training programs and development opportunities liked to specific performance dimensions. In addition, raters and ratees will pay more attention to the rating process and results when the items are known to reflect organizational expectations. For instance, they may be based on a model of desired management behavior that guides selection, training, appraisal, compensation, and outplacement policies. Also, the feedback results become more salient when the organization rewards continuous improvement and customer satisfaction and when facilitators are available to help employees interpret the feedback and incorporate it into development plans.

This model of multiple accountability constituencies, forces, and mechanisms makes three *assumptions about how these components work together*:

1. There are multiple ways to achieve the same end. Different constituencies operate to drive feelings of accountability and each may affect the actor's

behavior. One constituency is not, a priori, necessarily better than another constituency. As a result, interventions to enhance accountability should focus on accountability to the supervisor, to subordinates, to peers, to the organization, and to oneself.

2. Different forces and associated mechanisms are mutually reinforcing. They work together to enhance the salience of obligation to constituencies. Internal and external mechanisms may be important at the same time.

3. The actor may see functional and dysfunctional outcomes resulting from the same accountability constituencies. So, for instance, having to share and justify reactions to multisource feedback to one's supervisor may raise the ratee's feelings of accountability but increase the ratee's defensiveness, especially if he or she feels that the ratings are in some ways inaccurate. Also, survey items may focus attention on how work is done rather than on the outcomes of performance. Accountability mechanisms in multisource feedback may be most effective when they focus on means *and* ends (behaviors, process, and outcomes).

ENHANCING THE EFFECTIVENESS OF MULTISOURCE FEEDBACK

In performance appraisal and multisource feedback, raters are accountable to ratees to provide accurate meaningful information, and ratees are accountable to raters, management, and themselves to use the information. Multisource feedback can be made more valuable by establishing forces and associated mechanisms that reinforce accountability to oneself and others. These interventions influence raters by holding them accountable for the accuracy of their ratings, even if not identifying them to the raters. Other interventions hold ratees accountable for using the results by having to justify, explain, or demonstrate how they benefited from the feedback. We know, for instance, that managers respond positively to anonymous upward appraisals by improving their supervisory behaviors (Hegarty, 1974). But they respond more positively when a consultant reviews the upward performance ratings with them, encouraging them to use the information to improve their performance (Nemeroff & Cosentino, 1979).

Consider facilitating mechanisms that apply to different constituencies in the multisource feedback process: For raters, giving them the results of personality tests that suggest their interpersonal sensitivity may increase their self-reflection. Asking raters to participate in designing performance appraisal items may increase their understanding of, and commitment to, multisource feedback. For ratees, the frequency of self-assessment (e.g., regular surveys) may increase the salience of self-reflection. Asking ratees to make a explicit public commitment to use the feedback results for goal setting and performance improvement builds on the ratees' sense of integrity and desire to make a good impression. Such a commitment may be made during the course of a training session, in a meeting with a counselor or supervisor, or in a group discussion with subordinates. Work groups that spend time discussing their boss's feedback results increase subordinates' involvement in, and commitment to, these results. It should do the same for the managers who are the subject of the feedback. Incorporating peer ratings into teambuilding exercises and workshops enhances peer cooperation and learning from each other. Ratees' accountability to use performance information may also be increased when the performance review session is conducted by the supervisor in a constructive manner (e.g., nonthreatening, behaviorally based). The availability of average ratings across work groups may increase accountability by making highlighting comparisons and encouraging a discussion of standards. Training and rewarding supervisors' feedback and development behaviors support the importance of employee development in the organization and encourage employees to work seriously with the supervisor on learning from feedback.

CONCLUSION

This chapter described the ties between accountability constituencies, forces, and mechanisms. Accountability mechanisms require the feedback recipient to explain and justify use of the feedback, encourage employees to recognize the varying expectations of different constituencies, expect raters to provide accurate and meaningful ratings, and reward improved performance. Unfortunately, rating methods may not hold raters accountable for the accuracy of the information they provide or hold ratees accountable for using the feedback.

Here are the major conclusions from the chapter:

1. Increasing rater and ratee accountability improves the value of the information, enhances the ratee's sensitivity to the information, and increases the likelihood that the feedback will improve performance.

2. Accountability motivates the rater. People who feel accountable by having to justify their ratings to someone else generate more accurate ratings.

3. Accountability makes raters more susceptible to others' perceptions and feelings.

4. Accountability constituencies and associated forces and mechanisms stem from the individual (e.g., the desire for feedback and positive outcomes), society, the task, other people and how one is viewed by others, and the organization (e.g., through performance expectations and rewards).

5. The value of multisource feedback can be enhanced by establishing forces and associated mechanisms that reinforce accountability to oneself and others.

6. Mechanisms that increase accountability forces recognize that people may be accountable to different constituencies. Also, the mechanisms build

on underlying theoretical principles (reward, control, affiliation, self-presentation, impression management, and self-regulation) in relation to each constituency.

7. Multisource feedback can become part of the organization's management culture through interventions that support the use of the feedback.

The next, and final, chapter turns to reasons why feedback will continue to be an important part of successful management in the future.

12

Feedback Challenges in Emerging Work Settings

This chapter focuses on feedback issues in changing work settings. One issue deals with electronic performance monitoring. Advanced technology allows collecting abundant information at the expense of individual privacy. Another issue is the trend toward open learning methods that allow people to direct their own learning at their own pace. This raises the need for ways to learn about oneself through feedback and self-assessment and develop a program of learning based on this information along with a recognition of organizational requirements. Cross-cultural and diversity training provide other challenges for improving performance. New jobs and work group structures are evolving to meet organizational needs, changing technology, and fiscal pressures. As a result, employees will have to learn new competencies. So, I consider the components of job competency models that specify emerging performance dimensions for evaluation and feedback. I also address legal issues in the ever-changing regulatory climate. I conclude by describing how feedback fits into an integrated human performance system.

ELECTRONIC PERFORMANCE MONITORING

Being observed and evaluated is threatening enough for many people. Advanced computer technologies allow close tracking and scrutiny of employees' behaviors. In 1990, more than 10 million employees were subject to electronic performance monitoring (cited in Aiello & Kolb, 1995). Most of these were clerical workers, but electronic monitoring can also apply to management, technical, and professional employees. Consider the following jobs:

Truck driver. Remote monitoring can track location, speed, on-time deliveries, and even elements of the condition of the truck (e.g. tire pressure) and possibly driver (i.e., heart rate, response time, and attentiveness).

165

Hospital personnel. Detailed patient recording systems can determine amount and type of patient contact for each health care provider.

Factory worker. Work station monitoring can determine quality (accuracy) and quantity (pace) of output.

Educator. Student test score performance can be tracked and summarized by teacher, controlling for initial student abilities.

Office worker. Telephone systems can monitor time and location of incoming and outgoing calls. Network computer systems can monitor logged-on time and type of work.

Attorneys and other consultants involved in client service. Time tracking systems are important for billing. They also indicate the type and amount of work performed.

Although this book has emphasized when and how feedback can be valuable, an open question is how monitoring, especially electronic monitoring, affects the employee's productivity and feelings of stress. Several studies have found that electronic monitoring makes jobs seem more stressful (Gallatin, 1989; Irving, Higgins, & Safayeni, 1986). This may happen not because of the monitoring, per se, but because of other changes that accompany the introduction of the new observation method. Such changes may include increased workload and loss of control over the way they do their jobs (Smith, Carayon, Sanders, Lim, & LeGrande, 1992). However, monitoring may improve individual performance of people who are highly skilled because such people tend to perform better when they are observed. This is called the *social facilitation* effect (Zajonc, 1965). People who work in groups may not feel this stress if the group as a whole is monitored and the group is cohesive enough to provide members with social support. This was found in a study of students working on a data-entry task alone, as a member of a noninteracting group, or as a member of a cohesive group (Aiello & Kolb, 1995). (In the cohesive group, students spent some time getting to know each other prior to the task and were told that a test they had taken indicated they were highly compatible.) High-skilled participants performed better when they were monitored than when they were not. Low-skilled participants performed more poorly when they were monitored than when they were not, supporting the concept of social facilitation. The participants reported feeling least stressed when they were not monitored or were members of cohesive groups.

SELF-PACED LEARNING

Self-paced or *open learning* refers to people working on their own to learn new skills and acquire knowledge. Assessment and feedback are generally built into the process in order to help people determine what they should learn and whether they have learned it. Self-paced material may be presented in written form, through a computer with CD Rom, in audio or videotapes, or by an interactive video system (Warr & Bunce, 1995). Open learners have autonomy to decide what they study and how, when, where, and at what pace (Stewart & Winter, 1992). Learners control time spent on material, amount of review of material and revision of responses, and the way they explore and test new concepts.

Program Examples

Open learning can be incorporated into training programs on such topics as communications, problem solving, budgeting, hiring, and health and safety. Warr and Bunce described such a training process (Warr & Bunce, 1995). The topics were selected after extensive-needs analyses for first line managers in many different organizations. Designed for junior managers in a British firm, the trainees participated in the program during a 4-month period. They attended a 3-day introductory session, a 2-day workshop at the half-way point, and a 2-day review at the end. The rest of the time, trainees studied on their own, including 5 hours of paid time each week. Each module contained a workbook, an audio casette, and exercises to be completed along with self-testing questions and quizzes. Exercises and assignments were submitted to an assigned tutor for assessment.

Despite the self-paced design, this was a fairly structured program. Participants were given the modules and they merely had to go through them on their own. Tutors provided guidance and oversight. Other programs are less directive. They require the participant to select topics for study based on their own interests, views of their capabilities and knowledge, and assessment of career opportunities.

A Study-at-Home Skill-Enhancement Program. AT&T and its employee union, the Communications Workers of America, established a self-study-at-home program for occupational workers who wanted training in emerging areas of the telecommunications business and in general business skills. The program offered free learning materials on a variety of subjects. Interested employees could take their choice of topic and sign-up, and they were sent the materials. They received little or no feedback about their performance in the modules they chose.

Other programs are more attuned to helping employees work on their own to assess their skills, evaluate training needs, and track success over time. Here is an example:

On-Line Career Planning and Development. Computers provide avenues for individuals to direct their own development needs. One such program, called "Smart Software" has five components (James, 1994):

1. *Career review.* Asks questions about career progress and key learning experiences that occurred on the job.

2. *Motivation to develop and career aspirations.* Questions that promote the respondents' understanding of their future career direction—not specific jobs, but the creation of alternatives for where and how they could apply their skills.

3. *Competence-based job analysis.* Respondents can rate certain behavioral competencies in terms of their importance to their current role. This results in a weighted competence framework that allows the respondent to compare his or her assessment to his or her immediate supervisor's assessment.

4. *Competence-based self-assessment.* Uses insight questionnaires to evaluate strengths and weaknesses in areas identified as important in the prior job analysis.

5. *Development strategies.* The program asks the respondent to identify the three main areas they wish to develop. The software then offers appropriate literature that provides key principles in such areas as strategic thinking, problem solving, interpersonal communications, managing and motivating others, etc.

Overall, self-paced learning, often utilizing computer technology, is a cost-effective, flexible method. It can be accessed by the individual whenever he or she has the time and inclination. Also, it is applicable to small and large firms alike, because excellent software programs, videos, audio tapes, and written materials are increasingly available.

CROSS-CULTURAL TRAINING

Multinational firms must prepare managers to operate effectively in other cultures. As might be expected, cultural insensitivity leads to failure of expatriates. Different methods for cross-cultural training, which may be combined, include the following (Park & Harrison, 1993):

1. Description of the target culture through lectures, readings, videos, and other media.
2. Simulation and role plays of likely experiences and practice functioning in the new culture.
3. Self-awareness, based on the notion that understanding and acceptance of oneself leads to greater ability to adjust in another culture.
4. Cultural awareness, which helps people recognize their own values, analyzes contrasts with other cultures, and applies the insights gained to improve interpersonal effectiveness.

A popular method of cultural awareness uses role-playing encounters between a U.S. citizen and a person from another culture with contrasting values (Harris & Moran, 1987). The method highlights awareness of differences, but not necessarily skills for enhancing sensitivity.

Performance of people in new cultures is an increasingly important and exciting area for performance diagnosis and improvement. Cultural factors need to be incorporated into performance review programs. Human resource practitioners will need to assess the extent to which culture influences the introduction, use, and effectiveness of different review methods (e.g., the viability of self-assessment in paternalistic cultures). Also, cultural factors will need to be incorporated into performance competencies and standards (i.e., to evaluate the extent to which expatriates are successful in developing cross-cultural business relationships).

Diversity Training

Another form of cross-cultural training focuses on helping employees appreciate diversity within the organization (see Jackson, 1992, for descriptions of other methods of cultural diversity training). In general, firms are more likely to adopt diversity training when top management gives it a high strategic priority (Rynes & Rosen, 1995). Diversity training may take many forms. Consider the following:

Awareness Training.   Employees attend lectures and watch video tapes in which experts talk about the importance of valuing diversity and offer some guidelines for proper behavior. Video or in-person demonstrations may be provided with actors playing various scenes. Vignettes of situations involving discrimination and cultural conflict may be described.

Orientation Training.   All employees may be required to attend a session that describes the organization's policies about valuing and rewarding diversity and promoting equal employment opportunity. Also, the session may address negative consequences for sexual harassment, biased decisions, and other forms of discrimination.

Experiential, Shock Training.   Employees participate in role-playing exercises that give them the chance to feel what it is like to be in the minority. For instance, one such program divides employees into two groups. Employees assigned to one group wait for an extended period of time (maybe an hour or more) in an uncomfortable hallway. The other group has coffee and is briefed about the day. The group in the hallway is then led into a room and asked to sit on the floor surrounded by members of the privileged group sitting on chairs arranged in a circle. The leader proceeds to deride the behavior and characteristics of minority group members on the floor, addressing the privileged group members and avoiding eye contact with the others. The frustrated and angry minority group members cannot say a word. After an hour or more of this, the leader breaks set and debriefs the group. This powerful, frame-breaking technique drives home what it feels like to be treated with disrespect and disdain arising from negative group stereotypes.

For diversity training to work, the results must be measured. As such, the organization needs feedback mechanisms to track equal employment opportunity. This can be done at the organization level (e.g., minority group representation among new employees; number of grievances linked to discrimination). Similar statistics can be provided to managers of large units. The performance evaluation of individual managers at all organizational levels can include information about hiring practices in the group, attendance at diversity training sessions, and treatment of individuals.

NEW JOBS, ROLES, AND WORK STRUCTURES

Some fields are experiencing rapid changes in jobs, the creation of new positions and roles, and work team reconfigurations. Often these changes are imposed with minimal formal education or training. As a result, on-the-job training and feedback become critical to success, and existing employees need to learn how to give feedback to make the new employees effective as they all initiate new roles.

A good example is provided by the health-care industry. The nursing shortage in the late 1980s and the concern for lowering health-care costs in the 1990s led hospitals to begin changing the mix of licensed and unlicensed employees caring for patients. For instance, the Ochner Foundation Hospital in New Orleans developed the position of nursing-care technician, and the Presbyterian Medical Center of Philadelphia created the position of patient-care associate (King, 1995). These new personnel work with and for registered nurses (RNs) who delegate and supervise their work. After initial training from the hospitals, these unlicensed assistants learn new skills on the job from RNs. The RNs are trained to learn good delegation, communication, and teambuilding skills. Giving ongoing feedback is an essential part of enhancing the assistants' skills. Each assistant works with two or three RNs who have a chance to develop close working relationships with the assistant while allowing for flexible scheduling. Therefore, the RNs need to be consistent in their expectations and feedback, engage in ongoing evaluation of the assistants' role, and revise expectations and relationships as the assistants learn more skills that do not require licensed personnel.

Communicating Changes in Performance Competencies

As suggested in chapter 3, people judge others on the basis of mental categories. These categories help place the individual in our minds and form a conception of the individual's performance. A person's judgments can be influenced by category descriptions prior to making ratings. For instance, people who are asked to memorize or use either positive or negative personality-trait terms subsequently judge another individual as more attractive if they were previously exposed to favorable items than unfavorable items (Higgins, Bargh, & Lombardi, 1985; Higgins, Rholes, & Jones, 1977). People form distinct prototypes of effective and ineffective performance categories, and ratings of another individual are strongly related to the prototype the person resembles (Kinicki, Hom, Trost, & Wade, 1995). Thus, it may help people to have categories against which they can judge their own and other's performance. This produces an accurate *prototype*—a view of how the organization conceptualizes an effective individual and the benchmark against which people should compare themselves. The risk is that people are less accurate in discriminating actual behaviors when they have access to the prototype. The tendency is to match people to the category. Further, priming a person to think of negative information prior to rating another may produce a contrast effect such that positive information is evaluated more positively (Banaji, Hardin, & Rothman, 1993). As a result, it may be important that benchmark information be presented in neutral terms to produce a schema that establishes meaningful performance standards.

Developing a Competency Model

A competency model guides the development of a professional in an organization. The goal is to ensure that the firm has the best services available and provides its employees with the richest array of development options. The model recognizes that today's world requires that employees have up-to-date knowledge and continuous skill development.

A competency model defines *core competencies* for all professionals in the area. This is the minimum knowledge, skills, and experiences necessary to enter and remain in the discipline and serve the needs of the firm. It also defines the competencies within specialities. The model suggests ways to learn and measure each competency. As such, it explains the need and directions for continued growth and breadth of experience.

The core competencies and specialty areas help make the firm successful, pave the way for individual growth and opportunities, and show that enhanced, world-class professionalism leads to improved service. A competency model demonstrates how employees contribute to the firm's success, can gain broad (generic) experience in the profession as well as in various specialties, and have the chance to assume more responsibility. The model has implications for the selection and development of professionals into and within the firm, including logical career paths for development and advancement. It shows that development leads to a broad array of career opportunities within the company. Movement between and within the firm's business units is encouraged while the manager's expertise grows within the profession.

The model is a tool for professionals to assess gaps in their knowledge and set directions for further skill development. The firm expects its professionals to maintain and enhance their expertise. To that end, the firm supports continued learning in the profession and rewards development with increased responsibilities and advancement potential. The model shows different skill and experience requirements in different specialty areas within the discipline and at different organizational levels, with the principal focus on professional growth and development.

Employees are expected to fill gaps in their competencies to (a) do their current jobs better, (b) prepare for anticipated changes in competency requirements as their jobs evolve to meet changing business needs, and (c) consider areas for development that will enhance their career potential in the company. The competencies and specialty areas show that development is not an overwhelming task. Although learning is a continuous task, it needs direction and specificity. This tool offers the guidance needed for professionals to establish directions for career growth consistent with the company's expectations for continuous professional development.

There are multiple ways to acquire the same skills and reach the same level of expertise and proficiency. Indeed, a given competency should be developed in multiple ways (e.g., on-the-job experiences, short courses, certification programs, academic degree programs, professional literature, and conferences to name a few general sources of knowledge and skill development). The model suggests these different ways, but it is up to you, the individual professional, to choose directions for development that match your job and career goals.

There are synergies and dependencies among different skills and knowledge areas. Some are closely related and build on each other. This model helps professionals identify the complementary skills within their specialty areas, identify ways to expand these areas of competence, and obtain the education and experiences needed to branch off to new areas of expertise within the discipline.

Just as certain skills are interdependent, some processes and jobs are interdependent. This model helps the professional to understand these interdependencies. Avenues for development should build on these overlapping job requirements in order to enhance learning and job effectiveness.

This company's employees face increased challenges in the evolution and growth of the business. The company expects professionals to have the expertise to meet this continuously rising bar. Therefore, the model for professional development is flexible. It will evolve to meet changing needs of the firm and the profession. The competencies will change as the profession develops and becomes increasingly effective as a business partner. So, the current overview of competencies is a guideline that works for today. Professionals can go beyond the model to further enhance their competence. Moreover, they will contribute to the evolution and revision of the model.

All employees in the firm should be concerned about enhancing their performance and supporting the development of their work teams. This model will help employees of professionals be effective coaches, developers, and evaluators of the function and processes. It is also a vehicle for self-assessment and self-directed career development for employees.

In summary, the professionalism model shows the following:

- Being a professional entails significant skill and experience requirements.
- Professionals need increasing levels of competence to help the firm accomplish its goals.
- The professional in the firm can take advantage of considerable variability of opportunities for professional growth and development.
- The professional is expected to meet the challenge of a continuously rising bar of expertise to support continued organization transformation.

If we apply the model successfully, we will accomplish the following objectives:

- The firm will be viewed as both competitive and highly professional.
- The company's professionals will be sought after by customers for solving critical business problems.
- The company's professionals will be sought after by other organizations for their knowledge and expertise.
- The company's professionals will be recognized by their professions for their contributions and achievements both within and outside of the company.
- Company products, services, and systems will be recognized as "best-in-class" and serve as models for other organizations.
- The company's professionals will significantly affect the company's overall strategy and direction.

Competency Model Contents

1. The core competencies and specialty areas.
2. This is followed by a section that provides more information about each core competency and the central competencies that comprise each specialty area. For each competency, this includes:

- Definition and examples from different points in the associated process (e.g. program development, implementation, and outcomes) to show why the core competency is important to management in the firm.

- Suggestions for acquiring the competency including recommended reading, short courses, academic programs, and/or membership in, and material from, professional associations.
- Ideas for competency measurement to assess success in development and to aid in making staffing and assignment decisions.

3. This is followed by a section that explores the general implications of the core competencies and specialty areas for staffing, development, and career planning for professionals.

Edward Mone and I developed the example of a general competency model for human resource professionals in any organization is found at the end of this chapter. A similar format would be followed for other professions.

LEGAL ISSUES

Any performance appraisal system used to make an employment decision about a member of a protected class (e.g., based on age, race, religion, gender, or national origin) must be a valid system or it may be challenged in the courts (based, for instance, on the Title VII of the 1964 Civil Rights Act, the Civil Rights Act of 1991, and the Age Discrimination in Employment Act of 1975). Rating systems that depend on subjective criteria and personality trait evaluations rather than evaluations of behavior may very well be worse than having none at all. As pointed out earlier in this book (chap. 6), appraisals are subject to raters' subjective biases and prejudices. Appraisal systems linked to goal setting must be an ongoing procedure, such as the review process recommended here (chap. 7). If only an annual or semi-annual review meeting occurs that covers only the most recent performance information it is not a valid system. In addition to frequent performance discussions, documentation in behavior terms is recommended. However, remember that this material is discoverable in a court suit, so it better be accurate and factual. The supervisor should be clear with the subordinate at the outset of the performance period about how the appraisal will be used. Also, managers should review their appraisals of subordinates with the next level of supervision as a way of holding the manager accountable for a thorough and fair evaluation.

A related legal and social issue is sexual harassment. Harassment can easily masquerade as feedback. *Sexual harassment* involves sexual favors or the creation of an environment that tolerates unwelcome sexual advances or language. The organization should have a clear policy prohibiting such behavior. Moreover, the performance review guidelines and associated training should include reference to this policy and indicate that care should be taken to guard against creating a hostile environment in the review process. This includes any sexual advances, innuendos, or vulgar statements that the employee objects to or considers hostile.

DEVELOPING AN INTEGRATED HUMAN PERFORMANCE SYSTEM (HPS)

Feedback should be an integral part of a human resource system. Such a system should include human resource programs that support employee selection, training, job design, placement, appraisal, feedback, compensation, and outplacement. These functions should be integrated in the sense that they should be based on the organization's needs and employee competencies needed to accomplish the organization's goals. Personnel recruitment and selection criteria, development options and training modules, career planning programs, appraisal processes, and compensation should be targeted to the same set of organization objectives. These are "support" programs in that managers and employees make a human performance system work. They are responsible for using the system to manage their performance and enhance their subordinates' and coworkers' performances.

Consider how a human performance system supports changing organizational strategies. Mone and I described how such a system was designed in AT&T to support its transition from a regulated bureaucracy to a team-oriented, customer-responsive, competitive enterprise.

This new environment required employees to be responsive to multiple process team leaders, to balance work load responsibilities, and to be held accountable for meeting performance obligations of each work process. Employees now did not merely produce work output that would be used by different internal clients, but rather became integral parts of multiple teams. Consequently, the nature of work was obviously changing, performance demands were increasing, and skills such as leadership, empowerment, conflict resolution, negotiation and teamwork were emphasized.

The introduction of HPS began with in-depth training in goal setting as the precursor to development, performance management, appraisal and compensation. The training was made available to managers as quickly as possible. The goal setting workshop emphasized a customer focus, and employees were to be held accountable for both specific results and how those results were achieved. Setting both team and individual goals was expected, and a participative negotiation process between employees and their process support managers, process team leaders, and customers were encouraged. Goal setting workshops helped ensure that goals were tied to the new process management structure and expectations for quality improvement. These workshops were conducted throughout the organization top down by line managers as a way to introduce this new goal setting process and the Human Performance System as well. At the conclusion of the goal setting workshops, employees left with a preliminary set of performance goals to be reviewed and negotiated with their customers, as well as with an understanding of how their performance was to be evaluated, appraised and compensated. (London & Mone, 1993, pp. 118–119)

CONCLUSION

In this final chapter, I focused on some emerging areas in the work environment that suggest the continuing importance of giving and receiving constructive feedback. We will be challenged by new technologies that allow electronic performance monitoring. Employees will be left to their own devices to establish their training needs and a program for development and learning. This entails seeking feedback and incorporating the information with self-evaluations. It also entails being self-motivated to engage in learning, track one's progress, and apply the new knowledge and skills. Learning to manage in unfamiliar work settings will be a more frequent occurrence because of workforce diversity and market globalization. People will have to seek and deal with feedback about behaviors that they previously took for granted. Also, new jobs, roles, and structures give rise to new competencies and standards that must be understood and assessed. It is also important to attend to regulatory and legal issues that affect the performance review process. Finally, this discussion highlights the concept that feedback should be thought of as part of an integrated human performance system—a system of management practices, policies, and procedures that is geared to helping the organization achieve its objectives.

Here are some final conclusions:

1. We can expect abundant feedback from objective, technology-based sources of information. This poses some threat and raises the challenge to develop useful computer-based modes for involving people in self-management for continuous performance improvement.

2. People are increasingly responsible for their own assessment of their skills, evaluation of opportunities and needs, and acquiring the skills and knowledge required for continued success. Self-paced learners have autonomy to decide what they study and how, when, where, and at what pace. This poses exciting opportunities for cost-effective ways to deliver education effectively. However, these methods must take into account the need to motivate, evaluate their own strengths and weaknesses, learn on their own, set performance goals, and track their performance.

3. Increasing globalization in corporate operations and work-force heterogeneity suggest an expanded need for cross-cultural and diversity feedback and training.

4. Jobs, roles, and work group structures are being transformed to impose new demands on employees. These changes emphasize work processes that cross functions, departments, and organization levels. People need to learn new competencies to work in these environments. They must learn how to design new positions and support the feedback and development of employees in the new and evolving positions.

5. Competency models articulate performance requirements for these new positions. The models evaluate emerging job requirements, communicate core competencies, and outline specialty areas as guidelines for performance evaluation, feedback, and career planning.

6. Managers must know legal implications of how they deliver feedback. The performance review process must be conducted in a professional and fair manner, focused on behaviors and outcomes (not personalities), and free of discrimination that is unrelated to job performance.

7. Performance review and feedback processes should be part of an integrated human performance system that supports organizational goals. The system should include human resource policies and programs that support the same set of performance standards and objectives. Ensuring this linkage is not solely the responsibility of human resource professionals. A key component of every supervisor's job is human resource management. So all supervisors should recognize, and be accountable for, ongoing performance review and constructive feedback aimed at employees' development and continuous performance improvement.

EXAMPLE OF A COMPETENCY MODEL: CORE COMPETENCIES FOR A HUMAN RESOURCE PROFESSIONAL

The core competencies are organized into four areas of focus: (a) the individual employee, (b) the group focus, (c) the organization, and (d) competencies that cut across all functional areas.

All professionals in the firm are expected to have minimum knowledge in all of these core competencies. Minimum knowledge means a familiarity and general understanding of the concepts and their application to business practice. This minimum understanding is necessary for entry into the discipline.

Individual/Job Focus Competencies
Motivation theory (goal setting, feedback, reward mechanisms)
Adult learning theory principles/development
Job analysis
Health and safety

Group Focus Competencies
Supervision/interpersonal effectiveness
Quality principles
Employee attitude measurement and tracking
Group dynamics (team building/group development)

CHAPTER TWELVE

Organizational Focus Competencies
Organization and systems design
Strategy/policy development and implementation
Forecasting and planning
Accounting principles
Corporate culture
Information systems

Competencies That Cut Across Individual, Group, and Organization Foci
Theories of change and transformation
Leadership theories
Qualitative/quantitative research methods (measurement, research design,
    and program evaluation)
Organizational behavior (process management, inter–intraorganizational
    relationships)
Valuing diversity
Employment law
Labor relations (the meaning of collective bargaining and arbitration, nego-
    tiation, contract interpretation, labor law)
Benchmarking practices and structures
International dimensions of management

Human Resource Specialty Areas

1. Organizational effectiveness consulting: Expertise in change management, organizational design and transformation, developing effective work
group structures, team and work group facilitation, teambuilding, and cultural
diversity enhancement. Knowledge of the development and implementation
of support tools for organizational analysis, such as the design and use of
employee attitude surveys and multisource (360-degree) feedback methods.

2. Compensation and benefits: Expertise in pay and reward systems and
support tools, such as job evaluation and performance appraisal. Includes
understanding benefits administration and consultation.

3. Staffing/personnel selection: Expertise in job analysis, recruitment,
interviewing, testing, college relations, and outsourcing.

4. Performance management: Expertise in assessment for guiding employee development, performance appraisal methods and training, including
elements of person perception, ways to enhance rater accuracy, effective
performance feedback, goal setting, and performance management in a multinational firm (e.g., issues of managing and evaluating expatriates and in-coun-
try nationals).

5. Training and development: Expertise in instructional technology design
and delivery for employee orientation and socialization, training program
analysis and evaluation, training needs analysis, career planning programs, and

methods for facilitating movement of employees between and within business units and national boundaries.

6. Leadership development programs: Expertise in the early identification of high potential employees; managerial assessment methods; career planning for high potential employees; identifying, designing, and evaluating leadership development programs within and outside the company; coordination of leadership development policies and programs with other business units in the company.

7. Information management: Expertise in computer hardware and software involved in the development and maintenance of data systems, including local and corporate data bases for tracking and managing employees. These may include training registration systems, payroll and benefits processing, appraisal and salary management, attitude survey administration, and training registration and tracking.

8. Strategic planning and analysis: Expertise in using information to establish plans for human resource management that meets firm business objectives and track the success of these plans. This includes organization analysis to determine emerging human resource requirements; work force analysis to determine the extent to which the skills, knowledge, experience levels and work force demographics (e.g., retirement eligibility) resident in the firm match the emerging needs; and scans of the global, national, and local environment to identify the skills available in the labor force today and in the future. This also includes understanding and educating firm employees in cultural and legal factors that influence human resource management.

9. Partnership role: Expertise in providing the best client service for the firm community in areas such as planning, strategy, measurement, policy, advocacy, and team support. Requires understanding client service (responsiveness, knowledge of client's business objectives and work methods, and attention to client satisfaction).

[Sample Format For Explaining Competencies]
Core Competencies Explained

Individual focus
Motivation theory
Definition: Understanding psychological and environmental processes that energize, direct, and maintain behavior. Various theories of motivation have different implications for job design and reward systems to enhance performance. Motivation theories are important for designing challenging jobs, creating effective reward mechanisms, and promoting constructive supervisor-subordinate relationships.
Examples: *Content theories* describe what people want and distinguish between intrinsic and extrinsic needs (Maslow, Herzberg). *Process theories* describe how people decide what to do. These cognitive models emphasize

behavior-performance-reward linkages (Porter & Lawler's expectancy theory; House's path goal theory). Associated theories of goal setting and feedback (Locke) explain mechanisms that help keep people on target and evaluate their progress.

Learning the skill/acquiring the knowledge: Best sources are text books on management in general and motivation in particular (several good textbooks are listed at the end of this document). At the library and in periodical guides and abstracts, look up Hackman & Oldham on job design, Latham & Locke on goal setting, Herzberg on motivators and hygiene factors, and Porter & Lawler on expectancy theory. Management videos are available on the subject from the American Management Association and the Academy of Management.

Measurement: Able to describe examples of content and process theories. Able to describe how professionals use motivation theory in program design to enhance employee performance.

Understands reasons why goal setting and feedback are important to performance improvement.

Can specify dimensions of goal setting and feedback that make these techniques motivating.

Can explain implications of motivation theories for job design, compensation mechanisms, and supervisor/subordinate relationships.

Job Analysis

Definition: An examination of current or future job requirements and task specifications. Job analysis is used as the basis for a number of key human resource functions, such as job design, staffing, training, goal setting, appraisal, feedback, compensation, and career planning.

Examples: Job analysis methods collect information on where and how employees get information to do their jobs, physical and mental activities required to do the jobs, relationships with others, the physical and social job context, and other job characteristics (e.g., hours and responsibilities). Job analysis methods include structured questionnaires completed by job incumbents and task and behavior checklists completed by interviewers and observers. Job analysis collects critical incidents that describe what people do in performing the major components of their jobs. Future job analysis requires interviewing employees and engineers about job requirements for positions that have yet to be established or about new job dimensions for existing positions (e.g., new expectations for employees in light of changing business conditions).

Learning the skill/acquiring the knowledge: Introductory human resource texts cover the basics of job analysis.

Measurement: Understands how job analysis is used in job evaluation, test development, employment interviews, training design, performance appraisal design, and career path planning.

Recognizes that many programs cannot proceed without a thorough job analysis as the foundation.

Group focus
Quality principles (Techniques and tools)
Definition: Understands business applications of total quality management/continuous quality improvement. Includes an understanding of operations management (e.g., work flow analysis, and outcome measurement), group dynamics (e.g., team leadership and facilitation), and stages of quality improvement.

Examples: Quality structures (e.g., councils) within the company, quality improvement team operation, appraising employees' performance in quality efforts.

Learning the skill/acquiring the knowledge: Company documents on TQM. Numerous books on the subject are readily available in any bookstore, and articles are frequently published on the subject in professional journals.

Measurement: Can cite stages of a quality improvement team effort.

Can list several tools for measurement and group facilitation.

Can suggest how TQM can be applied within the department for improved services.

Can discuss how professionals can support quality improvement efforts in the firm.

Can describe the Baldridge Award process and COMPANY's success in winning the award.

Areas that cut across group and organization focus
Employment law
Definition: A general understanding of Federal laws and judicial rulings most frequently encountered in personnel. At the core competency level, this does not require knowing the laws by name or in detail. Rather, it requires recognizing the areas covered by the laws, understanding their implications for the selection and treatment of employees, and knowing sources of information when issues arise.

Examples: Principal areas covered by employment law include discrimination, disability related acts, and affirmative action rulings. Issues deal with selecting qualified applicants, accommodation for religious and physical handicaps, working conditions based on gender (issues of equal pay and sexual harassment), performance appraisal, promotion, age discrimination, benefit plan regulation, privacy rights and disclosure of information, employment-at-will doctrine, employee health and safety, and management malpractice. Key legislation includes the civil rights acts and their amendments, in particular Title VII; Americans with Disabilities Act; and the Family and Medical Leave Act of 1993, (note: labor law is covered under a separate core competency).

Learning the skill/acquiring the knowledge: Professionals should regularly follow current Federal and state legislation and court cases in the press.

Measurement: Able to enumerate areas of personnel practice covered by law (e.g., knows protected classes, relevant personnel actions, and areas of management decisions and actions for which management may turn to professionals for guidance).

Recognizes areas of employment, working conditions, and compensation and benefits applications covered by law and judicial rulings pertaining to discrimination, harassment, accommodation, privacy, and safety.

Can cite recent or pending legislation and court cases that address employment issues.

References

Abelson, R. P. (1976). Script processing, attitude formation and decision making. In J. S. Carroll & J. W. Payne (Eds.), *Cognition and social behavior*. Hillsdale, NJ: Lawrence Erlbaum Associates.

Aiello, J. R., & Kolb, K. J. (1995). Electronic performance monitoring and social context: Impact on productivity and stress. *Journal of Applied Psychology, 80*, 339–353.

Altman, I., & Taylor, D. A. (1973). *Social penetration: The development of interpersonal relationships*. New York: Holt, Rinehart & Winston.

Anderson, L. R. (1990). Toward a two-track model of leadership training: Suggestions from self-monitoring theory. *Small Group Research, 21*(2), 147–167.

Anderson, L. R., & Thacker, J. (1985). Self-monitoring and sex as related to assessment center ratings and job performance. *Basic and Applied Psychology, 6*, 345–361.

Antonioni, D. (1994). The effects of feedback accountability on upward appraisal ratings. *Personnel Psychology, 47*, 349–356.

Ashford, S. J. (1986). Feedback seeking in individual adaptation: A resource perspective. *Academy of Management Journal, 29*, 465–487.

Ashford, S. J. (1989). Self-assessments in organizations: A literature review and integrative model. *Research in Organizational Behavior, 11*, 133–174.

Ashford, S. J., & Cummings, L. L. (1983). Feedback as an individual resource: Personal strategies of creating information. *Organizational Behavior and Human Performance, 32*, 370–398.

Ashford, S. J., & Northcraft, G. B. (1992). Conveying more (or less) than we realize: The role of impression-management in feedback-seeking. *Organizational Behavior and Human Decision Processes, 53*, 310–334.

Ashford, S. J., & Tsui, A. S. (1991). Self-regulation for managerial effectiveness: The role of active feedback seeking. *Academy of Management Journal, 34*(2), 251–280.

Atwater, L., Rousch, P., & Fischthal, A. (1992). *The impact of feedback on leaders' performance and self-evaluations*. (Working Paper at SUNY-Binghamton School of Management). Binghamton, New York.

Babad, E. Y., Inbar, J., & Rosenthal, R. (1982). Pygmalion, Galatea, and the Golem: Investigations of biased and unbiased teachers. *Journal of Educational Psychology, 74*, 459–474.

Bailey, B. A. (1990). Developing self-awareness through simulation gaming. *The Journal of Management Development, 9*(2), 38–42.

Bales, R. F. (1950). *Interaction process analysis: A method for the study of small groups*. Cambridge, MA: Addison-Wesley.

Bales, R. F. (1988). A new overview of the SYMLOG system: Measuring and changing behavior in groups. In R. B. Polley, A. P. Hare, & P. J. Stone (Eds.), *The SYMLOG practitioner: Applications of small group research.* New York: Praeger.

Balzer, W., Doherty, M., & O'Connor, R., Jr. (1989). Effects of cognitive feedback on performance. *Psychological Bulletin, 106,* 410–433.

Banaji, M., Hardin, C., & Rothman, A. (1993). Implicit stereotyping in person judgment. *Journal of Personality and Social Psychology, 65,* 272–281.

Bandura, A. (1982). Self-efficacy mechanisms in human agency. *American Psychologist, 37,* 122–147.

Bandura, A. (1986). *Social foundations of thought and action: A social-cognitive view.* Englewood Cliffs, NJ: Prentice-Hall.

Baron, R. A. (1988). Negative effects of destructive criticism: Impact on conflict, self-efficacy, and task performance. *Journal of Applied Psychology, 73,* 199–207.

Barrick, M. R., & Mount, M. K. (1991). The big five personality dimensions and job performance: A meta-analysis. *Personnel Psychology, 44,* 1–26.

Bass, B. M., & Yammarino, F. J. (1991). Congruence of self and others' leadership ratings of naval officers for understanding successful performance. *Applied Psychology: An International Review, 40,* 437–454.

Bassman, E. S. (1992). *Abuse in the workplace: Management remedies and bottom line impact.* Westport, CT: Quorum Books.

Bateman, T. S., & Organ, D. W. (1983). Job satisfaction and the good soldier: The relationship between affect and employee "citizenship." *Academy of Management Journal, 26,* 587–595.

Baumeister, R. F. (1982). A self-presentational view of social phenomena. *Psychological Bulletin, 91,* 3–26.

Beach, L. R. (1990). *Image theory: Decision making in personal and organizational contexts.* New York: Wiley.

Beach, L. R., & Mitchell, T. R. (1978). A contingency model for the selection of decision strategies. *Academy of Management Review, 3,* 439–449.

Benedict, M. E., & Levine, E. L. (1988). Delay and distortion: Tacit influences on performance appraisal effectiveness. *Journal of Applied Psychology, 73,* 507–514.

Blakely, G. L. (1993). The effects of performance rating discrepancies on supervisors and subordinates. *Organizational Behavior and Human Decision Processes, 54,* 57–80.

Blau, P. (1964). *Exchange and power in social life.* New York: Wiley.

Boice, R. (1983). Observational skills. *Psychological Bulletin, 93,* 3–29.

Brockner, J., Derr, W. R., & Laing, W. N. (1987). Self- esteem and reactions to negative feedback: Toward greater generalizability. *Journal of Research in Personality, 21,* 318–333.

Caplan, R., Vinokur, A., Price, R., & van Ryn, M. (1989). Job seeking, re-employment, and mental health: A randomized field experiment in coping with job loss. *Journal of Applied Psychology, 74,* 759–769.

Carnevale, P. J. D. (1985). Accountability of group representatives and intergroup relations. *Advances in Group Processes, 2,* 227–246.

Cascio, W. F. (1986). *Managing human resources.* New York: McGraw-Hill.

Cascio, W. F., & Silbey, V. (1979). Utility of the assessment center as a selection device. *Journal of Applied Psychology, 64,* 107–118.

Casey, J. T., London, M., & Chatterjee, S. (1995, May). *Anticipated reactions to mixed performance feedback: Self-enhancement and loss aversion.* Paper presented at the annual meeting of the Society for Industrial and Organizational Psychology, Orlando, FL.

Cialdini, R. (1989). Indirect tactics of image management: Beyond basking. In. R. A. Giacalone & P. Rosenfeld (Eds.), *Impression management in the organization* (pp. 45–56). Hillsdale, NJ: Lawrence Erlbaum Associates.

Copeland, J. T. (1993). Motivational approaches to expectancy confirmation. *Current Directions in Psychological Science, 2,* 117–121.

Deutch, M., & Gerard, H. B. (1955). Study of normative and informational influence upon individual judgment. *Journal of Abnormal and Social Psychology*, *51*, 629–636.

Dobbins, G. H., & Russell, J. M. (1986). The biasing effects of subordinate likableness on leaders' responses to poor performers: A laboratory and a field study. *Personnel Psychology*, *39*, 759–777.

Drasgow, F., Olson, J. B., Keenan, P. A., Moberg, P., & Mead, A. D. (1993). Computerized assessment. *Research in Personnel and Human Resources Management*, 11, 163–206.

Drew, S. A. W., & Davidson, A. (1993). Simulation-based leadership development and team learning. *The Journal of Management Development*, *12*(8), 39–352.

Eden, D. (1992). Leadership and expectations: Pygmalion effects and other self-fulfilling prophecies in organizations. *Leadership Quarterly*, *3*, 271–305.

Eden, D., & Aviram, A. (1993). Self-efficacy training to speed reemployment: Helping people to help themselves. *Journal of Applied Psychology*, *78*, 352–360.

Eden, D., & Kinnar, J. (1991). Modeling Galatea: Boosting self-efficacy to increase volunteering. *Journal of Applied Psychology*, *72*, 770–780.

Eden, D., & Ravid, G. (1982). Pygmalion vs. self-expectancy: Effects of instructor-and self-expectancy on trainee performance. *Organizational Behavior and Human Performance*, *30*, 351–364.

Farh, J. L., Dobbins, G. H., & Cheng, B. S. (1991). Cultural relativity in action: A comparison of self-ratings made by Chinese and U.S. workers. *Personnel Psychology*, *44*, 129–147.

Fedor, D. B., Buckley, M. R., & Eder, R. W. (1990). Measuring subordinate perceptions of supervisor feedback intentions: Some unsettling results. *Educational and Psychological Measurement*, *50*, 73–89.

Fedor, D. B., Rensvold, R. B., Adams, S. M. (1992). An investigation of factors expected to affect feedback seeking: A longitudinal field study. *Personnel Psychology*, *45*, 779–805.

Feldman, J. M. (1981). Beyond attribution theory. Cognitive processes in performance appraisal. *Journal of Applied Psychology*, *66*, 127–148.

Fenigstein, A., & Abrams, D. (1993). Self-attention and the egocentric assumption of shared perspectives. *Journal of Experimental Social Psychology*, *29*, 287–303.

Ferris, G. R., Judge, T. A., Rowland, K. M., & Fitzgibbons, D. E. (1994). Subordinate influence and performance evaluation process: Test of a model. *Organizational Behavior and Human Decision Processes*, *58*, 101–135.

Festinger, L. (1954). A theory of social comparison processes. *Human Relations*, *7*, 117–140.

Fisher, C. D. (1979). Transmission of positive and negative feedback to subordinates: A laboratory investigation. *Journal of Applied Psychology*, *64*, 533–540.

Fleming, J. B. (1979). *Stopping wife abuse*. New York: Anchor Books.

Fletcher, C. (1986). The effects of performance review in appraisal: Evidence and implications. *The Journal of Management Development*, *5*(3), 5–6.

Ford, J. K., & Weldon, E. (1981). Forewarning and accountability: Effects on memory-based interpersonal judgments. *Personality and Social Psychology Bulletin*, *7*, 264–268.

Fried, Y., Tiegs, R. B., & Bellamy, A. R. (1992). Personal and interpersonal predictors of supervisors' avoidance of evaluating subordinates. *Journal of Applied Psychology*, *77*, 462–468.

Funder, D. C. (1987). Errors and mistakes. Evaluating the accuracy of social judgment. *Psychological Bulletin*, *101*, 75–90.

Fusilier, M. R. (1980). The effects of anonymity and outcome contingencies on rater beliefs and behavior in a performance appraisal situation. *Proceedings of the 40th Annual Meeting of the Academy of Management*, 273–277.

Gabarro, J. J. (1990). The development of working relationships. In J. Galegher, R. E. Kraut, & C. Egido (Eds.), *Intellectual teamwork: Social and technological foundations of cooperative work*. (pp. 79–110). Hillsdale, NJ: Lawrence Erlbaum Associates.

Gallatin, L. (1989). *Electronic monitoring in the workplace: Supervision or surveillance?* Boston: Massachusetts Coalition on New Office Technology.

Gangestad, S., & Snyder, M. (1985). To carve nature at its joints: On the existence of discrete classes of personality. *Psychological Review*, *92*, 317–349.

Gardner, W. L., III. (1991, April). *The impact of impression management on the performance appraisal process*. Paper presented at the sixth annual meeting of the Society for Industrial and Organizational Psychology, St. Louis, MO.

Gardner, W. L., III. (1992). Lessons in organizational dramaturgy: The art of impression management. *Organizational Dynamics, 21*(1), 33–46.

Geen, R. G. (1991). Social motivation. *Annual Review of Psychology, 42*, 377–399.

Gersick, C. J. G. (1988). Time and transition in work teams: Toward a new model of group development. *Academy of Management Journal, 31*, 9–41.

Gersick, C. J. G. (1989). Marking time: Predictable transitions in task groups. *Academy of Management Journal, 32*, 274–309.

Gersick, C. J. G., & Hackman, J. R. (1990). Habitual routines in task-performing groups. *Organizational Behavior and Human Decision Processes, 47*, 65–97.

Gifford, R. (1994). A lens-mapping framework for understanding the encoding and decoding of interpersonal dispositions in nonverbal behavior. *Journal of Personality and Social Psychology, 66*, 398–412.

Goldstein, A. P., & Sorcher, M. (1974). *Changing supervisory behavior*. Elmsford, NY: Pergamon Press.

Gouldner, A. W. (1960). The norm of reciprocity: A preliminary statement. *American Sociological Review, 25*, 161–178.

Graen, G., & Scandura, T. A. (1987). Toward a psychology of dyadic organizing. In L. L. Cummings & B. M. Staw (Eds.), *Research in organizational behavior* (pp. 175–208). Greenwich, CT: JAI Press.

Greenberg, J. (1990). Organizational justice: Yesterday, today, and tomorrow. *Journal of Management, 16*, 401–434.

Hackman, J. R. (Ed.). (1990). *Groups that work (and those that don't): Creating conditions for effective teamwork*. San Francisco: Jossey-Bass.

Harris, M. M., & Schaubroeck, J. (1988). A meta-analysis of self-manager, self-peer, and peer-manager ratings. *Personnel Psychology, 41*, 43–62.

Harris, P. R., & Moran, R. T. (1987). *Managing cultural difference*. Houston, TX: Gulf.

Heatherton, T. F., Polivy, J., Herman, C. P., & Baumeister, R. F. (1993). Self-awareness, task failure, and disinhibition: How attentional focus affects eating. *Journal of Personality, 61*, 49–59.

Hegarty, W. H. (1974). Using subordinate ratings to elicit behavioral changes in managers. *Journal of Applied Psychology, 59*, 764–766.

Herriot, P. (1989). Attribution theory and interview decisions. In R. W. Eder & G. R. Ferris (Eds.), *The employment interview: Theory, research, and practice* (pp. 97–110). Newbury Park, CA: Sage.

Higgins, T., Bargh, J., & Lombardi, W. (1985). Nature of priming effects on categorization. *Journal of Experimental Psychology: Learning, Memory, and Cognition, 11*, 59–69.

Higgins, T., Rholes, W., & Jones, C. (1977). Category accessibility and impression formation. *Journal of Experimental Social Psychology, 13*, 141–154.

Hill, C. E., & Corbett, M. M. (1993). A perspective on the history of process and outcome research in counseling psychology. *Journal of Counseling Psychology, 40*, 3–24.

Hillman, L. W., Schwandt, D. R., & Bartz, D. E. (1990). Enhancing staff members' performance through feedback and coaching. *The Journal of Management Development, 9*(3), 20–27.

Holt, K., Noe, R. A., & Cavanaugh, M. (1995). *Managers' developmental responses to 360-degree feedback*. Working paper, Department of Management, Michigan State University.

Hurley, A. E. (1993). *The effects of self-esteem and source credibility on self-denying prophecies*. Unpublished manuscript, Harriman School for Management and Policy, SUNY-Stony Brook.

Ilgen, D. R., Barnes-Farrell, J. L., & McKellin, D. B. (1993). Performance appraisal process research in the 1980s: What has it contributed to appraisals in use? *Organizational Behavior and Human Decision Processes, 54*, 321–368.

Ilgen, D. R., Fisher, C. D., & Taylor, M. S. (1979). Consequences of individual feedback on behavior in organizations. *Journal of Applied Psychology, 64*, 349–371.

Ilgen, D. R., & Knowlton, W. A. (1980). Performance attribution effects on feedback from supervisors. *Organizational Behavior and Human Performance, 25,* 441–456.

Irving, R. H., Higgins, C. A., & Safayeni, F. R. (1986). Computerized performance monitoring systems: Use and abuse. *Communications of the ACM, 29,* 794–801.

Jackson, S. (1992). *Diversity in the workplace: Human resources initiatives.* New York: The Guilford Press.

Jacobson, N. S., & Margolin, G. (1979). *Marital therapy: Strategies based on social learning and behavior exchange principles.* New York: Brunner/Mazel.

James, S. (1994). Recent advances in management development: Self-directed, continuous development through "Smart Software." *The Journal of Management Development, 13*(7), 35–39.

Johnston, S. (1986). How one organization uses "The Looking Glass, Inc." *The Journal of Management Development, 5*(4), 46–50.

Jones, E. E. (1964). *Ingratiation: A social psychological analysis.* New York: Appleton-Century-Crofts.

Jones, E. E., & Berglas, S. (1978). Control of attributions about the self through self-handicapping strategies: The appeal of alcohol and the role of underachievement. *Personality and Social Psychology Bulletin, 4,* 200–206.

Jones, R. G., & Whitmore, M. D. (1995). Evaluating developmental assessment centers as interventions. *Personnel Psychology, 48,* 377–388.

Judge, T. A., & Ferris, G. R. (1993). Social context of performance evaluation decisions. *Academy of Management Journal, 36,* 80–105.

Kahn, W. A. (1993). Caring for caregivers: Patterns of organizational care-giving. *Administrative Science Quarterly, 38,* 546.

Kanter, R. M. (1977). *Men and women of the corporation.* New York: Basic Books.

Kaplan, R. E. (1986). What one manager learned in "The Looking Glass" and how he learned it. *The Journal of Management Development, 5*(4), 36–45.

Kaplan, R. E. (1993). 360-degree Feedback PLUS: Boosting the power of coworker ratings for executives. *Human Resource Management, 32,* 299–314.

Karl, K. A., & Kopf, J. M. (1993, August). *Will individuals who need to improve their performance the most, volunteer to receive videotaped feedback?* Presented at the annual meeting of the Academy of Management, Atlanta, GA.

Kelley, H. H. (1972). Attribution theory in social interaction. In E. Jones, D. E. Kanouse, H. H. Kelley, R. E. Nisbett, S. Valins, & B. Weinere (Eds.), *Attribution: Perceiving the causes of behavior.* Morristown, NJ: General Learning Press.

Kelly, J. R., & McGrath, J. E. (1985). Effects of time limits and task types on task performance and interaction of four-person groups. *Journal of Personality and Social Psychology, 49,* 395–407.

Kenny, D. A., & DePaulo, B. M. (1993). Do people know how others view them? An empirical and theoretical account. *Psychological Bulletin, 114,* 145–161.

Keys, J. B. (Ed.). (1994). Practice fields for the learning organization. *The Journal of Management Development, 13*(8), 1–56.

King, B. A. (1995, June). Working with a new staff mix. *RN,* 38–41.

Kinicki, A. J., Hom, P. W., Trost, M. R., & Wade, K. J. (1995). Effects of category prototypes on performance-rating accuracy. *Journal of Applied Psychology, 80,* 354–370.

Kirk, M. O. (1995, June 25). When surviving just isn't enough. *New York Times,* F11.

Klarreich, S. (1993). RET: A powerful tool to turn a traumatic job termination into an enlightening career transition. *Journal of Rational-Emotive & Cognitive- Behavior Therapy, 11,* 77–89.

Klimoski, R., & Inks, L. (1990). Accountability forces in performance appraisal. *Organizational Behavior and Human Decision Processes, 45,* 194–208.

Kluger, A. N., & DeNisi, A. (1996). The effects of feedback interventions on performance: A historical review, a meta-analysis, and a preliminary feedback intervention. *Psychological Bulletin, 119,* 254–284.

Kopelman, R. E., (1986). *Managing productivity in organizations: A practical, people-oriented perspective.* New York: McGraw-Hill.

Kumar, K., & Beyerlein, M. (1991). Construction and validation of an instrument for measuring ingratiatory behaviors in organizational settings. *Journal of Applied Psychology, 76,* 619–627.

Langer, E. J. (1992). Matters of mind: Mindfulness/mindlessness in perspective. *Consciousness & Cognition: An International Journal, 1,* 289–305.

Larson, J. R., Jr. (1984). The performance feedback process: A preliminary model. *Organizational Behavior and Human Performance, 33,* 42–76.

Larson, J. R., Jr. (1986). Supervisors' performance feedback to subordinates: The impact of subordinate performance valence and outcome dependence. *Organizational Behavior and Human Performance, 37,* 391–408.

Larson, J. R., Jr. (1988). The dynamic interplay between employees' feedback-seeking strategies and supervisors' delivery of performance feedback. *Academy of Management Review, 14,* 408–422.

Latham, G. P., & K. N. Wexley (1981, 1994 2nd ed.). *Increasing productivity through performance appraisal.* Reading, MA: Addison-Wesley.

Leary, M. R. (1983). *Understanding social anxiety.* Beverly Hills, CA: Sage.

Lennox, R., & Wolfe, R. (1984). Revision of the self-monitoring scale. *Journal of Personality and Social Psychology, 46,* 1349–1364.

Levy, P. E. (1991). *Self-appraisal and attributional judgments.* Paper presented at the sixth annual meeting of the Society for Industrial and Organizational Psychology, St. Louis, MO.

Lindsley, D. H., Brass, D. J., & Thomas, J. B. (1995). Efficacy-performance spirals: A multilevel perspective. *Academy of Management Review, 20*(3), 645–678.

Locke, E. A., & Latham, G. P. (1990). *A theory of goal setting and task performance.* Englewood Cliffs, NJ: Prentice-Hall, p. 192.

Locke, E. A., & Latham, G. P. (1992). Comments on McLeod, Liker, and Lobel. *Journal of Applied Behavioral Science, 28,* 42–45.

Logue, A. W. (1995). *Self-control: Waiting until tomorrow for what you want today.* Englewood Cliffs, NJ: Prentice-Hall.

London, M. (1983). Toward a theory of career motivation. *Academy of Management Review, 8,* 620–630.

London, M. (1985). *Developing managers.* San Francisco, CA: Jossey-Bass.

London, M. (1988). *Change agents: New roles and innovation strategies for human resource professionals.* San Francisco, CA: Jossey-Bass.

London, M. (1995a). *Achieving performance excellence in university administration.* Westport, CT: Praeger.

London, M. (1995b). Giving feedback: Source-centered antecedents and consequences of constructive and destructive feedback. *Human Resource Management Review, 5*(3), 159–188.

London, M. (1995c). *Self and interpersonal insight: How people learn about themselves and others in organizations.* New York: Oxford University Press.

London, M., & London, M. (1996). Tight coupling in high performing ensembles. *Human Resource Management Review, 6*(1), 1–24.

London, M., & Mone, E. M. (1987). *Career management and survival in the workplace.* San Francisco: Jossey-Bass.

London, M., & Mone, E. M. (1993). Managing marginal performance in an organization striving for excellence. In A. K. Korman (Ed.), *Human resources dilemmas in work organizations: Strategies for resolution* (pp. 95–124). New York: Guilford, pp. 95–124.

London, M., & Smither, J. W. (1995). Can multi-source feedback change self-awareness and behavior? Theoretical applications and directions for research. *Personnel Psychology, 48,* 803–840.

London, M., Smither, J. W., & Adsit, D. J. (1997). Accountability: The Achilles Heal of multisource feedback. *Group and Organization Management.* In press.

London, M., Wohlers, A. J., & Gallagher, P. (1990). 360 degree feedback surveys: A source of feedback to guide management development. *Journal of Management Development, 9:* 17–31.

London, M., & Wueste, R. A. (1992). *Human resource development in changing organizations.* Westport, CT: Quorum.

Luft, J. (1970). *Group processes: An introduction to group dynamics.* Palo Alto, CA: National Press Books.

Mabe, P. A., & West, S. G. (1982). Validity of self-evaluation of ability: A review and meta-analysis. *Journal of Applied Psychology, 67:* 280–296.

Maier, N. R. F. (1958). *The appraisal interview: Objectives, methods, and skills.* New York: Wiley.

Martocchio, J. J., & Dulebohn, J. (1994). Performance feedback effects in training: The role of perceived controllability. *Personnel Psychology, 47,* 357–373.

Maurer, T. J., & Tarulli, B. A. (1994). *Acceptance of peer and upward performance appraisal systems: Considerations from employee development, job analysis, and leadership.* Unpublished manuscript.

McAfee, R. B., & Champagne, P. J. (1993). Performance management: A strategy for improving employee performance and productivity. *Journal of Managerial Psychology, 8*(5), 24–32.

McCall, M. W., & Lombardo, M. M. (1983). *Off the track: Why and how successful executives get derailed.* (Technical Report No. 21). Greensboro, NC: Center for Creative Leadership.

McCauley, C., & Lombardo, M. (1990). Benchmarks: An instrument for diagnosing managerial strengths and weaknesses. In K. E. Clark & M. B. Clark (Eds.), *Measures of leadership* (pp. 535–545). West Orange, NJ: Leadership Library of America.

McClelland, D. C. (1965). Achievement motivation can be developed. *Harvard Business Review, 43*(6), 6–14, 178.

McGill, M. E., Slocum, J. W., Jr., & Lei, D. (1992). Management practices in learning organizations. *Organizational Dynamics, 21*(1), p. 5.

McLeod, P. L., Liker, J. K., & Lobel, S. (1992). Process feedback in task groups: An application of goal setting. *Journal of Applied Behavioral Science, 28,* 15–41.

Mero, N. P., & Motowidlo, S. J. (1995). Effects of rater accountability on the accuracy and the favorability of performance ratings. *Journal of Applied Psychology, 80,* 517–524.

Meyer, H. H. (1991). A solution to the performance appraisal feedback enigma. *Academy of Management Executive, 5*(1), 68–76.

Mitchell, T. R., & Wood, R. E. (1980). Supervisor responses to subordinate poor performance: A test of an attributional model. *Organizational Behavior and Human Performance, 25,* 123–138.

Mitchell, T. W., & Klimoski, R. (1984). *Accountability bias in performance appraisal.* (Working Paper Series in Industrial/Organizational Psychology). Columbus: The Ohio State University.

Morrison, E. W., & Bies, R. J. (1991). Impression management the feedback-seeking process: A literature review and research agenda. *Academy of Management Review, 16*(3), 522–541.

Morrison, E. W., & Vancouver, J. B. (1993, August). *The effects of source attributes on feedback seeking.* Presented at the annual meeting of the Academy of Management. Atlanta, GA.

Munchus, G., III, & McArthur, B. (1991). Revisiting the historical use of the assessment centre in management selection and development. *Journal of Management Development, 10*(1), 5–13.

Murphy, K. R., Balzer, W. K., Kellam, K. L., & Armstrong, J. G. (1984). Effects of the purpose of rating on accuracy in observing teacher behavior and evaluating teaching performance. *Journal of Educational Psychology, 76,* 45–54.

Murphy, K. R., & Cleveland, J. N. (1991). *Performance appraisal: An organizational perspective.* Needham Heights, MA: Allyn & Bacon.

Nadler, D. A. (1977). *Feedback and organization development: Using data based methods.* Reading, MA: Addison-Wesley.

Nadler, D. A. (1979). The effects of feedback on task group behavior: A review of the experimental research. *Organizational Behavior and Human Performance, 23,* 309–338.

Napier, N. K., & Latham, G. P. (1986). Outcome expectancies of people who conduct performance appraisals. *Personnel Psychology, 39,* 827–837.

Neale, M. A., & Bazerman, M. H. (1991). *Cognition and rationality in negotiation.* New York: The Free Press.

Nelson, T. D. (1993). The hierarchical organization of behavior: A useful feedback model of self-regulation. *Current Directions in Psychological Science, 2,* 121–126.

Nemeroff, W. F., & Cosentino, J. (1979). Utilizing feedback and goal setting to increase performance appraisal interviewer skills of managers. *Academy of Management Journal, 22,* 566–576.

9 to 5, Working Women Education Fund (1990). *Stories of mistrust and manipulation: The electronic monitoring of the American workforce.* Cleveland, OH: Author.

Nisbett, R. E., & Wilson, T. D. (1977). Telling more than we know: Verbal reports on mental processes. *Psychological Review, 84,* 231–259.

Organ, D. W. (1988). *Organizational citizenship behavior: The good soldier syndrome.* Lexington, MA: Lexington Books.

Oz, S., & Eden, D. (1994). Restraining the Golem: Boosting performance by changing the interpretation of low scores. *Journal of Applied Psychology, 79,* 744–754.

Padgett, M. Y., & Ilgen, D. R. (1989). The impact of ratee performance characteristics on rater cognitive processes and alternative measures of rater accuracy. *Organizational Behavior and Human Decision Processes, 44,* 232–260.

Park, H., & Harrison, J. K. (1993). Enhancing managerial cross-cultural awareness and sensitivity: Transactional analysis revisited. *The Journal of Management Development, 12*(3), 20–29.

Perkins, D. N. (1981). *The mind's best work.* Cambridge, MA: Harvard University Press, p. 206.

Reilly, B. A., & Doherty, M. E. (1989). A note on the assessment of self-insight in judgment research. *Organizational Behavior and Human Decision Processes, 44,* 123–131.

Reilly, B. A., & Doherty, M. E. (1992). The assessment of self-insight in judgment policies. *Organizational Behavior and Human Decision Processes, 53,* 285–309.

Reilly, R. R., Warech, M. A., & Reilly, S. (1993). *The influence of self-monitoring on the reliability and validity of upward feedback.* Paper presented at the annual meeting of the Society for Industrial and Organizational Psychology, San Francisco.

Rosenberg, M. (1965). *Society and the adolescent self-image.* Princeton, NJ: Princeton University Press.

Rosenthal, R. (1991). Teacher expectancy effects: A brief update 25 years after the Pygmalion experiment. *Journal of Research in Education, 1,* 3–12.

Rosenthal, R., & Jacobson, L. (1968). *Pygmalion in the classroom: Teacher expectations and pupils' intellectual development.* New York: Holt, Rinehart & Winston.

Rousch, P. E., & Atwater, L. E. (1992). Using the MBTI to understand transformational leadership and self-perception accuracy. *Military Psychology, 4,* 17–34.

Russo, J. E., & Schoemaker, P. J. H. (1992). Managing overconfidence. *Sloan Management Review, 33*(2), 7–17.

Rynes, S., & Rosen, B. (1995). A field survey of factors affecting the adoption and perceived success of diversity training. *Personnel Psychology, 48,* 247–270.

Saavedra, R., Earley, P. C., & Van Dyne, L. (1993). Complex interdependence in task-performing groups. *Journal of Applied Psychology, 78,* 61–72.

Salancik, G. R., & Pfeffer, J. A. (1978). A social information processing approach to job attitudes and task design. *Admnistrative Science Quarterly, 23,* 224–253.

Salvemini, N. J., Reilly, R. R., & Smither, J. W. (1993). The influence of rater motivation on assimilation effects and accuracy in performance ratings. *Organizational Behavior and Human Decision Processes, 55,* 41–60.

Sanders, M. M. (1993). Situational constraints through the cognitive looking glass: A reinterpretation of the relationship between situations and performance judgments. *Human Resource Management Review, 3,* 129–146.

Schmit, M. J., & Ryan, A. M. (1993). The big five in personnel selection: Factor structure in applicant and nonapplicant populations. *Journal of Applied Psychology, 78,* 966–974.

Senge, P. M. (1990). *The fifth discipline: The art and practice of the learning organization.* New York: Doubleday.

Shrauger, J. S., & Shoeneman, J. (1979). Symbolic interactionist view of self-concept: Through the looking glass darkly. *Psychological Bulletin, 86,* 549–573.

Silverman, S. B. (1991). Individual development through performance appraisal. In K. N. Wexley, (Ed.), *Developing human resources* (pp. 120–151). Washington, DC: The Bureau of National Affairs, Inc.

Simonson, I., & Nye, P. (1992). The effect of accountability on susceptibility to decision errors. *Organizational Behavior and Human Decision Processes, 51,* 416–446.

Slovic, P., & Lichenstein, S. (1971). Comparison of Bayesian and regression approaches to the study of information processing in judgment. *Organizational Behavior and Human Performance, 6,* 649–744.

Smith, M. J., Carayon, P., Sanders, K. J., Lim, S.-Y., & LeGrande, D. (1992). Employee stress and health complaints in jobs with and without electronic performance monitoring. *Applied Ergonomics, 23,* 17–28.

Snyder, M. (1974). Self-monitoring of expressive behavior. *Journal of Personality and Social Psychology, 30,* 526–537.

Snyder, M. (1987). *Public appearances, private realities: The psychology of self-monitoring.* New York: W. H. Freeman.

Snyder, M., & Gangestad, S. (1986). On the nature of self-monitoring: Matters of assessment, matters of validity. *Journal of Personality and Social Psychology, 51,* 125–135.

Stamoulis, D. T., & Hauenstein, N. M. A. (1993). Rater training and rating accuracy: Training for dimensional accuracy versus training for ratee differentiation. *Journal of Applied Psychology, 78,* 994–1003.

Steele, C. M., Spencer, S. J., & Lynch, M. (1993). Self-image resilience and dissonance: The role of affirmational resources. *Journal of Personality and Social Psychology, 64,* 885–896.

Steiner, D. D., Rain, J. S., & Smalley, M. M. (1993). Distributional ratings of performance: Further examination of a new rating format. *Journal of Applied Psychology, 78,* 438.

Stewart, G. L., Carson, K. P., & Cardy, R. L. (1996). The joint effects of conscientiousness and self-leadership training on employee self-directed behavior in a service setting. *Personnel Psychology, 49,* 143–164.

Stewart, J., & Winter, R. (1992). Open and distance learning. In S. Truelove (Ed.), *Handbook of training and development* (pp. 197–229). Oxford: Blackwell.

Stinson, L., & Ickes, W. (1992). Empathic accuracy in the interactions of male friends versus male strangers. *Journal of Personality and Social Psychology, 62*(5), 787–797.

Storms, M. D. (1973). Videotape and the attribution process: Reversing actors' and observers' points of view. *Journal of Personality and Social Psychology, 27,* 165–175.

Stowell, S. J. (1988). Coaching: A commitment to leadership. *Training and Development Journal, 42*(6), 34–41.

Stumpf, S. A., & Dutton, J. E. (1990). The dynamics of learning through management simulations: Let's dance. *The Journal of Management Development, 9*(2), 7–15.

Stumpf, S. A., Watson, M. A., & Rustogi, H. (1994). Leadership in a global village: Creating practice fields to develop learning organizations. *Journal of Management Development, 13*(8), 16–25.

Summers, D. A., Taliaferro, J. D., & Fletcher, D. J. (1970). Subjective vs. objective descriptions of judgment policy. *Psychonomic Science, 18,* 249–250.

Sundstrom, E., De Meuse, K. P., & Futrell, D. (1990). Work teams: Applications and effectiveness. *American Psychologist, 45,* 120–133.

Surber, C. F. (1985). Measuring the importance of information in judgment: Individual differences in weighting ability and effort. *Organizational Behavior and Human Decision Processes, 35,* 156–178.

Taylor, S. M., Fisher, C. D., & Ilgen, D. R. (1984). Individuals' reactions to performance feedback in organizations: A control theory perspective. In K. M. Rowland & G. R. Ferris (Eds.), *Research in Personnel and Human Resources Management, 2,* 81–124.

Tetlock, P. E. (1983). Accountability and the perseverance of first impressions. *Social Psychology Quarterly, 46,* 74–83.

Tetlock, P. E. (1985a). Accountability: The neglected social context of judgmenet and choice. *Research in Organizational Behavior, 7,* 297–332.

Tetlock, P. E. (1985b). Accountability: A social check on the fundamental attribution error. *Social Psychology Quarterly, 48,* 227–236.

Tetlock, P. E., & Kim, J. I. (1992). Accountability and judgment processes in a personality prediction task. *Journal of Personality and Social Psychology, 52,* 700–709.

Tetlock, P. E., Skitka, L., & Boettger, R. (1989). Social and cognitive strategies for coping with accountability: Conformity, complexity, and bolstering. *Journal of Personality and Social Psychology, 57,* 632–640.

Thompson, L. (1991). Information exchange and negotiation. *Journal of Experimental Social Psychology, 27,* 161 179.

Thompson, L., & DeHarpport, T. (1994). Social judgment, feedback, and interpersonal learning in negotiation. *Organizational Behavior and Human Decision Processes, 58,* 327–345.

Thompson, L., & Hastie, R. (1990). Social perception in negotiation. *Organization and Human Decision Processes, 47,* 98–123.

Thornton, G. C., III, & Byham, W. C. (1982). *Assessment centers and managerial performance.* New York: Academic Press.

Tice, D. M., & Baumeister, R. F. (1990). Self-esteem, self-handicapping, and self-presentation: The strategy of inadequate practice. *Journal of Personality, 58,* 443–464.

Tornow, W. W. (1993). Perceptions or reality: Is multiperspective measurement a means or an end? *Human Resource Management, 32,* 221–230.

Tsui, A. S., & Ohlott, P. (1988). Multiple assessment of managerial effectiveness: Interrater agreement and consensus in effectiveness models. *Personnel Psychology, 41,* 779–803.

Ury, W. I., Brett, J. M., & Goldberg, S. B. (1988). *Getting disputes resolved.* San Francisco: Jossey-Bass.

Van Velsor, E., & Leslie, J. B. (1991). *Feedback to managers, Vol. I: A guide to rating multi-rater feedback instruments* (Report 149). Greensboro, NC: Center for Creative Leadership.

Vinokur, A. D., van Ryn, M., Gramlich, E. M., & Price, R. H. (1991). Long-term follow-up and benefit-cost analysis of the Jobs Program: A preventive intervention for the unemployed. *Journal of Applied Psychology, 76,* 213–219.

Warr, P., & Bunce, D. (1995). Training characteristics and the outcomes of open learning. *Personnel Psychology, 48,* 347–375.

Wayne, S. J., & Kacmar, K. M. (1991). The effects of impression management on the performance appraisal process. *Organizational Behavior and Human Decision Processes, 48,* 70–88.

Wells, L., Jr. (1992). Feedback, the group unconscious, and the unstated effects of experimental methods. *Journal of Applied Behavioral Science, 28,* 46–53.

Whitney, K. (1994). Improving group task performance: The role of group goals and group efficacy. *Human Performance, 7,* 55–78.

Williams, K. J., DeNisi, A. S., Blencoe, A. G., & Cafferty, T. P. (1985). The role of appraisal purpose: Effects of purpose on information acquisition and utilization. *Organizational Behavior and Human Performance, 35,* 314–339.

Woehr, D. J., & Feldman, J. (1993). Processing objective and question order effects on the causal relation between memory and judgment in performance appraisal: The tip of the iceberg. *Journal of Applied Psychology, 78,* 232–241.

Wofford, J. C. (1994). An examination of the cognitive processes used to handle employee job problems. *Academy of Management Journal, 37,* 180–192.

Wohlers, A. J., & London, M. (1989). Ratings of managerial characteristics: Evaluation difficulty, coworker agreement, and self-awareness. *Personnel Psychology, 42,* 235–260.

Yammarino, F. J., & Atwater, L. E. (1993). Understanding self-perception accuracy: Implications for human resources management. *Human Resource Management, 32,* 231–249.

Yammarino, F. J., & Dubinsky, A. J. (1992). Supervisor-subordinate relationships: A multiple level of analysis approach. *Human Relations*, *45*, 575–600.

Yu, J., & Murphy, K. R. (1993). Modesty bias in self-ratings of performance: A test of the cultural relativity hypothesis. *Personnel Psychology*, *46*, 357–363.

Zajonc, R. B. (1965, July). Social facilitation. *Science*, *149*, 269–274.

Zalesny, M. D., & Highhouse, S. (1992). Accuracy in performance evaluations. *Organizational Behavior and Human Decision Processes*, *51*, 22–50.

Author Index

Subject Index